D1566719

Coming of Age in Nineteenth-Century India

In this engaging and eloquent history, Ruby Lal traces the becoming of nineteenth-century Indian women through a critique of narratives of linear transition from girlhood to womanhood. In the north-Indian patriarchal environment, women's lives were dominated by the expectations of the male universal, articulated most clearly in household chores and domestic duties. The author argues that girls and women in the early nineteenth century experienced freedom, eroticism, adventurousness and playfulness, even within restrictive circumstances. Although women in the colonial world of the later nineteenth century remained agential figures, their activities came to be constrained by more firmly entrenched domestic norms. Lal skillfully marks the subtle and complex alterations in the multifaceted female subject in a variety of nineteenth-century discourses, elaborated in four different sites – forest, school, household and rooftops.

Ruby Lal is Associate Professor in the Department of Middle Eastern and South Asian Studies at Emory University. She has written extensively on women and gender relations in Islamic societies in the precolonial and colonial world. In addition to numerous academic articles and political commentaries, she is the author of *Domesticity and Power in the Early Mughal World* (Cambridge University Press, 2005). She is currently writing *Uncrowned Empress*, a historical biography of the iconic Mughal Empress, Nur Jahan.

For Fanny, Aashna, Ananya –
My dazzling nieces, who give me the vital clues to this history

For Rita Costa Gomes –
With love for sharing my American journeys

For Gyan –
Life companion and critic

Coming of Age in Nineteenth-Century India

The Girl-Child and the Art of Playfulness

RUBY LAL

Emory University

To, President Carter —
In appreciation of your
work on African children!
Best,
Ruby Lal
11/12/14

CAMBRIDGE
UNIVERSITY PRESS

CAMBRIDGE UNIVERSITY PRESS
Cambridge, New York, Melbourne, Madrid, Cape Town,
Singapore, São Paulo, Delhi, Mexico City

Cambridge University Press
32 Avenue of the Americas, New York, NY 10013-2473, USA

www.cambridge.org
Information on this title: www.cambridge.org/9781107030244

First published 2013

Printed in the United States of America

A catalog record for this publication is available from the British Library.

Library of Congress Cataloging in Publication data
Lal, Ruby.
Coming of age in nineteenth-century India : the girl-child and the
art of playfulness / Ruby Lal.
p.   cm.
Includes bibliographical references and index.
ISBN 978-1-107-03024-4 (hardback)
1. Women – India – Social life and customs – 19th century.   2. Girls – India –
Social life and customs – 19th century.   3. Domestic relations – India –
History – 19th century.   I. Title.
HQ1742.L346 2013
305.235'2095409034–dc23
2012023652

ISBN 978-1-107-03024-4 Hardback

Contents

Photos

Maps

Acknowledgments

I began writing a book on the nineteenth century, shifting (temporarily) from my earlier work on the Mughal world, in order to enrich my understanding of the history of women in India. Every step of the way, the making of this book has been a gratifying, rewarding, and at once, humbling experience. *Coming of Age in Nineteenth-Century India* became what it is only because of the extraordinary generosity of a large number of colleagues, friends and acquaintances.

My primary academic debt is due to several scholars who have written on nineteenth-century northern India: "the first generation" writing on the North Western Provinces (NWP). I steal David Lelyveld's beautiful title of his first book in order to emphasize the significance of the work of these scholars, which made my charting of a history of feminine figures possible. Barbara Metcalf, C. M. Naim, David Lelyveld, Gail Minault, Francis Robinson – and along with "the first generation," in very special ways, Michael Fisher and Wendy Doniger – have supported me at each stage of my thinking and writing, from a discussion of the nineteenth-century north-Indian world and its archival complexities to reading various drafts of this work.

In the United States, deepest thanks to Lynne Huffer, Rita Costa Gomes, Michael Fisher, V. Narayana Rao, Colin Johnson and Gyan Pandey, for their continuous, exacting criticism and unwavering support since the inception of this work. Each one of them gave me enormous amounts of time, patience, affection – and immediate reactions in dire times! – for which I am extremely grateful. Since my arrival at Emory in 2005, I have been part of two fabulous writers' groups: one with Lynne Huffer and Gyan Pandey, and the other with Laurie Patton, Leslie Harris and Lynne Huffer. Both these creative spaces, and the reactions of each of my friends, have been critical to my thinking, writing and being! I learned a great deal from conversations with several colleagues, who persuaded me to take my work in some of the directions it now follows: thanks to Barbara Ramusack, Gyan Prakash, Gayatri Reddy, Wendy Doniger, Mary Odem, Martha Fineman, Mark Jordan, Joyce Flueckiger, Bruce Knauft, Kamala Visveswaran, Anjali Arondekar, Mrinalini Sinha, Muzaffar Alam, Ulrike Stark, Rashmi Bhatnagar, Rupert Snell, Thomas Trautmann, Peter Stearns, Ruth Vanita, Jonathan Prude, Veena Oldenberg, Stephen Dale, Shalom Goldman and Suzanne Raitt. My colleagues in the Department of Middle Eastern and South Asian Studies at Emory University in Atlanta have helped with ideas, archival material and translations of difficult passages. Special thanks to Rkia Cornell, Vincent Cornell, Gordon Newby, Oded Borowski, Ofra Yeglin, Benjamin Hary, Devin Stewart, Hussein Samei, Roxani Margariti, Scott Kugle and Robert Phillips. I am grateful to the Emory administration for its generous support; to the former dean, Bobby Paul, for two most-needed research leaves; and to Lisa Tedesco, Robin Forman, Michael Elliott and Wendy Newby for their consistent help, encouragement and interest. Emory's commitment to the arts and humanities makes its landscape an exciting and rewarding one, and for that I recognize the special efforts of my colleagues in the Emory administration.

In England, long-term gratitude is due to Francis Robinson and Tapan Raychaudhuri, who have been steady sources of ideas and models of intellectual generosity. Francis read many drafts of this book, including some very shoddy ones, for which I am especially grateful. I owe special thanks to Susan Stronge and Robert Skelton for their long-term, invaluable help and terrific leads on Indian images; to Carolyn Steedman for an important discussion of the possible directions my work could take; to Christopher Pinney for a wonderful conversation on the pictorial representations of the Indian girl-child; and to the late Ralph Russell for his guidance, engagement and appreciation of the work he saw me begin. In Australia, thanks to Peter Reeves for introducing me to *The Bride's Mirror* and for giving me his own copy. And to Jim Masselos for a long discussion at the British Library and the gift of an early nineteenth-century volume on Hindi and Urdu. In Germany, to Monica Juneja and Margrit Pernau, and in the Netherlands, to Peter Geschiere and Willem Van Schendel, my appreciation for their reactions and warm support.

In India, a very special thanks to Suraiya Masud and C. M. Naim for hosting me in their Barabanki home in December 2004. Much gratitude to Naim Saheb for making December 2004 a most memorable time for me – not least because he first asked me to meet Azra. I have the privilege of an enormous gratefulness to Azra Kidwai: her boundless energy, exceptional generosity with time and candid expression of her feelings are all rare gifts that she gave me. The soul of this book would have been missing without Azra as the interlocutor. Milind Wakankar persuaded me to keep the forest as a heuristic space. The "woman of the forest" in this book comes from his engagement with my work. And the insistence that I keep all the other spatial configurations as central to the history of the figure of the girl-child is Gyan Pandey's. Saleem Kidwai, my friend, brother of Azra Kidwai (historically, our turn to turn things around!), has always been there for me: I cherish his suggestions, gentle disagreements and his love. To Saleem and Sufia Kidwai, my deep appreciation for hosting me in their home in Lucknow in December 2010; special thanks to Sufi Baji for that unforgettable trip to Baragaon and Paisar.

Sadiq-ur-Rahman Kidwai, Romila Thapar, Mushirul Hasan, Ram Advani, Alok Bhalla, William Dalrymple, Shashank Sinha, Mubarak Ali, Prathama Banerjee, Sudhir Chandra and Geetanjali Shree have been very generous with archival suggestions, offering unstinting support in my intellectual endeavors. To Chiki Sarkar, Bridget Wagner, and Alane Mason, very special thanks for their keen interest in my new biography of Nur Jahan – ensuring circuitously that I finish this book.

Parts of *Coming of Age in Nineteenth-Century India* were presented at a variety of academic seminars and workshops. Thanks to the organizers for the invitations and to all the participants and commentators who asked me questions that have been important. To Juan Cole and Minnie Sinha at the University of Michigan; K. Sivaramakrishnan and Inderpal Grewal at Yale; Gail Minault, Kamala Visveswaran and Kamran Ali at Austin, Texas; Anjali Arondekar and Geeta Patel for the timely invitation to the Madison Feminist Pre-conference where I first presented parts of this work; Rochona Majumdar at Chicago; Deanne

Williams at York (Canada); Anand Yang and Priti Ramamurthy at the University of Washington, Seattle; Crispin Bates and Aya Ikegame at the University of Edinburgh; Ruth Vanita at the University of Montana; Nariaki Nakazato at the Institute of Oriental Culture, the University of Tokyo; Nobuko Nagasaki at Ryukoku University, Osaka, and the University of Kyoto; Mahesh Rangarajan at the Nehru Memorial Library, New Delhi; and Gyan Pandey for the invitation to present a paper from my current work at the Subalternity and Difference Workshop, first at Emory and then at four workshops in India in the summer of 2009. A note of appreciation is due to my doctoral students, Debjani Bhattacharyya, Durba Mitra, Aditya Pratap Deo and Kelly Basner for their reading and critique of my work. Special thanks to Kelly for locating Bhavna Sonawane's *Sleeping Beauty*, the image on the cover of this book, and for her help in preparing the index. I should make a special acknowledgment of the enthusiasm for this book expressed by my students in the spring 2010 senior seminar, "Women in India."

I thank the librarians and staff of the Indian Institute Library and the Center for Islamic Studies at Oxford University (Oxford), the British Library and the library of the School of Oriental and African Studies (London), The National Museum (New Delhi), The University of Chicago Library, The University of Amsterdam Library and the Woodruff Library at Emory University for their outstanding service. Thanks to Tim Bryson of the Emory University library for chasing the most obscure references. For research assistance and technical support, I am thankful to Connie Kassor (Religion) and to Juana McGhee and Tarje Lacy of my department at Emory.

The following grants and fellowships made possible the research and writing of this book: Research Grant from the Institute of Comparative and International Studies, Emory University, in 2006 and 2007; Senior Fellowship, International Institute of Asian Studies, Amsterdam, Netherlands, summer 2007; and University Research Council for Arts and Sciences Fellowship, Emory University, 2011; a grant in March 2012 from the subvention fund of Emory College facilitated the production of this book.

I am grateful to Marigold Acland, my astute editor at Cambridge University Press for her support and suggestions over the years, especially for our conversations on the title of this book. It is because of

Marigold that this book is called *Coming of Age in Nineteenth-Century India*. My historical and conceptual concerns, as well as my methodology, are radically different from Margaret Mead (*Coming of Age in Samoa*, 1928) and Anne Moody (*Coming of Age in Mississippi*, 1968). Yet, I am delighted to be sharing this title, and with it, hopefully advancing several crucial debates in matters of gender and history. Special thanks to the two anonymous readers for their very insightful and gracious comments. And to painter Bhavna Sonawane for giving me permission to use her image *Sleeping Beauty* as the cover of this book. A small set of materials from Chapter 5 were used in an early article entitled "Gender and *Sharafat*: Rereading Nazir Ahmad," *Journal of the Royal Asiatic Society*, Vol. 18, Part I (January 2008): 15–30. I then published "Recasting the Woman Question: The 'Girl-Child/Woman' in the Colonial Encounter," *Interventions* Vol. 10 (3) (2008): 321–339, which became the basis for Chapter 1. This article was reproduced as "Recasting the Woman Question: The 'Girl-Child/Woman' in the Colonial Encounter," in Gyanendra Pandey (ed.), *Subaltern Citizens and Their Histories: Investigations from India and the USA* (London and New York: Routledge, 2010): 47–62. Both the journal and the edited volume are productions of Routledge Press, London.

David Page and Ruth Kirk-Wilson have always given me a home in London, alongside inspiring conversations on unbaked projects. I am grateful for their love, as I am for the new friendship with Sally and Bruce Cleghorn. Rita Costa Gomes is not only a "court friend," but a friend with whom I walk the various facets of American life, year after year, in inspiring ways. Rita, and Richard Semba, chef par excellence, my Baltimore friends, spoil me each year with sumptuous food, thrilling conversations and silent films, for which we write scripts as we savor many glasses of wine! Sue Hunter, my yoga and sushi friend, an Atlanta enthusiast, has generously shared her knowledge of the urban history of this city, my new home. Kiran and Ani Agnihotri, Joyce Flueckiger, Laurie Patton, Leslie Harris, Benny Hary and Martha Fineman are cherished Atlanta friends. Lois and Don Reitzes, Bobby and Leslee Paul, Lynne Huffer, Allan Sealy, William Dalrymple, Anish and Susan Mathai are friends one can only dream of – curious, enthusiastic, loving, unpretentious, secular intellectuals.

My sisters, Gudiya and Reena, and my brother-in-law, Prabhakar, have given me so much love that I wonder how I got so lucky. My nieces, Fanny, Aashna and Ananya, are the superstars of my life. Given how much affection, sheer joy and fun I have with them, it is not surprising that playfulness has become my fundamental intellectual engagement. My parents, Prabha and Manmohan, are delighted to see all their girls being themselves. I am grateful for their dignified acceptance of the ethos of modern times and I always look at them with admiration. I can hardly thank Gyan for his enthusiasm for the worlds I want to open up, his intellectual sympathy and love and companionship. I couldn't have written this book without the nurturing affection of my dear ones.

Ruby Lal
Atlanta, March 2012

Note on Transliteration, Translation and Citations

There is no standard practice of transliteration from Persian, Urdu and Devanagri to English.

For Urdu, I use the system practised by *The Annual of Urdu Studies* http://www.urdustudies.com/pdf/22/01TitleTranslit.pdf.

For Devanagri, I rely on the discussion on the conventions of Hindi and Urdu in the following volumes: Christopher Shackle and Rupert Snell, *Hindi and Urdu Since 1800: A Common Reader* (London, 1990); and R. S. McGregor, *The Oxford Hindi-English Dictionary* (New Delhi, 1993).

For Persian, I use a modified version of the IJMES (*International Journal of Middle East Studies*) system developed by Layla S. Diba and Maryam Ekhtiar for their edited volume, *Royal Persian Paintings: The Qajar Epoch, 1785–1925* (New York, 1998).

*I have chosen to omit all diacritical marks. For nonspecialists, this removes a source of visual distraction, making the text less cumbersome. The specialist, in any case, should have no difficulty in recognizing the Urdu, Hindi and Persian terms.

*I have retained the common English form of well-known places and persons.

*Original spellings have been retained in quotations. As a result certain names or places appear with two spellings: differently in citations and in my text.

*All translations of Urdu, Devanagri and Persian texts are mine unless indicated otherwise. I have made it a consistent practice to provide the reference to the available translation in English even where I have relied extensively on my own translation of texts.

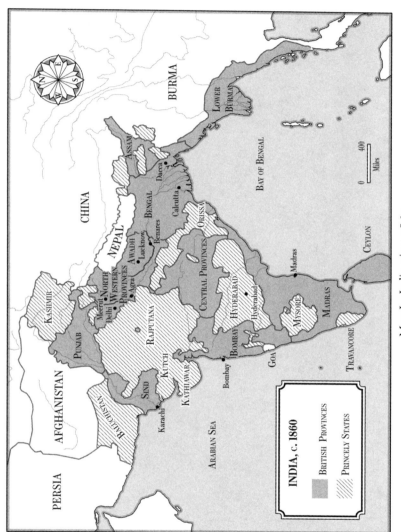

Map I. India, circa 1860.

Prelude

Opening the Door

In December 2004, I went to Lucknow and Barabanki in the company
of the renowned Urdu literary scholar and critic, C. M. Naim. My first
book had gone to press and I was beginning to explore ideas for a second book. The obvious sequel to my book on the early Mughal domestic world, indeed the demand of several colleagues and a number of
senior scholars, was that I write a second book on the later Mughals.
I decided, however, to break what I feared would be a simple chronological extension and perhaps a repetition of my argument, now trans-
posed to the structures (that I had already described) of the later, more
visibly imperial, architecturally and archivally accessible period of the
Grand Mughals. I knew I would certainly return to the Mughals at
some stage. I needed first, while continuing to explore feminine forms
and women's cultures, to challenge my own thinking by writing a book
about female figures and domestic life in a rather later period on the
brink of late Mughal and early colonial society. It was in this context
that I had sought out C. M. Naim.

Naim Saheb gave me the most wonderful feedback a young scholar
can dream of. Over the four days that I spent in his and his sister
Suraiya Masud's Barabanki home, he spoke to me at length about the
Hindi and Urdu literature of the nineteenth century and discussed the
spatial setting of respectable life in that time. He also took me to see
a number of other localities and respectable homes in the vicinity of

I

Barabanki. And then he brought up a name that was new to me, and suggested that it would be invaluable (the word he used was "critical") for me to speak with Azra Kidwai.

I found out that Azra Kidwai was the older sister of the noted historian and gay rights activist Saleem Kidwai. I had known Saleem for over a decade and had a professional-personal friendship with him. On our return to Delhi, Naim Saheb introduced me to Azra. When Azra and I began meeting, she was already aware of my friendship with Saleem, and my communication with her grew rapidly from there (I have seen Azra each winter since 2004, over extended periods in her Delhi home).[1]

In our first meeting itself I had the feeling of something special about my conversations with Azra. Here was a thoughtful and articulate interlocutor of the elite world I was interested in – although she is very much a twentieth-century woman, and the focus of my research is the nineteenth century. Statuesque and bold, she spoke clearly about her views. Our early exchanges were respectful, even a little formal – not the later, more sharing, affectionate and intimate ones that came with time and greater trust. Azra knew the earlier writing and research I had done and asked me about the work I wished to do. And she began working with me in a very organized, almost diligent fashion: drawing the very complicated kinship charts of the Kidwai family, explaining the relationships among the various branches of the family and simultaneously giving me a tender portrayal of her girlhood and womanhood.

Why Azra? A scholar, teacher, mother, who has lived in Delhi since her marriage in 1966, Azra was born in 1945 in an eminent, *sharif* (respectable) family of Paisar and Baragaon, aristocratic and landed groups on the outskirts of Lucknow in the modern province of Uttar Pradesh in northern India. The Kidwais are one of India's great

---

[1] With Azra's permission, I recorded all our conversations and took detailed notes. She spoke in a mixture of Urdu and English. All transcriptions and translations of the interviews are mine. Azra has seen all my writings related to this project. I have her permission to use her name in this prelude and in the book. The conversations cited above date between December 2004 and December 2010. This book project has been a central part of my discussions with Saleem, each time I met him in Delhi on various visits and again in December 2010 in Lucknow. He has also seen the two early pieces I have written on the subject of the girl-child and woman in the nineteenth century.

families: the Barabanki branch of the Kidwai family is known to have been present there since the eighteenth century.[2] The family has several branches – Baragaon, Daryabad, Gadia, Masauli and Jaggaur – and smaller ones in other villages. There were also twenty to twenty-five Kidwai Sufi saints.[3] The Baragaon family maintained close relations with the Farangi Mahall family of Lucknow, one of India's leading learned families.[4] Over the past two centuries, the Kidwais have produced many important politicians, lawyers, intellectuals and literati – men and women.

Azra was brought up in a highly literate environment, reading the literature and being educated in the models of the nineteenth-century and early-twentieth-century didactic books. As both a participant and an analyst of the literary and material worlds in which she has lived, she narrates her upbringing in the light of the ethical literature and well-defined spaces of the elite homes in which she grew to womanhood. Four years into our conversation, Azra told me that she had been writing a memoir in the form of a diary (still unpublished). For her, she said, our conversations were an extension of several issues that she had already been thinking through over the years. She added that my questions were hers.

In what follows, I draw on Azra's reminiscences in order to suggest how these become a compelling invitation for structuring the arguments of this book. Azra becomes a guiding voice, providing the framework of what follows in the subsequent chapters. This book is about the nineteenth century. And it is not my intention to extrapolate

---

[2] The Kidwais draw their lineage from Qazi Qidwa (Qidwa meaning "elevated" in Arabic). He is placed by some in the fifty-fourth generation of Adam and by others in the fifty-seventh. Qazi Qidwa traveled through Syria, Iraq, Bustan and Mawra-un-Nahr in Central Asia before arriving in Hindustan. Khwaja Muin-ud-Din Chishti, the famous Sufi saint, advised him to go to the province of Avadh to propagate Islam. The initial settlement of the Kidwais was in the Barabanki, Lucknow and Faizabad districts of Avadh – in the central portion of Uttar Pradesh. The present family of Baragaon started with the migration of Qazi Muhammad Aman (fifteenth generation from Qazi Qidwa) from Rasauli to Baragaon sometime in the eighteenth century. For these details and an extensive discussion including family charts, see Riaz-ur-Rahman Kidwai, *Biographical Sketch of Kidwais of Avadh: With Special Reference to Barabanki Families* (Aligarh, 1987), pp. 5, 6, 11, 14, 85.
[3] Ibid., pp. 49–84.
[4] For an excellent study of the Farangi Mahall, see Francis Robinson, *The `Ulama of Farangi Mahall and Islamic Culture in South Asia* (New Delhi, 2001).

from Azra's experiences and impose her feelings and responses on the nineteenth-century world.[5] Yet, her analysis alerts us to vital issues like the constraining role of physical spaces and the force of literary conventions in the making of a girl-child and a woman. Azra opens the door, as it were. Following her invitation, I chart a history of becoming woman through an exploration of diverse paradigmatic spaces, as well as a range of didactic literature, which I have called "lived" literature, since it has been in circulation for generations and is fundamental to the upbringing of respectable Muslim and Hindu girls from at least the latter half of the nineteenth century.

Another important aspect of my investigation has been an attempt to think through those dimensions of feminine lives and cultures that were nonexistent in my earlier conversations with Azra. There was no discussion, for example, of aspects of her life unrelated to domestic duties, anything tranquil and playful, until she heard me speak in 2009 at a workshop in Jamia Millia Islamia, Delhi, on the concept of "playfulness" (that is, resourcefulness, creativity and vision within confining arrangements). From then on, another narrative emerged in our conversation, almost a shadow discourse on pleasure and playful asides, close relationships and spontaneous, transgressive activities among women, very much a part of Azra's life. Following the 2009 interruption, and Azra's articulations, I have foregrounded the theme of playfulness in this book. My conceptual engagements with this and other themes will be clarified in the next chapter.

Although this prelude is written in an ethnographic mode, based on conversations with Azra spread over five years, beginning in December 2005, it must be emphasized (as Azra also put it to me) that Azra has already done the analysis that I present here. The frame and the narration is hers. What I wish to suggest is that part of what is implied in such a manner of history writing – where women (Azra and I) in the present hold the keys for the readings of the past that follow in the book – is that we challenge habits of historical narration in which we are chronologically bound. In the received disciplinary practice, the criss-crossing of chronological divisions (the nineteenth century, the early twentieth

---

[5] I am grateful to Barbara Metcalf for an extended discussion on the importance of this prelude for the book. And to David Lelyveld, who encouraged me to break chronological boundaries in thinking about women's worlds in our first conversation in New York City as I began exploring the nineteenth-century feminine worlds.

century, the late twentieth century, the twenty-first century and so on), and the hypothetical different historical-cultural ethics of different times, to understand particular historical moments and figures, is not generally accepted. It is not within the domain of the general academic practice to challenge conventional periodization: to argue that a person in the present, as in the historical past, has ways in which s/he opens and shuts worldviews both of the past and the present, and that their views become the legitimate grounds for writing a historical past.[6] The way we think today, I argue, constitutes the past; it is not only the past that constitutes us. Hence the case for Azra's and my collaborative work.

On many occasions, Azra has said to me that it is because of me that she thinks back to her childhood. Azra is my accomplice who enables me to countersign the origins of a history in which women were rendered "nameless," in which they played but were taught not to play. Thus, the example of playfulness (creativity, almost an art of taking initiative within restrictive circumstances and domains) in a range of paradigmatic physical spaces (the forest, the school, the household, the rooftops) becomes a central trope in this book as I explore the

---

[6] Audre Lorde's call in *Sister Outsider* to employ non-master's ways of knowing, so to speak, has been quite central to my thinking as has been the case with a major strand of feminist methodology; Audre Lorde, *Sister Outsider: Essays and Speeches by Audre Lorde* (Berkeley, 1984; rpt. 2007). In a review of the field for the journal *Signs*, Patti Lather locates feminist ethnography alongside the emergence of the literary turn in the 1980s and concerns about reflexivity, textuality and a questioning of the disciplinary boundaries of history. Lather describes feminist methodology as seeking "counterpractices of knowing in personal voices, archival resources such as diaries and journals, dialogic and interactive interview formats, reflexivity regarding interpretive imposition, practices such as cowriting." Patti Lather, "Postbook: Working the Ruins of Feminist Ethnography," *Signs*, Vol. 27, No. 1 (Autumn 2001), p. 203. There have been several other debates. For example, Ruth Behar's *Translated Woman: Crossing the Border with Esperanza's Story* (Boston, 1993), where she claimed to record a Mexican street peddler named Esperanza's story "in her own words." This of course raised the important question, *a la* Spivak, "Can the Subaltern Speak?" And further, critically, can a feminist scholar record the story of a subaltern subject? This issue was taken up in feminist ethnographies that concerned the problem of power imbalances and thinking through experimental writings. Kamala Visweswaran's *Fictions of Feminist Ethnography* (Minneapolis, 1994) is invested in charting how each new epistemic ground signals a new direction, in other words, how feminist ethnography's failures are in fact "productive." Visweswaran asks us to pay attention to women scholars' work with ethnographic dialogues and their difficulties as important strategies. Taking up Laura Bohannon's notion of ethnographer as trickster, Visweswaran conceptualizes the feminist ethnographer as a "trickster ethnographer" who knows she cannot master the dialogical hope of speaking with nor the colonial hope of speaking for; Visweswaran, *Fictions of Feminist Ethnography*, p. 100.

simultaneity of constraint, wisdom and desire in girls and women. Azra's explorations, and by extension, our social formations (Azra's and mine), become framing devices in the investigation of respectable, modern Indian womanhood and of feminine cultures. Azra's life, and her telling of it, provides an arc that enables me to think about the place and production of girl-child and woman in the nineteenth century – giving clues to an understanding of the past and of our present in complex and deeply contested ways.[7]

For the nineteenth-century northern Indian world of the girl-child/woman that my book focuses on, pictures of this "other life" of the girl-child and woman emerge in the popular tales in circulation, in the didactic texts, pamphlets, novels and manuals of comportment that sketched out the models to which women were meant to aspire. Azra grew up reading several of these books, and while her specific interpretations – in her girlhood and today – are obviously significant, and I turn to these later, another equally significant point comes through in her discussion of literary texts. "The world of books gave me access to worlds outside my own," she said at one point. "Unwittingly my father gave me these books [although it was her mother who handed them to her]. My horizon grew from there. Some kind of idealism was created." "Unwittingly," Azra's father gave her the clues to think and interpret the world for herself, but the deliberations, translations and inferences were Azra's.

---

[7] Several historical writings have informed the writing of this book. The literature from South Asia will be discussed at length in the historiographical section of Chapter 1. On the making of women in the Muslim world, and practices and ethics of ethnography, there is now a vast literature. See the following works as important examples: Cynthia Nelson, "Public and Private Politics: Women in the Middle Eastern World," *American Ethnologist*, Vol. 1, No. 3 (August 1974); Fatima Mernissi, *Beyond the Veil: Male-Female Dynamics in a Modern Muslim Society* (Cambridge, MA, 1975); Lois Beck and Nikkie Keddie (eds.), *Women in the Muslim World* (Cambridge, 1978); Soraya Altorki and Camilla El-Solh, *Arab Women in the Field* (Syracuse, 1988); Lila Abu-Lughod, *Veiled Sentiments: Honor and Poetry in a Bedouin Society* (Berkeley and Los Angeles, 1999, 2nd edn.); Lila Abu-Lughod, *Writing Women's Worlds: Bedouin Stories* (Berkeley and Los Angeles, 1993); My debt to the anthropologists writing a range of impressive ethnographies on South Asia is great, and it is impossible to cite all the accounts that have informed my work. I am grateful to Visweswaran, *Fictions of Feminist Ethnography* and Gloria Goodwin Raheja and Ann Grodzins Gold, *Listen to the Heron's Words: Reimagining Gender and Kinship in North India* (Berkeley, 1994), among many other important volumes.

Azra's recounting of her experiences makes palpable several registers of "namelessness," a term used by the great Urdu writer Qurratulain Hyder in an interview she gave me on January 20, 2007. Azra arranged this meeting and was with me during the conversation. "Don't forget. Make this a central proposition of your work," Hyder said to me. "It's a deep feminist point. *Naam ka pardah tha*; at this time there was a veiling of names. Women were nothing but mother of such and such, wife of such and such." It was over a period of five years of interviewing Azra that I began to appreciate the multiplicitous character of namelessness that Qurratulain Hyder had invoked and that Azra had unfolded in her poignant recollections of a burdensome girlhood.

Through much of the late 1940s when Azra was growing up, her father was her chief instructor. What she read, what languages were important for her education and maturity, and even how she dressed, what she cooked, what her responsibilities were: much of this was decided by him. The responsibilities apart from keeping up with her school curriculum were steady: looking after her younger siblings, the management of cooking, sewing and knitting. Standing testimony to how respectable girlhood is produced. In Azra's extraordinary descriptions of the girl-child she was not, we find her father conjuring up the world that *he* wanted.

What also emerged in Azra's narration is that the world that the patriarch designed, however, opened up in unexpected ways. The abstract blueprints for women's lives, articulated by and for the convenience of the male, could never take away the life of the woman. Despite the order and regime of how a woman must conduct herself, there were spaces that a man could not access. In Azra's plays and games, in her interactions with other women, in her reading and thinking, in her anguish, in the physical separation of spaces between men and women, things were ordered in ways subtly or markedly different from ideal (male) prescriptions. There is a sense of another life, not outside the patriarchal demands and prescriptions, but within the confines of the social and familial structures, a non-male trace (even in the invocations and characterizations of male authors) of the more "undisciplined" life of the girl-child and woman that Azra leads us to consider.

Two kinds of images pervade Azra's narration. One is spatial. She constantly refers to her four "homes": the apartment in Lucknow where she spent a large part of her girlhood; Baragaon (the paternal, ancestral house of a *Zamindari* or landlord family), and Paisar (the maternal, ancestral home of a *Taluqdari* family, part of a historically distinguished landed gentry, more aristocratic in demeanor and wealth than the Zamindars of the region) where she went during her summer vacations; and Matia Mahal, the mansion in Old Delhi where she went as a young bride. Azra's homes and the spirit of the four settings in which she lived enliven for us the different stages of her life. A second continual presence in Azra's recollections is the models of praiseworthy life drawn from literary texts and ethical digests that were repeatedly cited to her. "*Tum Akbari banna chahti ho ya Asghari?* You want to be like Akbari or Asghari?" she was asked, for example, in reference to the exemplars of Nazir Ahmad's famous book, the *Mirat al-`Arus* (*The Bride's Mirror*, 1868–9).

In both the spatial and the textual ordering of Azra's world, one gets a visceral feel for the place of nineteenth-century literature and didacticism in the life of a *sharif* family and woman in the mid-twentieth century that I analyze in the section entitled "Living Creatures in my Mind." This goes alongside and frames Azra's everyday life: how she set about the tasks she had to accomplish each day (besides keeping up with her school work), what she made of the books she was asked to read (the models were constantly displayed for her), what games she could play (different in Baragaon, in Paisar and in Lucknow), the spaces she inhabited and the intimacies and friendships she forged. I follow Azra's recollections on the importance of spaces and moments of pleasure in the sections entitled "Spaces Become Your Universe" and "The Pleasures of Paisar." I have chosen to detail Azra's telling under these three headings in order to remain faithful to her conceptions and the separations she makes in emphasizing what she calls "time and space" on one hand and "literary invocations" on the other when speaking about her life. However, the spatial and the textual cannot be separated in any strict sense of the term: in Azra's and in my analysis, these overlap and inform each other. These discussions are followed by a set of concluding thoughts in which I reflect on the invitation that Azra gives us though a construction of her life.

"SPACES BECOME YOUR UNIVERSE"

"We were a big family in a big house. We were a big family in a small house." Azra describes succinctly how her family and space were linked in Barabanki and Lucknow. Speaking about Lucknow and her girl-hood, she says, "Physical spaces produce childhoods: from the front yard (*ghar ka baraamda*) to the shops and shopkeepers of Hazratganj to the boundary of my school. I recall the tamarind tree in my school, and picking up tamarind. Between classes four and eight, I had the same place in the class room. I could see the playground, I could see the clock tower and the post office. I didn't have a wrist watch."

Alongside this opening on her girlhood, Azra puts what she calls "invocations of the past" by her mother, Ruqayya, which had "great significance (*ahmiyat*)" for her: "There were invocations of the past all the time, wherever we went. My mother would always be saying (on visits to Paisar), 'this was our [Ruqayya's] father's English drawing room.' 'This settee (*takht*) has an enormous value for us; each evening our mother [Azra's grandmother] used to sit here. Boxes of betel leaves would be prepared, water would be sprayed on this settee.' 'Where the goats are now kept, this used to be the quarter of my *ustani* (teacher).'" Azra explains: "I am living back in time. I am imagining the grandeur of my mother's time. How do I narrate? Only by going back in time."

Azra goes back: remembering different generations, their ways and how "spaces designed life and consciousness," as she put it. "Spaces become your universe," she said on one occasion. She asked me to con-sider this: "two generations living in two different times – in one space." Azra explains: "my mother had a much more aristocratic upbringing. She was a *taluqdar* [aristocratic landlord]'s daughter, the fifth of nine children. There were three or four women to teach and look after her. Her training was left to Bua (a caretaker) and others [Bua – a term of kinship referring to the father's sister – was central in the upbringing of Azra's mother, Azra and her siblings and then Azra's two sons]. Bua came with my mother's trousseau. Bua's mother, one of five girls, was bought by my family in 1857. She never took any salary, never sat close to any of us; yet, she had close ties with us. After my marriage, she came to Delhi with me. She said she would leave my door only after her death. And she did. She died on 1st January 1986."

"From this [aristocratic life]," Azra continues the life story of her mother, "my mother shifted to a [relatively] humble establishment. Cooking, stitching. But she never complained. *That* was part of the training [Azra's emphasis]." In giving glimpses of the lifestyle of her parents' generation, Azra begins to dwell on the ethics of their generation, at the center of which was her father. "Father, brother, husband: a woman was supposed to be under their protection." Clearly implied in the histories of the older generation and its ways was a statement on how boys and girls must be brought up, how they must behave, what they should and should not do – all of this differently from each other.

This is what Azra means by "two generations" living in "two different times in the same space." The males of one generation laid down the tracks of life and insisted that the next generation behave exactly in line with the commands of the first. The women and girls of the second generation were followers and the older women the carriers of these directions: "My father insisted on my cooking from very early on. *'Hisaab ki kaapi dikhao'* [show me the accounts], he would ask all the time. *Itni Badi*: a term that used to be in my consciousness way before I went to High School. I had to bathe and dress two younger sisters and a brother. Hugging, kissing for me came much later. They were part of the boys' domain (*vo ladkon ke hisse ki cheezein thee*)."

Itni Badi is the phrase that Azra Kidwai recalled repeatedly when we began our first conversation on December 14, 2005. Her father used the phrase to describe Azra even before she went to high school, stressing not a girl's growth (*itni badi*, literally meaning "so big"), but more significantly the physical maturity that is deemed dangerous. And with the threat of the sheer physicality of the becoming woman came a whole host of constraining and disciplining measures, expressed in the emphasis laid on her being a *sharif* (respectable) girl, required to perform the part of a *sharif* woman, which included distinct responsibilities and distinctly gendered ways of behaving from a very early stage in life.

On the gendering of honor, Azra says: "the male [child] is the heir to the family. Tradition, prestige – all of this has to be expressed in the power that the male exercises. Mother and children form one unit, with distinctions between the male and the female [children]. The girl is the most fragile as far as the honor and name of the family are concerned. The fear of dishonor and loss of name [prestige]: in and outside the family. She must be a proper embodiment of all values. Men are cocooned: dishonor in relation to them can be covered."

The structure of the Lucknow apartment where Azra spent her girlhood is instructive for the ways in which the spaces themselves were organized to preserve the principles of respectable (gendered) ways. "It was a rented flat with two rooms and a small gallery in between. Kitchen with asbestos sheets on it, at one end of the gallery. Outside was an open space with a tap: here we kept a stove on one side. One room was given to a male and a female cousin and their mother [the female cousin was two months younger than Azra]. The second room, one bathroom and a latrine was for Ammi [mother] and us [Azra, her two sisters, two brothers, of whom the older has passed away]. There was a second flat: a flat wall divided the first flat from the second, a window broken open between the two. This second flat had the same lay-out as the first. Here, one was my father's room. The other was the drawing room. The dog also stayed here and often littered the front yard of this flat. Mother would sleep in father's flat once a week. It was only later that we shifted to our own house on Shah Najaf Road." Strikingly, Azra's narration never dwells on the house on Shah Najaf Road. This apartment does not exist anymore. The building in which it was located is now a commercial establishment.

The space allotted to one man equaled the space given to several women and children: "one whole flat for my father, and one for us," says Azra. In the first flat, in Azra's mother's room, stood a bed and a divan. In the gallery that connected the two rooms was another divan for Bua to sleep on. "There was no bedroom, but multi-purpose rooms. Few people used to go to the drawing room, except Abbu's [father's] friends who listened to the radio. We were not allowed to listen to film songs on the radio. We could listen to the radio, but not while Abbu was around.[8] No concept of dining rooms. No space for it in the flat. Our activities were confined to this limited space. The needs

---

[8] Growing up in the late 1940s, Fatima Mernissi, a Moroccan feminist scholar, points out that the women of the haram and the girl-children were not allowed to listen to the radio. Men and boys listened to the radio in their quarters and when the men went out, on several occasions, the women stole the radio and enjoyed listening to it. Fatima Mernissi, *Dreams of Trespass: Tales of Harem Girlhood* (Reading, MA, 1994), p. 7. I discuss *Dreams of Trespass* in the last chapter.

Photo 1. Azra Kidwai, with her mother and father in the Lucknow flat, pre-1958. Reprinted with permission from Azra Kidwai.

of childhood were accommodated by this space. In the summer, the rooms were emptied out for us to play: cards, ludo, monopoly, carrom board. And in the open yard, we played marbles, cricket, and spinning the top. There was hopscotch and skipping. But we were not allowed where the boys flew kites." All this, so different from Paisar, her maternal home.[9] As she put it poignantly: "*Vahan ke palang khaskaye nahin jaate the*: the beds there were not shifted [unlike in the Lucknow apartment where different rooms acquired a different character according to the moment's requirements]."

[9] The Paisar mansion was built by Azra's maternal grandfather. Soon after the death of the grandfather, Azra says that the house was divided among the families of his four sons, two of whom died in the lifetime of their father. These sons were survived by their widows and a daughter as well as a son of Azra's mother's uncle (father's brother), who was married to Azra's aunt (mother's sister). The splendid mansion housed five families, but with very little interaction. There were continuous property disputes between them, which remain unsolved to this day. Azra's mother kept good relations with all her relatives. Azra says, "We were equally welcome in all homes. I spent the time with three of my cousins, one my age and two a little older, and that friendship still continues though each one of us is living a very different life."

The summer of 1958, when Azra visited Baragaon, her great-grandfather's house, is a momentous time in her telling. She was thirteen. Before detailing the events that transpired that summer, let me provide a brief indication of the setting. Baragaon is an enormous aristocratic estate (in Barabanki district), thirty miles or so from Lucknow, with four splendidly kept residential sections divided among four brothers of Azra's great-grandfather: Azra calls it a "big family in a big house."[10] There are some sections in the *haveli* (mansion) that Azra did not see until the wedding of her younger son that took place there in December 2003: the *mardaana hissa* (the male section) was a part that Azra was not allowed in at all.

As children, while Azra stayed in her great-grandfather's portion, she and her cousins often went from one section of the *haveli* to another, playing about. Usually, Azra went across from an inner passage and over the rooftop, but "it was very complicated." This is what happened one day in the summer of 1958. "So I was going from my great-grandfather's house to the other. I went out and then went into the other house. Not alone, there were cousins too. My father was sitting out in the lawn with his uncles and other people of the village. He saw us going from one house to the other. There was no *dupatta* [stole] on my head, yet. After we went back to Lucknow, my father told my mother, 'These girls are shameless (*Besharm ho gayi hain ladkiyan*). They go to schools in tunic. They do not realize that the people of the village were sitting. Just came out and went from one house to another. Take them out immediately from Christchurch and send them

---

[10] As you enter through the gate of the Baragaon haveli, you see a semicircular, imposing building divided into four residential sections: these four independent households belonged to the descendants of Azra's paternal great-grandfather and his brothers. Azra belongs to, in her words, "the fourth generation of the founding father, and my husband is the great-grandson of the eldest of the four brothers." One family of each descendant lived in Baragaon, but during summer holidays and for marriages all relatives living in different parts of India came together. They were housed and hosted in the household of their ancestor. This congregation brought together kids and adults of all ages, for instance, in Azra's age group of female cousins there were six of them who "managed to have a good time together. We mixed freely with male cousins, but were not permitted to play outdoor games with the male cousins outside the house. We were permitted to go with them to the farm house of our grand uncle, and spend time playing cards and other indoor games. It was here that older cousins organized picnics and concerts." I have visited all the homes of Azra, except the Lucknow apartment that does not exist any longer. I have included the information in this and the previous footnote at Azra's request made in an e-mail dated June 20, 2011 that Azra sent me after reading this prelude.

to Karamat Husain. They will only realize when their attire [*libaas*] changes. Going to school with bare legs!"

Until then, Azra had gone to a Christian missionary school, Christchurch: upon her return to Lucknow, she was put in Karamat Husain College, where a more formal Urdu and "Islamic" education was mandatory. The affairs of the home that Azra had to manage kept increasing, not to mention the embroidery and stitching. Her father insisted she cook and run the general household affairs as well. He would go out hunting, kill the birds and small animals and then organize parties. He demanded that Azra cook particular dishes. At one point, Azra was getting ready to take her board exams (a critical annual exam in Class XII, the last year of senior high school, which was the gateway for admission to an undergraduate college), and he asked that Azra cook "raspberry mince and meat." Her mother suggested, "Don't ask her. Her exams are on. I'll cook." He replied: "Has she gone mad? Just because her exams are on, she won't cook? I'll pull them out of the school if they show such guts."

In 1959, Azra's father insisted that she wear a *burqa*. "Till she wears the *burqa*, she will not recognize what honor and shame is (*sharm-o-haya*)." Later Azra wanted to drive; she was told, "Do it with a *burqa*." She did, accompanied by Bua and the woman friend who taught her how to drive. In recounting these incidents over and over again, Azra notes: "Before [my] marriage, time moved slowly. From college onwards the movement [of time] was rapid." The slowness of the time that Azra speaks about is also articulated, as she says, in "not having much sense of time." Much of her girlhood and young adulthood was spent in everyday chores, what she also calls "tedious responsibility, routine, same kind of life [day after day]." Each day, this is what Azra did: writing the household accounts, measuring ingredients to be given to the cook, distributing food to the servants – all this besides cooking herself and keeping up with her school curriculum. And cooking was no fun: the spices had to be ground freshly every day; the cooking itself was done on a coal stove. Azra got a gas stove only after her marriage. Besides, she was asked to read the Quran whenever she had any spare time, "as part of the duty to others. For parents, for *barakat* (blessings)."

Two different spaces, both in the patriarchal realm, encouraging different possibilities: Azra becoming a woman variously in these spaces.

Photo 2. Azra Kidwai, dressed for a play, Karamat Husain College, 1959/60. Reprinted with permission from Azra Kidwai.

The Lucknow apartment brought duties, more and more chores and monotony. And constant recrimination: "Disgraceful! Where are you going? *Dupatta*? [A wrap thrown over the upper body] Have you no shame jumping about?" "These naked legs; you've been made shameless." Azra enjoyed whistling. She was stopped. A friend saw Azra's hands laden with flour. "What, were you playing with flour?" she asked Azra. "No. I was helping Bua cook." Despite the constraints and the smallness of space, there was enriching proximity: "lack of privacy creates intimacy. Sleeping next to your mother, your sister. Production of attachment when guests come. Beds are shared. How these held my world! I cannot imagine how we lived in such a small space," Azra muses. "And then we went to a bigger home. There were bigger spaces, but my world was the same."

In Baragaon, where the saga of the change of school and the demand to keep herself "covered" arose, girls and women had to stay away from older men and from where boys would be playing cricket. For Azra, Paisar, her maternal home, remains a space of freedom where she experienced the "pleasures" of girlhood. Playing, running, chatting. And the games were different too: "we made tamarind cakes. We played on the swings all day long. Then there were *budkuniyan*: 'little-little' utensils to cook food in. There was an annual picnic in the mango grove. We kids recited poetry; we danced. The family [women] was the audience, we the performers. In spending long holidays together, there was a lot of bonding between women and girls."

In the third space that is central to Azra's recounting – her marital home, Matia Mahal in Old Delhi where she came as a young bride – she speaks about a sense of uncertainty and constraint to begin with: she had to adjust to new hierarchies and arrangements, but there was a feeling of this "rapid movement" of time as well. "A life, I never imagined I could have," says Azra almost nostalgically. Azra's husband descended from the same familial ancestor as she. Of the four main lines that came from the ancestor of Baragaon, Azra's husband descended from the first brother and Azra from the second (Azra and her husband are first cousins as is common in many respectable Muslim circles). She explains how her marriage was arranged: "As a good daughter, I knew I would abide by the choice of my parents. Wherever they married me, I would agree. But when it happened, it was very strange. My feeling was very different from what my mind was saying. It was at that time, I suddenly recognized myself." Further: "I felt I was selected for marriage on the basis of objective criteria: sewing, knitting, speaking English – a 'good girl' label." As it happened, she married an open-minded young man who did not want her to wear the *burqa*. A man with whom she built life in unexpected ways, with an air of freedom, but within the constraints of the familial and household traditions, furthering her education while rearing and bringing up her children – and now her grandchildren.

Azra arrived in Matia Mahal after her marriage in 1966. To imagine the setting of the still splendidly kept Matia Mahal, we have to direct our imagination to what seventeenth-century Delhi might have been like. This was the capital of the Mughal emperor, Shahjahan, builder of Shahjahanabad (the walled city in present-day Old Delhi) and the Taj Mahal. Stephen Blake provides an instructive account of this setting:

> The cityscapes of Shahjahanabad ... were dominated by the palaces and mansions of the emperors and their nobles. The imperial palace fortresses were enormous structures, covering between 125 and 2,700 acres... In addition to the household troops of the emperor, they held merchants, artisans, servants, poets, painters, musicians, clerks, and administrators ... [also] workshops, stables, stores, treasuries, state records, mints and weapons. They were the most important neighborhoods or quarters ... and set the pattern for the mansions of princes and nobles. The residential complexes of the great men ordered the urban system, the palace-fortress directing the life of the city as a whole and the noble mansions the affairs of their sectors.[11]

Matia Mahal is one among the different kinds of noble mansions that Blake discusses, located behind a complex of lanes specializing in particular goods – women flatbread sellers (*nan baiyon walan*), bangle sellers (*chudi walan*) and so on – across from the Jama Masjid. Onion pink in color, the mansion has a regal entrance made of a carved wooden door. The entrance leads to the first floor with several rooms devoted to an education center called Balak Mata Center. An adult education center, this was started by Azra's mother-in-law, a devout propagator of women's education, who after years of hardship on account of her husband's early death eventually became a member of the Delhi Legislative Council and was then nominated as a member of the Rajya Sabha (the upper house of the Indian parliament). The school was later maintained and supervised by Azra's husband's aunt (married to his mother's brother), fondly called Dammi (short form of *dulhan-ammi*, the bride-mother) by the family, who was also invested in Muslim women's education and was later elected to the Delhi Corporation and the All India Congress Committee. It was she who was in charge of the Balak Mata Center when Azra arrived there.

The second floor of the Matia Mahal is reached by a stone staircase adjacent to the left-hand side of the entrance. The second floor has

[11] Stephen P. Blake, *Shahjahanabad: The Sovereign City in Mughal India 1639–1739* (Cambridge and New York, 1993), p. xiii. See also, Eckart Ehlers and Thomas Krafft (eds.), *Shahjahanabad/Old Delhi: Traditions and Colonial Change* (New Delhi, 1993, 2nd edn.). Azra's husband, Urdu literary critic Sadiq-ur-Rahman Kidwai, discussed the spatial setting of Matia Mahal with me after our visit there in January 2008.

three beautiful rooms on one side: in front of these runs a narrow gallery from which one can view the ground floor and the goings-on of the school children. (The central space of the mansion is an open space: courtyard at the ground level and the sky above, and intricately carved buildings on the four sides). Tucked away in another corner of the second floor is another large room, where Azra spent the first six months of her married life. Adjoining this room is a narrow spiral staircase that leads to the highest room on the terrace, where Dammi lived.

"It was a cultural shock," says Azra. When she arrived in Matia Mahal, she was decorated with a garland of rupees. Her room was decorated with new utensils. "Wherever I went [in the lanes and by-lanes of Old Delhi], children of the streets would follow me. That's when I missed my *burqa*," she says. "Matia Mahal was exposed. People looked at me with curiosity. I used to be surrounded by people. 'So, here you are.' 'What is this you're wearing?' 'You have come from Lucknow?' 'What is this?'" She continues: "Until the excitement died, it was difficult to handle the attention." The atmosphere of the *mohalla* (an old urban neighborhood with closely knit residences, connected by rooftops, set in a maze of market lanes) was different from anything she had envisioned before. There were "songs all through the night, sounds of the `azan from the mosque, so many sounds of conversations, steps of people going in and out ... there was a workshop that made the frames of reading glasses. I could hear frames being moved on the table, individually and several together, *khad-khad, khadadadadad*." At the same time, the young bride Azra was taken to be an expert in cooking from the word go. Dammi, who was always involved in the activities of the Balak Mata Center, would just "give orders": "Azra do make *suji halva*."

Here was Azra, living in Matia Mahal in Old Delhi. No more *burqa*, and her husband suggesting they meet for movies. "'Meet me at the Odeon,' he would say. 'Where is the Odeon?' I would ask. 'Near Connaught Place.' 'How will I get there?' 'Take a bus,' he would say. I had never sat in a bus in Lucknow. 'Take a scooter [three-wheeler],' he would say." Azra recalls: "New roads, new atmosphere, new people. Without a *burqa*, something was missing. I used to feel naked, as if completely exposed (*jaise exposed hain bilkul*)." She did meet her husband for films, and went with him to music concerts. Sometimes they saw two films in a day during the film festivals. She continued

Photo 3. Azra Kidwai, early 1970s. Reprinted with permission from Azra Kidwai.

her university education and commuted to Delhi University, changing buses at the Red Fort, a couple of miles from Matia Mahal. Later, she taught in a college; she wrote; she researched. "Good times," she says, recalling the early years of her marriage.

"LIVING CREATURES IN MY MIND"

"The Old culture had a model way for training their children." Even before Azra was sent to Karamat Husain College in 1958 for formal education in Urdu, she explains, she had already learned Urdu and recited the Quran regularly at home. Three things were central to Urdu learning at home: *aamukhta* (yesterday's lesson), *sabak* (lesson), and `imla* (dictation). Azra was asked to read the Surah-al Ya Sin and Surah-al Rahman, the thirty-sixth and fifty-fifth Surat respectively from the Quran. Ya Sin is read especially in the mornings, or when there's a difficult situation, or simply for *barakat* (blessings). The main purpose of reciting the Rahman is to give manifestation to Allah's mercy and grace, evident from the beginning until the end. Reading the Quran was, she was told, "part of the duty to others. For parents, for *barakat*." By the time her siblings were growing up, the emphasis that her father laid on this kind of training was reduced.

"Boys read the Quran too, but they could take liberties," Azra clarifies. "Girls were treated more strictly. Their [boys'] achievements were applauded. The reading and training and upbringing of boys and girls were different. There were different responsibilities. The difference was emphasized constantly." Azra recalls how partial their governess (an English woman named Linda Ohern) was towards her younger brother. Azra also found her mother inclining in favor of her sons. At one point Azra's mother was very ill. When she started to recover, she called out to her dead son and then to her younger son. Azra was astonished and said to her mother: "You are only remembering your sons; even in your subconscious!" Azra felt "dismissed." "Just like that," she says. In addition, "I used to be scared that [all the time] I'll get scolded. What will Abbu [father] say?"

The magazines, books and novels that Azra read set the terms for her behavior: what she was supposed to do, what kind of woman she was supposed to become. The ideal women of these texts were always quoted for her: the "good" heroines were literate, good cooks, excellent account keepers and house managers, clean and healthy. Azra was surrounded by these lessons: other women were reading the same literature and discussing the episodes and characters familiar to many generations.[12]

---

[12] Azra's mother read several of the books that she then reread with Azra, which I discuss above. Her favorite, however, was A. R. Khatoon's *Shama*. A 'social novel,' it was an Urdu best seller of the early twentieth century and was very popular among several generations of Muslim women in north India. A. R. Khatoon pioneered a genre of fiction dominated by women characters. In *Shama*, the main story is that of the protagonist Shama's struggle to keep her independence despite many odd and sad turns in her life. The story also focuses on Shama's father, who as a single parent did not want wealth to be the only inheritance for Shama. Set in the 1930s, it is the story of an extended family's transition from rural to urban Uttar Pradesh, accompanying a new professional lifestyle. The questions that were fundamental to Shama's family at this time were women's education, *purdah* and appropriate social behavior, vital issues also in Azra's family. Saleem Kidwai has just finalized a translation of this book. Saleem Kidwai (tr.), A. R. Khatoon, *Shama* (New Delhi, forthcoming).

As a girl, Azra read the following magazines, mostly concerned with the education and training of children: *Khilona* (*Toy*), *Kaliyan* (*Buds*), *Gulcha* (*Bouquet*), *Phool* (*Flower*). The titles of these children's magazines are indicative of the need to mold children (particularly impressionable at this stage in life) in precise ways. While Azra was reading these Urdu magazines, her younger brother was reading English books. He also read Urdu books, such as the stories of the Prophet, entitled *Pyaare Nabi ki Pyaari Batain*; stories about Noah's Ark, Hazrat Isa and Ibrahim, and so on. But "the models of behavior" urged on him did not necessarily come from books. "For men, what mattered was hunting [*shikar*], driving, dogs and dog shows. And temper, expression of annoyance, was only allowed to men. Men's anger was legitimized, tolerated, pampered [all words in English are Azra's]." Azra captures the atmosphere (*maahaul*) of the familial at this time in one word: *zamindarana* (feudal), which implied calling servants with authority (*hukm se naukar ko pukaarna*) and an authoritative style (what she calls *authoritative lehja*).

The books that Azra read time after time – as her mother had – were Nazir Ahmad's *Mirat al-'Arus* (*The Bride's Mirror*), composed in 1869, and the *Banat-un-Na'sh* (*The Daughters of the Bier*, a name for the constellation of Ursa Major), composed in 1872. C. M. Naim makes the point that these books formed "a syllabus for the instruction of women" for Nazir Ahmad: *Mirat al-'Arus* for teaching household arts (*umur i khanadari*) and *Banat un-Na'sh* for teaching useful facts (*ma'lumat i dururi*).[13] Of all the books that Azra read, she says, characters from these two became "living creatures in my mind."

The story of *Mirat* centers on two sisters named Akbari (the great one) and Asghari (the small one), these names being an efficient device in Nazir Ahmad's building of his ideal woman character. Akbari is never great; Asghari becomes great in her everyday, wise acts. The author marks Akbari's unsuitability for respectable married life by showing

---

[13] C. M. Naim, "Prize Winning Adab: A Study of Five Urdu Books Written in Response to the Allahabad Government Gazette Notification," in Barbara D. Metcalf (ed.) *Moral Conduct and Authority: The Place of Adab in South Asian Islam* (Berkeley, 1984), p. 300. The third book in this set, *Taubat an-Nasuh* was meant for teaching piety (*khuda parasti*), which I discuss in Chapter 5 along with the other two listed here.

her *behunari* (lack of talent) and *badmizaji* (ill-temperedness),[14] her disrespectful attitude in relation to her mother-in-law and sister-in-law and her persistent engagements with the younger women of the *mohalla* (neighborhood) who were not from *sharif* families. By contrast, Asghari is shown to be gifted with *hunar aur saliqa* (talent and proficiency), *adab* (good comportment), *qa`ida* (the right way) and *nekdili* (kindness), and is lauded for keeping her family together.[15] She has a courteous association with her mother-in-law and is an efficient household manager. She never mixes with the lower-class women of the neighborhood, but she does educate the girls of the *mohalla*. Asghari, already set as an example, and her sister-in-law Mehmooda, both educating the girls of the neighborhood, thinking about a curriculum for life, as it were, is what Nazir Ahmad narrates beautifully in his *Banat-un-Na`sh*.[16]

Akbari, the argumentative, hot-tempered, badly behaved figure of the *Mirat* was often cited when Azra did not behave well. "*Phir tumne Akbari ki batain kin?*" ("Again you behaved like Akbari"), she was told by her father on many occasions. Her mother asked on several occasions: "*To tum yeh banna chahti ho ya ye?* Would you like to be this or that?" [invoking Akbari and Asghari].

Gudar ka Lal: Khawateen aur Ladkiyon ke liye ek Naseehatkhez Novel (*Ruby in Rags: A Novel with Advice for Women and Girls*) by Akbari Begum (d. 1929), published in 1907[17] often given in marriage as part of brides' dowries, is another novel that Azra recalls reading, although the characters of this book do not seem to have as prominent a space in her recollections as do Nazir Ahmad's Akbari and

---

[14] I use the following Urdu edition of this text: Nazir Ahmad, *Kulliyat-e Diptee Nazir Ahmad* (Lahore, 2004); hereafter, Mirat Urdu edn. All translations are mine unless otherwise stated; Mirat Urdu edn., p. 65. Maulvi Nazir Ahmad, *The Bride's Mirror, Mirat ul-`Arus: A Tale of Life in Delhi a hundred years ago*, G. E. Ward (tr.), (New Delhi, 2001). Hereafter, *The Bride's Mirror*.

[15] These are the adjectives with which Asghari is introduced in the *Mirat*, qualities with which she subsequently manages most affairs of her married life, as the author demonstrates. Mirat Urdu edn., p. 98.

[16] I use the following Urdu edition of this text: Nazir Ahmad, *Kulliyat-e Diptee Nazir Ahmad* (Lahore, 2004); hereafter, Banat Urdu edn. All translations are mine.

[17] Akbari Begum was the *momani* (wife of maternal uncle) of Nazr Sajjad Hyder, mother of the well-known Urdu writer Qurratulain Hyder. She wrote *Godar ka Lal* under the pseudonym of Valida-e Afzal Ali (Mother of Afzal Ali). Qurrat-ul-Ayn Hyder mentions that the book was published in 1907.

Asghari.[18] Azra, and her mother, also read Rashid-ul-Khairi's (1868–1936) novels and some issues of *'Ismat* (modesty, chastity or honor), the Urdu literary magazine for women that he started in 1908. Rashid-ul-Khairi, nephew of Nazir Ahmad, was one of the most prolific novelists of the early twentieth century, who became very popular for women's stories. His two novels, *Hayat-e Saliha* or *Salihat* (1902) and *Manazil us Saira* (1905) were concerned with social reform and written "in imitation of Nazir Ahmad's [novels], describing women's lives, using the highly colloquial language of Delhi women in the dialogue, and emphasizing the importance of women's education for the happiness of their families."[19]

Since the establishment of *Mirat* as a best seller, women's literature, often using Nazir Ahmad's device of good woman/bad woman, was noticeably concerned with two goals: education for women and the place of the literate woman in the family. Or perhaps it would be better to describe the goals of such novels and stories not as two separate ones, but rather as one: making the argument for having an educated woman at the helm of domestic affairs. The first issue of *'Ismat* was candid about such aspirations. Apart from emphasizing that it would be an Urdu journal for "respectable Indian women" (*sharif Hindustani bibiyan*), *'Ismat* listed specific items such as: "To make the sanctuary sanctified (*haram ki harmat qa'im rakhna*), or 'as the English saying goes, to make the home a castle'" [written in English in the original].[20]

To produce the good woman, "who could [in Azra's words] never criticize, even symbolically," was the point of reading this literature. A

---

[18] *Gudar ka Lal* was written in three volumes, and the novel deals with literacy and education of women, incompatible marriage and polygamy. It revolves around multiple plots, especially around the fate of the children of two sisters and one brother: Zinat-un-nisa and Qamar-un-nisa, the two sisters, and a brother, whose name is not mentioned. Qamar's son, Yusuf Raza's, first marriage is with Maqbool, who has practically no education and proves to be an ill match to the educated Yusuf Raza. He therefore marries a highly educated woman, Mehr Jabeen. The dynamic of the relationship between Mehr Jabeen, his second wife, and Maqbool, his first wife, and the qualities that emerge in the negotiations between these two women comprises most of the novel. Asiya Alam writes extensively about *Gudar Ka Lal* in her M.A thesis, *Polygamy, Family and Sharafat: Discourses amongst North Indian Muslims, circa 1870–1918.*

[19] For an excellent introduction to Rashid-ul-Khairi's writings, see Gail Minault, "'Ismat: Rashid ul Khairi's Novels and Urdu Literary Journalism for Women," in C. Shackle (ed.), *Urdu and Muslim South Asia* (London, 1989), p. 130.

[20] Minault, *'Ismat*, p. 133.

good woman, literate, keeping the home well, doing things for others' happiness, was the model in most of the stories that Azra was asked to read and remember. The English books that Azra read – Jane Austen, Georgette Heyer, and *Little Women* (these are Azra's terms) were also about "good wives." While being told to read these books, Azra was also continually reminded (as if the message of the stories themselves was not enough): "What is the use of education if you don't know household work (*padhai kis kaam ki agar ghardaari na aaye*)."

Azra's subtle contesting of what she was made to read, however, flows into her narration unexpectedly and powerfully. She explained to me at one point that she had given up reading the Quran after her marriage. Much later, after her father had passed away and her mother was older, she would coax Azra to read the Quran. Azra would say, "I live in Jamia Nagar [a Muslim majority neighborhood, built around the secular Muslim university, Jamia Millia Islamia]. There's *Quran-khani* [invocations and reading of the Quran] all the time. Sometimes I read there." Her mother replied: "It is *your own* reading that matters" [mother's emphasis; in Urdu, *tumhara apna padhna*]. The older woman urged the younger woman to read *for her own sake*: Azra has never stopped her daily recitations from the Quran since then!

"THE (SHORT-LIVED) PLEASURES OF PAISAR"

As I indicated earlier, it was only after my talk at the Jamia Millia Islamia (in the Jamia Nagar area of Delhi where Azra lives and is an active participant in the activities of the university) in August 2009 that Azra briefly reminisced about the pleasures of her maternal home, Paisar. "The Pleasures of Paisar" emerged as a short-lived, fleeting moment in Azra's recollection of her girlhood and young womanhood. The "Pleasures of Paisar" emerged again in our last conversation in December 2010.

The paper that I gave in 2009 was about a story composed in 1803 by the brilliant writer Insha-allah Khan. In fact, this story was first mentioned to me, almost in passing, by Azra's husband. Like Gulbadan Banu Begum's vital place in my first book, Insha-allah Khan has become the pivot for my current work, bringing into view the rich worlds of girl-child and woman in the early nineteenth century. (His story is the focus of Chapter 3, "The Woman of the Forest").

Photo 4. Azra Kidwai, 1992. Reprinted with permission from Azra Kidwai.

The point that I made in my presentation at Jamia was this: in the late-nineteenth-century debate on "the woman question," images of women's life stages and self-creativity were substantially erased and a static girl-child/woman appeared as symbol and victim. Going back to an earlier time, however, reveals discussions, linguistic enunciations, figures (daughter, wife, mother, lover, friend, matriarch, queen) that are multifaceted and fluid and that pose a challenge to the idea of the already known respectable woman of nineteenth-century India. Through Insha, then, I suggested that in considering what I call classic spaces, such as the forest (embodying freedom) and the palace (standing for pedagogy), the playfulness, agency and creativity of women reappears. Additionally, I illustrated Insha's playfulness in his experimentation with languages and use of literary techniques derived from a diverse literary and linguistic milieu (themes I address in the next two chapters).

Suffice it to say about my Jamia presentation that the idea of playfulness immediately struck a chord in Azra, and the audience, which was generous with its questions, suggestions and active encouragement to me to extend and deepen the concept. As a footnote, I should add that I believe it is after that workshop that the engagements of this book became clear to me and an arc for its arguments fell into place. What followed in my conversations with Azra the next day and in my later meetings with her in December 2010 was at variance with all that had gone before. Except for a casual mention of the games in the Lucknow apartment, which never came up in our conversation again, there was no talk of any play in Azra's telling of her life until August 2009. Her account of the games in Paisar (and a mention of picnics and concerts in Baragaon) that I discussed earlier came after the Jamia workshop.

In my last conversation with Azra in December 2010, just before I left for Lucknow to visit Baragaon and Paisar, she reiterated several "facts" that she had covered in the last five years. In addition to helping me understand, one more time, the distinction between her two ancestral homes, Baragaon and Paisar, she spoke in some detail about leisure and nondomestic activities. Noticeably, it was in Paisar, the grander and more "imperial" of her childhood homes, with its disciplinary structures, where "*parda* was strict (*parda bahut tha*), [and] the routine [was] rigidly governed by the *namaz* (daily prayers)," that Azra found a lot of pleasure. Azra and her female relatives would go about in a carriage (*taanga*). There were mango groves where they played, talked and relished the succulent fruit, though they were told not to pick mangoes, only to take the fallen ones. "All these were the pleasures of Paisar (*yeh maze Paisar mein the*)."[21] Along with this

---

[21] It was during these visits to Paisar that Azra became especially close to her two aunts, in whom she confided about the ways in which she suffered at the hands of her father. The aunts in turn shared their own feelings, including the suffering they experienced

recollection, Azra wanted to emphasize that "a child remains a child. Certain spaces, occasions and periods during the day are granted to you [to be a child]." But there were restrictions for girls: such as playing only inside the house or the courtyard. She remembers the reprimands: "Do not play in the open. Make sure you have your *dupatta* on." And demands: "If it was meal time, we [girls] had to leave [that is, stop playing to go and help serve food], not the boys."

AZRA'S INVITATION

By summoning spaces of girlhood and young womanhood, harking back to the earlier literary characters, underlining recurrently the fundamental role that her father played in designing her life, Azra invites us to think about the domestic space and gender relations, and how in the performance of gendered roles laid out by the respectable male, boys and girls, men and women are made: in thinking the history of being woman (or man), the question for us is also what gets emphasized (woman, the producer and the nurturer of the family) and what gets erased (girl-child, pleasure, the individuality of women).

An immediate appeal of Azra's account lies in drawing our attention very directly to the literature she read. As mentioned before, the nineteenth- and twentieth-century books, magazines and novels that she recalls constitute a "lived" literature, and Azra's case demonstrates its centrality in the disciplining of women subjects and the ordering of everyday relations within the physical spaces and the social landscape of respectable households. The texts that Azra harks back to became the staple texts for generations of new girls and women in a radically reconstituted *sharif* world from the 1870s and 1880s. The famous didactic pieces by Nazir Ahmad, the *Mirat*, and the *Banat*, to which Azra ascribes a "specialness" – and other texts that I examine in the chapters that follow (Raja Shiv Prasad's *Vamamanranjan* and the *Gutka*, various renditions of Shakuntala, Gauridatt's *Devrani-Jethani ki Kahani*, Hali's *Majalis-un-Nissa* and numerous others[22]) – center on the *ta'lim-u-tarbiyyat* (education and upbringing) of children. This

---

at the hands of their husbands. Azra notes repeatedly that these women "despite their husbands, despite the system, were very strong."

[22] For a fuller list, references and a discussion of the archive for this book, see Chapter 1.

involves training in the art of how to live as a good *sharif* man or woman. The education of women, who nurture children as a nurturing of *sharif* culture itself, is critical here. What we see in many of the didactic texts of the late nineteenth century is the consolidation of one kind of ideal of the girl-child/woman. I investigate several other figurations of the girl-child/woman in this book that in fact point to the prehistory of the firm, bounded women figures widely circulated and recognized in the late nineteenth century.

There are also important suggestions in Azra's account about a reconstituted domestic space, itself critical to the changed relationships and regulations of the reconstituted *sharif* world. The domestic space of both the Baragaon and of the Lucknow apartment seems very clearly marked off from the extended world of the *mohalla* (neighborhood), perhaps more than ever before. The *mohalla* was not completely shut out, but its intersection with the *zamindar*'s (landlord's) world had changed considerably from the traditional setting in which the landlord's domain extended to the village, and servants, travelers, workers, relatives and friends and the poor, within the confines of distinct male and female spaces, were regular presences within the landlord's house, even if the *zamindar*'s immediate family occupied an inner sanctum. The interaction with the wider community seems greatly reduced by the later nineteenth century, and more emphatically in the twentieth, in the context of increased urbanization and the consequent constriction of living spaces, the newly emerging modern (often bureaucratic) class consciousness and the need for a private familial space that was especially emphasized in the colonial discourse. There is an increasing separation between the inner sanctum (inhabited primarily by immediate relatives, people with blood and kinship ties) along with one or two old servants such as Bua, and that of the outer space (in which interactions continue with a wider social segment, but not as closely as before). The relationship with the *mohalla* and its inhabitants continues to be vital to the life of the *ashraf*. Strikingly, Azra's Old Delhi home, the Matia Mahal mansion, reflects the spirit of the old *mohalla* in the networks of relationships that she details. Even as this engagement with the *mohalla* is outlined, Azra's "home" comes to be much more distinctly cordoned off.

In Azra's case, what we see is a newly segregated domestic world institutionalized in a new way. In the professional elite's increasing separation of itself (and of the *sharif* family) from the dirt and the dust (but also the people and the festivals and the practices) of the surrounding habitations of the less privileged, in town and country, we have the emergence of "the home as a castle" to hark back to `Ismat's goal. It is in this sense that we may speak of a more clearly segregated, institutionalized, and "embattled" domestic sphere, even though the domestic world of the elite – and the women of this world – will always (or at least from long ago) have been sequestered as sacred and protected.

Another conspicuous feature in Azra's recollections is the centrality of the male head of the household. Azra's girlhood was dominated by her father. He laid down the rules of the household and ensured they were followed. This male centrality is reflected in the repeated entries and exits of her father in her account: in his decisions about which schools Azra would go (or not go) to, when she would wear the *burqa*, in his insistence on her cooking and keeping household accounts and so on. His *zamindarana adab* (feudal comportment), his *sakhti* (strictness) towards Azra and his insistence on making sure respectable life was upheld emphatically makes the point about the overarching presence of the patriarch. When Azra's father visited her after her marriage, he observed with pleasure that she would finish cooking for the morning and organize several other household chores before leaving for the university, for her M.A. classes, at 7:30 AM. As he said to Azra's mother: "If I had not been strict, if I had not trained her this way, could your daughter have accomplished all this?" Thus, alongside the continuance of homosocial spaces for men and women, boys and girls, there seems to be a greater physical intrusion by the man in female quarters and in female activities.

The place of older women is also noteworthy in Azra's multifaceted and at times paradoxical narration. While the older women (Azra's mother; Dammi; her mother-in-law) are clearly not invisible or absent in the day-to-day domestic affairs, they seem to be like the king's vice regents, administrators of the familial arrangements worked out by men, advancing the ways of *sharif* life emphasized by them. Azra speaks about her mother with great admiration and affection, yet her mother comes into our conversation only now and then, a fragmentary appearance, almost always in relation to her father. "My mother was very weak," says Azra. It is important to underline the absence of any challenge by Azra's mother to the authority of her father: like the older women, says Azra, her mother had come to "accept and implement the rules laid down by the men, as part of the need of the sociеty and maintenance of social structures. Patriarchy is maintained via matriarchs." Or as Azra wrote to me on March 25, 2010 in response to a draft of this prelude: "Father was the instructor. But the instructions were followed and implemented by mother. Interactions with father were very limited, and the communication of father's instructions, orders, displeasures were communicated by mother most of the time. Father was a revered figure."

In Azra's story, the playfulness of girlhood is referred to infrequently. Her warm recollections of Paisar or even those of Baragaon and the Lucknow apartment are still burdened by the memory of chores to which she keeps returning: spaces of freedom are fleeting. She experiences "freedom" in her marriage, but it remains within the terms of her duties and responsibilities as a wife, daughter-in-law, mother and now grandmother. Nonetheless her account invites us precisely to think about such fragments of contest and play (within the patriarchal, within the familial) that allow other possibilities, other figures and other histories to emerge.

Several fictional and nonfictional texts from the early nineteenth century reveal the ongoing contests, the pleasures and joys of girlhood and the play at work in living (and narrating) the different stages of life. Such narrations of "freedom" and creativity are eroded once the concern with modernity and respectable life in a colonized land takes over in texts of the later nineteenth century onwards: the girl-child and woman comes to be constrained by increasingly fixed notions of community, caste and religion – in both colonial and noncolonial discourses.

In the chapters that follow, I turn to a history of girlhood and womanhood by engaging unattended, varied, playful, contestatory figures and their complex and contradictory articulations. I investigate the history of women figures (girl-child, girl, woman) in northern India, *circa* 1800–70, in order to detail and historicize female lives and spaces and to complicate the transition from girlhood to womanhood that I call *becoming woman*. My hope is to write a history "freeing" the constricted woman subject found in received scholarly writings, where the female always leans forward into a future belonging to someone else (husband, children, family, nation) or clings to a child-centered past that she effectively never enjoyed. In such an historical unfolding, I should underline, the feminine figures, forms and cultures is not always a given. As Azra's narration so powerfully reminds us, the subterranean, shadow discourse of "play" is very much a part of writing such a history, as is documenting the more apparent traces of women's life stages, agency and self-creativity: both processes are, to use Sedgwick's words from another context, "a painstaking process of accumulative reading and historical de- and recontextualization."[23]

[23] Eve Kosofsky Sedgwick, *Epistemology of the Closet* (Berkeley, 1990), p. 12.

I

Texts, Spaces, Histories

As is well known now, the figure of the girl-child and woman emerged as the center of wide-ranging debates on education, reform and modernity that raged through much of the nineteenth century in India. In the Hindi-Urdu speaking region, as well as beyond, this was a significant departure from the earlier courtly traditions (under the Great Mughals and their successors) in which the prince/male child was the focus of education and ethical literature. Yet, importantly, while the "woman question" became the central symbol of the colonial encounter, the girl-child/woman appeared only as object, as site of contestation and improvement. Attendant questions of women's life stages, agency, and self-creativity largely disappeared.

The major colonial and reformist texts of the 1860s and after presented a set of rather fixed and static female figures. Fundamental to these female figures were clearly defined tracks of respectable domesticity, which were accorded a pivotal position in the animated debate on social reform. Inevitably, therefore, what has had to be negotiated in historical writings is the problem of a "static" woman, confined to the space of the household, duty bound with familial obligations, even as the drive to make her literate grows ever more insistent. In spite of the limitations of the archive, recent scholarship has engaged in an innovative and sustained investigation of the debates surrounding the "woman question" as it played out in the nineteenth and early twentieth centuries, producing a powerful critique of the various sites of reform, as well as the meaning of respectability and education.[1]

The period of mature colonialism, following the Mutiny and civil uprising of 1857 and the establishment of more direct British rule, has been the focus of much of this recent historical inquiry, which excavates a time when reformists and publicists sought to establish the quite ahistorical essence of the good "Hindu" and "Muslim" woman, who was of course located in modern middle-class, or more broadly respectable, culture.

In attempting to further historicize women as subjects, I retain this focus on aristocratic, respectable families, which have been central to the debate on the woman question. A departure I make while doing this, however, is to begin investigation from the early 1800s. Going back to an earlier time reveals debates and figures (daughter, wife, mother, lover, friend, matriarch, queen) that are complex and fluid, and that pose a challenge to the idea of the already known respectable woman of traditional India. Attention to these richer and less programmed lives also troubles the typical progress narrative of women's increasing liberation with the passage of time, where *later* is, somehow, always *better*. By going back to the writings and perspectives of the early nineteenth century, what we see more clearly are female subjects in a range of life stages (childhood, girlhood, womanhood) inhabiting diverse worlds of duty, aspiration, fantasy and freedom.

I argue in this book that although "making" a "woman" – *Coming of Age in Nineteenth-Century India* (as in other early modern and modern societies) – was a male project, regularly conceived and promoted in terms of a male universal, the "becoming" woman was always the product of a greater negotiation. Thus, the point about an unknowable future for a girl-becoming-woman is central to my argument. In other words, "becoming woman" is not a teleological proposition – a linear progression of an individual moving on from being a girl, then a young woman and then a mother. In fact, most of the literary and reformist discourses of the nineteenth century deluge us with a liminal figure, which I shall call girl-child/woman (I elaborate this concept later in this chapter).

---

[1] I discuss these contributions at greater length in a subsequent section of this chapter.

My inquiry rests on an exploration of a number of paradigmatic spaces of yearning, activity, potential and discipline: forests, schools, households, neighborhoods and rooftops. In my investigation, these spaces may be seen as the grounds for the establishment and improvement of gender relations. These diverse spaces not only interrupt the stagist accounts of becoming woman; they also help destabilize the fixed, programmed and predictable woman figure. In organizing my book around lived spaces, and in line with a major strand of feminist scholarship, I foreground the theme of "playfulness" that binds the social and the sexual together and allows room for intervention and critique even within authoritarian structures.

Three concepts – the *girl-child/woman, becoming* and *playfulness* – are central to the writing of this book. Before I elaborate these, a few words are necessary about a more familiar concept also central to this work: the colonial modern. Several scholars have made the argument, persuasively, that modernity and colonialism go hand in hand – and not only in the colonies. The establishment of the regime of modernity is dependent on the colonial (imperial) carving up of the world in terms of time, space and civilization. It is in the carving up of the globe, and of time past and present – in other words, in the long, drawn out cultural, economic and political colonization of the world in the era of capitalism and Enlightenment – that the universal (male) modern itself is constituted. In that sense, all modernity is a colonial modernity.[2] However, the resources out of which, and methods by which, this modern condition is worked out by colonizing and colonized peoples in different parts of the world are obviously diverse; the history of the modern necessarily takes on different forms and articulations in separate locations. It is one such location and one significant contest over the construction of the modern female that I investigate in the present study.

The point I wish to underline in this exploration of nineteenth-century India is that there is specificity to the colonial encounter, and hence to the texture of the modernity produced by the colonized people in

---

[2] On this point, among recent writings on South Asia, see Prathama Banerjee, *The Politics of Time: 'Primitives' and History-Writing in a Colonial Society* (Delhi, 2006) and Anjali Arondekar, *For the Record: On Sexuality and the Colonial Archive in India* (Durham and London, 2009); Milind Wakankar, *Subalternity and Religion: The Prehistory of Dalit Empowerment in South Asia* (London and New York, 2010).

the subcontinent. It is in the shadow of an overweening colonialism and of scathing colonial attacks on their values, traditions and history that the colonized articulate and rearticulate their vision of respectable, honorable and useful life and what constitutes civilization and progress in a modernizing world. The particular colonial encounter or clash over civilization in nineteenth-century northern India that I examine is obsessively concerned, among other important issues, with the so-called "woman question." In revisiting this issue, I introduce the concept of the girl-child/woman.

In the colonial representation of the culture and civilization of the colonized population of northern India – past and present – the woman question occupied a central place. "The condition of the woman is one of the most remarkable circumstances of the manners of nations," says James Mill in his *History of British India* (1817).[3] He culls the truth of "the Hindu family" from Manu: "Then only is a man perfect when he consists of three persons united, his wife, himself, and his son."[4] Mill quotes Manu to suggest that the Hindu man is urged to choose "for his wife the girl, whose form has no defect; who has an agreeable name; who walks gracefully like a phenicopteros, or like a young elephant; whose hair and teeth are moderate respectively in quantity and in size; whose body has exquisite softness." Among other injunctions, a man must avoid marrying the daughter of a family "which had produced no male children."[5] In this classic statement, the daughter has no place at all. The perfect family is a man, his wife and his son. When a female appears, she is already a woman: a wife from a family known to produce male children. There is obviously no room then for any discussion of a girl's training, education or upbringing.[6]

---

[3] James Mill, *The History of British India Volume I* (1817; rpt London, 1997), p. 309.
[4] Ibid., p. 258.
[5] Ibid., pp. 308–309.
[6] For an elaboration of this point, see my "Recasting the Woman Question: the 'Girl-Child/Woman' in the Colonial Encounter," *Interventions*, Vol. 10, No. 3 (2008). Wendy Doniger notes that the question of girl being dependent on father, wife on husband and old woman on son is mentioned twice in Manu. It is not mentioned in the *Mahabharata*. The later commentaries increasingly resort to a characterization such as Manu's. For a detailed discussion of commentaries on Manu, see Wendy Doniger, *The Laws of Manu* (New York, 1991).

Numerous colonial portraits reaffirmed this picture as a special feature of the East.[7] The colonial critique of the position of Indian women and a concomitant emphasis on reform, education and the uplifting of women was a central part of the colonizers' discourse – from Mill, to Katherine Mayo's *Mother India*, and beyond.[8] It is scarcely surprising that the woman question also became central to the discourse of the reformers and spokespersons of the colonized, who took up the challenge of responding to the colonial indictment. Consequently, the issue of reform, focusing on the education of girls and women, became fundamental to the issue of modernity and civilization in India, especially in the second half of the nineteenth century, once British colonial rule had come to be securely and, as it seemed, irreversibly established.

I have felt it necessary to reconceptualize the woman question as the question of the girl-child/woman for a number of reasons. In Mill, as in other writings from the nineteenth century, the girl-child was merely the shadow of woman, imagined in – and solely as – the mother, and the mother of boys and men at that. Further, this girl-child/woman could do nothing of her own at any stage: "By a girl, or by a young woman, or by a woman advanced in years, nothing ... must be done, even in her own dwelling-place, according to her mere pleasure. In childhood must a female be dependent on her father ['absolutely at the disposal of their fathers, till three years after the nuptial age'], in youth, on her husband; her lord being dead, on her sons: a woman must never seek independence."[9] Dependent in childhood, in youth and in old age, the girl-child/woman could never exist on her own, let alone exercise independent agency. The separation of a distinct stage called childhood is practically impossible in such a scenario.

At the same time, while the girl-child was already a woman, the woman remained something of a girl. Such an imbrication of the girl-child and woman is one inflection of the general problem of namelessness or "*naam ka parda*" (the veiling of names, a term used by Qurratulain Hyder), which I referred to in the prelude. In this

---

[7] For details, see Lal, "Recasting the Woman Question," especially pp. 325–327.

[8] For a fine analysis of Katherine Mayo's *Mother India* as an important chapter in the history of women and colonialism, see Mrinalini Sinha, *Specters of Mother India: The Global Restructuring of an Empire* (Durham and London, 2006).

[9] Mill, *British India*, pp. 311, 317.

connection, consider the following observation from Gayatri Spivak: the most detailed record of women's names in early colonial India is in the context of widow self-immolation. "There are many lists of pathetically misspelled names of the satis of the artisanal, peasant, village-priestly, money-lender, clerical, and comparable social groups from Bengal, where *Satis* were common... There is no more dangerous pastime than transposing proper names into common names."[10]

Qurratulain Hyder's articulation *naam ka parda* refers not only to the literal erasure of names, which happens in much of the writing of history and of social life more generally, but also to the very denial to women of agential position, reflection and playfulness, not to say history. The so-called Rani of Sirmur circulates, as Spivak compellingly shows, without archival traces. No papers, a few rumored stories, nothing in traditional archival terms. Spivak charts an unofficial genealogy around the figure of the Rani: in Spivak's reading, she emerges "nameless," resting in the constant twist between "patriarchal subject-formation and imperialist object-constitution" in much of which "the track of the sexual difference is doubly effaced."[11]

Namelessness is a wide-ranging cultural proposition that extends to the broader woman's domain, to the duties she performed and to her aspirations and assessments in the rich and contradictory worlds she inhabited. As I show in the pages that follow, the female adult and child are frequently collapsed into one another in the discourses of the nineteenth century. Reformist writings of the late nineteenth century, British as well as Indian, often erase the potential for spontaneity and discovery, as befits the stage of girlhood, while simultaneously constricting the space for the exercise of critical reasoning and the capacity for autonomy and self-governance that the "new woman" could be expected to possess.

By introducing instability into the object of reform and education, my compound phrase girl-child/woman challenges the givenness of these categories from the very beginning of a consideration of the question of the colonized woman. I hope it works also to undo the static – and unhistorical – quality of the figure of woman that British

---

[10] Gayatri Chakravorty Spivak, *A Critique of Postcolonial Reason: Toward a History of the Vanishing Present* (Cambridge, MA, 1999), pp. 231–232.

[11] Ibid., pp. 231–232, 235, 274.

colonialists and Indian reformers alike worked with. For neither individual historical women, nor the figure of the girl-child and woman, could be contained as the frozen symbol of some cultural norm.

Essential to my argument about historicizing women is the concept of *becoming*. Problematizing progression/regression, this draws attention to the pauses, interludes and intervals in the production of feminine figures, as well as historical females, spaces and cultures. To the philosophers who speak about becoming, the fact that a variety of possibilities (linguistic, spatial, and cultural) have not been realized for women is the fundamental problem.[12] For the history that I write in this book, my argument is as follows: it is not only that the potential of women has not been realized; it is also that the very possibility of becoming is denied.

Consider this: the vast majority of the sources for the writing of this book were composed by male authors: reformers, inspectors of schools, storytellers. Although several women figures in their texts challenge the prescriptions and strain towards lives different from what their authors spelled out, it is male authors who underline the models and ethics of life that women must follow. Men "birth" women: it is through their writings that women acquire centrality in the nineteenth century.

While this fact reinforces the point that historically the universal is male and that everything to do with female/feminine is constructed in the terms of the universal (male),[13] it is nonetheless a provocative

---

[12] Deleuze and Guattari signify virtual powers when they speak about becoming woman in the context of an ever-evolving contingent world. Giles Deleuze and Felix Guattari, *A Thousand Plateaus*, Brian Massumi (tr.), (Minneapolis, 1980), pp. 233–242; 298–309. Luce Irigaray differs with Deleuze on the concept of becoming. For her, she says, "It does not mean becoming another thing with respect to my own being, as it seems to be the case in Deleuze's discourse … about 'becoming woman' or 'becoming animal.'… I have to keep, and even to conquer, this individuation in spite of an undifferentiation I meet with. 'Becoming Woman' or 'becoming animal' appears to me as a search for undifferentiation, instead of overcoming it." Luce Irigaray, *Conversations* (New York, 2008), p. 48.

[13] A critique of a single, masculine subjectivity is central to Irigaray's writing. As a first articulation of this, see Luce Irigaray, *Speculum: Of the Other Woman*, Gillian C. Gill (tr.), (Ithaca, 1985). She has continued to spell out the mediations, to use her words, "which permit a feminine subjectivity to emerge from the unique and so called neutral Western culture, and to affirm herself as autonomous and capable of a cultivation and a culture of her own." More recently, as she says, she has devoted her work to "defining and rendering practicable the ways through which masculine subjectivity and feminine subjectivity could coexist." Irigaray, *Conversations*, p. 124.

invitation for a feminist investigation to consider the audacious work-ings of the (male) universal: how it produces, what it catalogues, how and what it erases, in each instance. In nineteenth-century north-ern India, entire stages and spaces of female lives, as I have noted, were wiped out. This book aims to reinstate such figures, spaces and critiques to history – and the possibilities that come with them. And in doing so, hopes to dwell on what might be – and what might have been – feminine cultures.

Finally, to emphasize the historical concerns discussed above, I fore-ground the idea of *playfulness* in thinking about the girl-child/woman, since in arguments about women as silenced and long-suffering vic-tims, individual subjects, child, girl, woman and their varied capabil-ities and inclinations disappear in a rhetoric of recovery, civilization and progress. Playfulness is in keeping with the feminist position of rethinking selves that implies social and sexual interaction without asserting authority, and allowing forms of self-expression and literary creativity that are not dependent on masculinist definitions of fulfill-ment. In emphasizing play, I also wish to focus on authorial playful-ness, the room for maneuver, innovation and creativity even where the constraints appear overwhelming, for such literary "undecidability" critically affects the production of the figure of girl and woman, in nineteenth-century India as anywhere else.

I elaborate these concerns in the sections that follow, first through a slightly more extended discussion of contemporary writings and later scholarly debates on education and social reform in nineteenth-cen-tury northern India, and then by reference to a number of important nineteenth-century texts that allow us to explore the concept of girl-child/woman, becoming and playfulness a little more fully.

THE WOMAN QUESTION IN THE METROPOLIS AND THE COLONY

The question of woman, or women's reform, has loomed large in writ-ings on the colonial encounter in nineteenth- and twentieth-century

That is, Irigaray does not wish to *become* woman in terms of the undifferentiated human (man). Rather, she stresses the differentiation of humankind and calls for the making of women in women's terms (which would also probably make for a better, richer, more egalitarian culture of humankind).

India. The debate has covered a large chronological span, as indicated in the dates of some of the legislation central to these debates: the prohibition of the practice of burning Hindu widows alive (*sati*) in 1829; the legislation allowing remarriage of Hindu widows in 1856; and in 1891 (and again in 1929), the raising of the age of consent within and outside marriage.[14] I point to this extensive history of legislative reform in order to suggest that for the colonial period as a whole, we have repeated meditations, via the figure of woman, on the qualities of Indian civilization, its fallen state or its excellence.

By way of context, it is instructive to juxtapose comments on Indian civilization and the need for urgent reform with parallel calls for moral reform in nineteenth-century Britain. A wholesale condemnation of the colonized world goes hand in hand with the construction of a modern idea of civilization in Britain. In the late nineteenth century, moral reformers in Britain campaigned to defeat the Contagious Diseases Acts, passed in the 1860s to control the spread of venereal disease by subjecting prostitutes to compulsory examinations. New approaches to moral reform superseded the efforts at reform and control that had targeted the prostitute. Social purity especially focused on youth and the working classes and what was seen as their dangerous sexual potential. Such "moral reforms" proliferated in the 1880s. Control of children was the key to this "radical transformation." "Control over children also afforded authorities and reformers enormous leverage over other members of the working-class household and community... The Criminal Law Amendment Act [1885], which was supposed to raise the age of consent, was mainly enforced to control adult sexual behaviour."[15]

Reform in Britain speaks to criminality: note that the 1885 act was called The Criminal Law Amendment Act. In the colonized world,

---

[14] See, notably, Lata Mani, *Contentious Traditions: The Debate on Sati in Colonial India* (Berkeley, 1998); Sudhir Chandra, *Enslaved Daughters: Colonialism, Law and Women's Rights* (Delhi, 1998); Tanika Sarkar, *Hindu Wife, Hindu Nation: Community, Religion, and Cultural Nationalism* (London, 2001); Rajeswari Sunder Rajan, *The Scandal of the State: Women, Law and Citizenship in India* (Durham and New Delhi, 2003); Sinha, *Specters of Mother India*; Kamala Visweswaran, "'My Words Were Not Cared For': Customary Law, Criminality and the 'Woman Question' in Late Colonial India," Unpublished paper.

[15] Judith R. Walkowitz, *Prostitution and Victorian Society: Women, Class, and the State* (Cambridge, 1980), pp. 1, 246, 251.

criminality gets translated as depravity. So when the Indian respondents took on the question of civilization, it became crucial to them to clarify the meaning of reform. No longer was this about the correction of the criminal. Rather it was about the resuscitation of the "true" scientific basis, and the assuredly civilized character, of Indian social customs and practices.

Late-nineteenth-century Indian reform efforts focused on women and the education of the young, and through that on civilization. Only now the issue becomes *our* civilization (rather than the lack of it), and in that context, *our* women and *our* girls. In the Indian reformists' constructions, women and girls were accorded high respect. They were positioned differently from their Western counterparts in that the reformers emphasized an intrinsically *dharmic* quality in Indian women's lives: dutiful, disciplined, oriented towards the good: *dharm* and *farz* – translatable as *duty* – are mentioned repeatedly in the contemporary Urdu and Hindi texts dealing with women's place and their lives.

Behind the reformers' propositions were specific ideas of civility and respectability that, in their view, needed preservation and sustenance.[16] At the same time, Indian commentators expressed the need to develop certain other facets of life that a modern age demanded, such as institutionalized Western-style education. The authors of several Hindi and Urdu books wrote about the education of children and the ethics of their upbringing. Strikingly, it was the education and upbringing of the girl-child that drew pointed attention, even if this was, in the end, primarily in the interests of the training of boys and young men. There was no escape from the focus on girls, for their centrality had emerged clearly in the ongoing colonial critique of Indian civilization.

Childhood as a concept and as a distinctly separated stage in the evolution of the individual emerges in Europe in the late seventeenth

---

[16] Barbara D. Metcalf, "Islamic Reform and Islamic Women: Maulana Thanawi's Jewelry of Paradise," in Barbara Metcalf (ed.), *Moral Conduct and Authority: the Place of Adab in South Asian Islam* (Berkeley, 1984); Partha Chatterjee, "The Nationalist Resolution of the Women's Question," in Kumkum Sangari and Sudesh Vaid (eds.) *Recasting Women: Essays in Indian Colonial History* (New Jersey, 1997); Gail Minault, *Secluded Scholars: Women's Education and Muslim Social Reform in Colonial India* (Delhi, 1998); Mushirul Hasan, *A Moral Reckoning: Muslim Intellectuals in Nineteenth-Century Delhi* (New Delhi, 2005), Ruby Lal, "Gender and *Sharafat*: Reading Nazir Ahmad," *Journal of the Royal Asiatic Society*, Vol. 18, No. 1 (2008).

and eighteenth centuries. The circumstances of the emergence of this stage have been investigated and discussed extensively.[17] A point evident in the scholarly discussion of European childhoods is the uncertainty, the tentativeness, even the ad hoc character of the new notion of childhood.[18] After the first flush of writing in the mid- to late 1960s on the new sense of childhood and on the introduction of a gentler approach to children's upbringing, a further revision appeared in the historiography. The new writings disputed the idea that traditional Europeans lacked a conception of childhood as a stage of life, and rejected the notion that most parents were not affectionate to their children, providing evidence of parental and familial affection through letters, diaries and other materials. Abandonment of children in traditional European societies had been viewed as rejection by several scholars; to the revisionists, this was a reflection of poor material conditions. For the former, wet nursing was an indication of lack of parental interest; revisionists noted that whatever the case in a handful of aristocratic families, most urban families turned to wet nurses only because of work demands – in the family business, for example.[19]

Thus, even in the case of Europe, one has to ask: Among which classes, from which period, and until when – given today's world of child soldiers and child prostitution – does the "natural" condition of childhood (and the normal practices of nurturing, education and play associated with it) exist? For all the uncertainty and contradictoriness of the idea of childhood at home, however, colonial writers in India mounted a derisive critique of the absence among the colonized of the innocent, delightful stage of life called childhood.

[17] Philippe Aries, *Centuries of Childhood: A Social History of Family Life* (New York, 1962); David Hunt, *Parents and Children in History: The Psychology of Family Life in Early Modern France* (New York, 1970); Lawrence Stone, *The Family, Sex, and Marriage in England, 1500–1800* (New York, 1972); John Demons, *Past, Present, and Personal: The Family and the Life Course in American History* (New York, 1986); Phillip Graven, *Spare the Child: The Religious Roots of Punishment and the Psychological Impact of Abuse* (New York, 1991); Carolyn Steedman, *Strange Dislocation: Childhood and the Idea of Human Interiority, 1780–1930* (Cambridge, MA, 1995); Peter N. Stearns, *Childhood in World History* (New York and London, 2006).

[18] Aries, *Centuries*, p. 13.

[19] Stearns, *Childhood*, pp. 45–46.

Part of the specifics of writing *Coming of Age in Nineteenth-Century India* is the necessity of engaging with this colonial critique about the missing child. The question of civilization in colonial India is haunted by the figure of the girl-child, even (I argue) in its "absence." Ironically, this is an absent figure despite its newly emerging centrality in the literature of the time. The girl-child might even be said to dominate the debates on the woman question. In colonial and noncolonial discussions on child marriages, child widows, female infanticide, and so on, the education, the rights, the pleasure, the oppression of the girl-child is a major site of contestation. Given how centrally the girl-child figures in all these debates over colonial reform in India, one might think that the British came to save the Indian girl, even though they could scarcely find her!

THE DEBATE ON THE GIRL-CHILD/WOMAN

Let me turn for a moment from the nineteenth-century debate to recent scholarly engagements with the colonial critique of Indian civilization and the woman question. In his influential essay, "The Nationalist Resolution of the Women's Question," first published in 1989, Partha Chatterjee noted that, contrary to received scholarly opinion, the women's question did not disappear from the nationalist agenda in India at the end of the nineteenth century, but rather came to be folded into it – and thus "resolved" – as the "spiritual," "inner" content of the nation, a domain of cultural and spiritual sovereignty presided over and preserved by women.[20] The question that other scholars have asked since, and that I revisit in this book, is what kind of figure is this woman who (in the words of Chatterjee) becomes the spiritual symbol of the nation? What are the specific processes of cultural or spiritual sublimation or (as I suggest) erasure that go into its making? Or to put it somewhat more polemically, might one argue in an extension of Chatterjee's point that it was not the disappearance of the women's question, but *the disappearance or erasure of women as historical subjects* that was the issue – and the centerpiece – of the nationalist resolution of the women's question?

[20] Chatterjee, "The Nationalist Resolution of the Women's Question," cited previously.

A good deal of the scholarly output on women's reform and education in late-nineteenth-century India has been based on evidence drawn from Bengal and northern India.[21] A number of scholarly writings on the woman question in late colonial India refer to child wives, child brides and infant marriages. In the case of sati, we are told that women "not under the age of puberty" were allowed to perform it.[22] And puberty was marked as follows: "*garbhadhan* made it obligatory for a girl to have intercourse with her husband within sixteen days of her first period."[23] Of course, "to ensure the performance of this rite, marriage was essential in early infancy, for the exact moment of puberty was both uncertain and very early in warm climates."[24] In 1890, Phulmonee, an eleven-year-old girl, died of marital rape by her husband.[25] She was just one among many.

Consider again the matter of raising the age of consent for marriage, another central issue in the debate on the woman question. In 1860, the criminal code set the age of consent for both married and unmarried girls at ten. In 1891, the Child Marriage Restraint Act raised the age of consent to twelve. In 1927, Rai Sahib Harbilas Sarda introduced his Hindu Child Marriage Bill, also known as the Sarda Act. This was passed in 1929 and raised the minimum age of marriage to sixteen for boys and fourteen for girls.[26]

The girl-child is a key figure throughout these debates, yet she is missing as a historical presence. In the context of the debates over sati and the age of consent, Tanika Sarkar asks "whether the woman, as a person, enjoyed protection from violent death when the community laws allow such a death to occur. The question was also whether she was, in fact, legally and politically, a person at all whose claim to life would be self-authenticating because of her personhood."[27] Further, she asks importantly: "Were they [reformers or revivalists] talking

---

[21] See notably the writings of Metcalf, Naim, Mani, Minault, Sarkar, Sinha and others cited earlier.

[22] Mani, *Contentious Traditions*, p. 35.

[23] Tanika Sarkar, "A Prehistory of Rights: The Age of Consent Debate in Colonial Bengal," *Feminist Studies*, Vol. 26, No. 3 (2000), p. 601.

[24] Tanika Sarkar, "Enfranchised Selves: Women, Culture, and Rights in Nineteenth-Century Bengal," *Gender and History*, Vol. 13, No. 3 (2001), p. 552.

[25] Sarkar, "A Prehistory of Rights," p. 601.

[26] Geraldine Forbes, *Women in India* (Cambridge, 1996), pp. 83–85.

[27] Sarkar, "A Prehistory of Rights," pp. 605–606.

about a woman or a mere child yoked to untimely marriage? Was there a separate stage in the woman's life as childhood, and if so, was it compatible with marriage?"[28]

The question, however, has remained unexplored. I outline the strategic and interested ways in which masculinist logic minoritizes women by denying them, somewhat ironically, their very minority, which is to say their status as girl-children. Colonial patriarchalism – here I include the discourses of both the colonizers and the colonized – erases the figure of the girl-child by only ever acknowledging her as a woman in the future tense, that is, as wife, mother and nurturer, even as it erases women by infantilizing them and binding their claim to personhood to others – fathers, husbands, sons – most of all to the children they are obliged to produce and care for under the terms of what Adrienne Rich calls "compulsory heterosexuality."[29] Women's social and historical dispossession happens, in part at least, through a kind of temporal displacement that always constructs the female as leaning forward into a future that more rightly belongs to some-one else (husband, family, nation, etc.), or projecting backward into a child-centered past they themselves never enjoyed.

In the writings of British observers like James Mill (1773–1836), Fanny Parks (1794–1875) and Mrs. Meer Hassan Ali,[30] but also in the prescriptions and reflections of Indian writers and educators such as Nazir Ahmad (1830–1912), Raja Shiv Prasad (1823–1895) and Pandit Gauridatt (1836–1906), among others whose writings I take up in this study, the girl-child when she appears, is almost always, already a woman. Of course, the manifestations and logic of this appearance vary in colonial and noncolonial articulations. By placing colonial and reformist discourses adjacent to each other, I want to indicate a variety of articulations on girl-child and woman figures – pictures

[28] Ibid., pp. 613–614.
[29] Adrienne Rich, "Compulsory Heterosexuality and Lesbian Existence" in Henry Abelove, Michele Aina Barale and David M. Halperin (eds.), *The Lesbian and Gay Studies Reader* (New York, 1993), pp. 227–254.
[30] Now identified as Biddy Timms of Adiscombe, Surrey, not many details are available about the author's life, except that she was married to a Mr. Meer Hassan Ali, a man of Sayyid origin, and lived with his family for twelve years from 1816 to 1828. She composed her observations in 1832. Mrs. Meer Hassan Ali, *Observations on the Mussulmauns of India*, W. Crooke (ed.), (Karachi, 1973, rpt.); and http://www.columbia.edu/itc/mealac/pritchett/00islamlinks/mrsmeerhassanali/index.html.

of feminine life that circulate, that are invoked in different contexts and alongside new ones, and that change in meaning according to the context in which they appear – that manage, nonetheless, to produce the girl-child/woman as a static, ahistorical figure. In the civilizing discourses that dominated the colonial world in the nineteenth and twentieth centuries, the figure of the girl-child appears fleetingly, as shadow, only to disappear quickly into the compound figure of the child/adult.

For all that, it is important to note, the iconic Indian/Hindu/Muslim girl/woman could not be contained or frozen, even in the prescriptive texts of Indian reformers. As the compound phrase girl-child/woman suggests, the figure of the girl or woman is always more than the category allows. Other figures are implicit in this one: wife, mother, and, in this period, teacher and guide with civic consciousness, since claims of education and citizenship become increasingly important. One needs also to underline the diachrony implicit in the figure of the girl-child/woman. Since education and improvement were hailed as the signs of the time, and these had built into them the possibility, indeed the inescapability, of change, growth and maturity (improvement), the girl-child/woman could not just be the self-same, constant compound person. Such a figure was always liable to overflow the boundaries of the construction of girl-child, woman or both.

THE LONG NINETEENTH CENTURY

Within a decade of the Indian mutiny of 1857, when debates on civilization and respectability became more focused, several texts set the parameters of a new, yet traditional, Muslim and Hindu womanhood. By the 1870s, Akbari and Asghari of Nazir Ahmad's famed *Mirat al-`Arus (The Bride's Mirror)*,[31] Anandi of Gauridatt's *Devrani-Jethani ki Kahani (The Story of the Sisters-in-law)*, the Shakuntala of the bardic tradition and many other such figures had emerged as foundational symbols of the new traditional woman (or girl-child/woman).[32] I

---

[31] *The Bride's Mirror* and *Mirat* Urdu edn., cited earlier.
[32] Take the very visible story of Shakuntala that I discuss extensively in Chapters 2 and 3: in the late nineteenth century, the most popular version of this tale was the one told by Kalidasa. Here Shakuntala is submissive, rarely speaks and exudes a sense of quiet acceptance, what Romila Thapar calls "the ideal *grhini*." Romila Thapar,

conceptualize this moment in terms of what I call the "Woman of the Household" in Chapter 4. The debates on education and reform produced a "new woman" in a new kind of domestic world, with the male strikingly, indeed physically, present at the center of the household. The reformist texts do hold the potential of opening up future spaces; nonetheless what we see are rather firm, almost de-historicized women models – fully formed and isolated in the late-nineteenth-century world, products of just *that* time, elaborating the domestic proposals their male guides were laying down.

In the 1870s, new articulations and essences regarding the "good woman," "*sharif* life," and "domestic life" acquired fixity. Specific features of respectable life were elevated. Through the male head, male reformers/authors continually rehearsed the ethics of this new domestic world. The problem is that the sharply etched models of the texts of the later nineteenth century are considerably removed from the confusing and contradictory worlds in which historical beings live and historical subjectivities are made (and thus removed from a sense of the discursive production of truth and from the histories of production and travels of cultural and literary forms and models). It is important to return to the educated Indian/Hindu/Muslim woman that becomes clearly discernible, well formed, concretized and institutionalized as a foundational figure, to ask what are the ways in which erasures of specific figures and spaces took place.

Even in the late-nineteenth-century texts, the girl-child was sublimated but could never be completely erased. The shadow of the girl-child reappeared every so often to worry the disciplined figure of the respectable woman. More strikingly still, many different kinds of feminine figures, which speak to many ways of being, emerge from the texts predating the 1870s. As I have argued in the preceding pages, these other images have largely been expunged from the historical record. Naming those erased figures and spaces may be a first step in writing a history of the foundational myths of Hindu or Muslim

Sakuntala: Texts, Readings, Histories (London, 2002, rpt.), p. 255. The critical point to which Thapar is drawing our attention is that Shakuntala of the bardic tradition of *Mahabharata* gets lost, and what becomes popularly disseminated is the heroine of Kalidasa, who becomes an "icon of Hindu culture" by the nineteenth century, a model who now "epitomized the virtues of a good Hindu woman." Ibid., pp. 236, 240.

(or Indian) womanhood, and of the struggles of the historical women these myths attempt to de-historicize.

Central to my propositions is a text from 1803, Insha-allah Khan's (1756–1817) tale of Rani Ketki, which I analyze in Chapter 2 ("Woman of the Forest"). The narrative brings into view different kinds of female subjects (girl, daughter, friend, woman) in a variety of situations, saturated with conflicting possibilities, tendencies and desires. It is a rare text in that it is the only one of its kind available to us in writing from the early nineteenth century. At the same time, given its placement in a variety of Indic traditions, it represents a form of storytelling widely popular at the time. This is seen in the way in which the hero and the heroine meet, for example, and in the spatial locations of the tale (forest and palace, representing freedom and pedagogy, in conversation with each other) – very much a part of old traditions of storytelling found, for instance, in the epics, the Ramayana and the Mahabharata. The unusual feature of this story is that, in 1803, Insha decides to write it down and the tale moves from an oral into a written tradition.[33]

What is conspicuous in Insha's tale, transcribed from an oral world to a written word, is that the girl and the woman are centered to address a versatile moral universe. The female characters are not final, fully formed or confined to regimented respectable domestic ethics. The women in Insha's tale speak within the limits of the palace; nonetheless, they generate a play within the system by expressing their wishes, by going to the forest, playing on the swings and even transgressing in obvious ways. While these are not historical figures with precise locations and dates, these are an author's ideas of potential: the characters embodying such ideas emerge out of – and speak to – the codes of the society of Insha's time.

When reproduced later, in a different physical location in the *Gutka* (collection of stories) designed for junior officers of the Raj by an influential inspector of schools in the NWP, Raja Shiv Prasad (1823–1895), the tale of Rani Ketki comes to be read as an account of a perfect woman. In Shiv Prasad's *Gutka*, an anthology in Hindi put together in 1867 and printed in the Devanagri script,[34] Rani Ketki's story – along

[33] Personal communication from Urdu literary scholar and critic, Sadiq-ur-Rahman Kidwai, August 2009.

[34] I searched for several years before I located an 1852 Perso-Arabic script of this story. I take up the question of the loss of Insha's tale in the next chapter and discuss how

with that of Shakuntala, Damyanti, Queen Victoria, Nur Jahan and many others – becomes part of a collection of stories of historically verifiable exemplary women written in praiseworthy Hindi. It is to the question of what constitutes excellence in the use of the Hindi language, and to the plenitude of ideal women in history, conforming to the great societal norms, that attention is now directed.

Strikingly, in the first school textbook in Hindi for girls from the NWP, *Vamamanranjan* (tales for the entertainment of women), also composed by Raja Shiv Prasad, and published in 1859, which I turn to in Chapter 3 ("Woman of the School"), the tale of Ketki was not included. The very placement, framing and inclusion or exclusion of stories in these recuperative times and in these recuperative texts (the moment of reform and the abundance of reformist texts) transforms the ways readers read stories, what they choose, what they notice, what they overlook – what becomes grounded, stabilized, and what gets lost. We also see this in the elaboration of other literary and reformist texts of the period.

The writings of Nazir Ahmad, referred to earlier, a Muslim publicist and a prolific writer who published numerous books in diverse genres, to take one example, shows the respectable domestic world as an idealized haven constructed in the interest of children and their upbringing (*ta`lim-u tarbiyat*). In this production of the fantasy of the good life, the domestic is constructed as a desexualized domain. In Nazir Ahmad's famous novel, the *Taubat al-Nasuh* (*Repentance of Nasuh*), composed in 1873, Nasuh, the hero, blackens out sections of Sadi's *Gulistan* (a thirteenth-century ethical digest) before his wife, Fahmidah, reads them because he finds them unfit for her to read. The "extravagance" of Nasuh's son, Kalim, is another matter of contention in the *Taubat*. After a heated exchange with Kalim, Nasuh goes to his son's quarters and finds a cabinet of books written in Persian and Urdu. After examining these books, which he calls false and

---

Insha's story was claimed by Hindi scholars as a piece of excellent Hindi. Raja Shiv Prasad (1823–1895) was a school inspector under British rule. He was centrally concerned with education, designing school curriculum, setting up schools in rural areas of northern India and writing a wide range of books in Hindi and Urdu. For Raja Shiv Prasad's *Gutka*, I use an 1882 edition of the Indian Institute Library, Oxford: *Gutka or Selections, Part I, II, and III* (Hindi Misc. B 17 1/2/3). *Rani Ketki ki Kahani* is included in the third part. All translations are mine.

degrading (*jhuthe qisse, behuda batain, luchche mazmun*), he throws them into the flames.[35]

What exactly are these unfit texts? Prominent among them is Sadi's *Gulistan*, a section of which Nasuh blots out. It is most likely the notorious chapter V, "Youth and Love," that is targeted.[36] In her *Observations on the Mussalmauns of India* (1832), an excellent source for portraits of *sharif* familial life in the early nineteenth century, Mrs. Meer Hassan Ali says about Sadi's book that it was "the standard favourite of all good Mussulmauns ... 'Goolistaun' (Garden of Roses), is placed in the hands of every youth."[37] *Gulistan*, completed in 1258, and other similar "mirrors" were not meant to be gender specific. Michael Fisher notes that Begum Sombre (1778–1836) of Sardhana kept a copy of "the famous thirteenth-century Iranian poet Sadi's works always by her bedside."[38] Muzaffar Alam says that writings such as the *Akhlaq-i Nasiri*, a thirteenth-century ethical treatise in which the father is the center of the worldly domains, inner and outer, were very much part of the north Indian Islamicate milieu for numerous generations.[39] As were, C. M. Naim notes, Sadi's *Gulistan* focusing on ethical and moral issues; the *Qabus-Nama*, which related to rules and practices of specific occupations; and other courtesy books.[40]

[35] Nazir Ahmad, *The Repentance of Nussooh (Taubat-al-Nasuh): the Tale of a Muslim Family a Hundred Years Ago*, M. Kempson (tr.), (Delhi, 2004), p. 11. I use the following Urdu edition: Nazir Ahmad, *Kulliyat-e Diptee Nazir Ahmad* (Lahore, 2004). Hereafter Taubat Urdu edn. (translations mine). Taubat Urdu edn., p. 163.

[36] E-mail communication with C. M. Naim, May 2009. Several other scholars in India whom I have spoken with about this passage in the *Taubat* agree that it is chapter V of Sadi's *Gulistan*.

[37] Meer Hassan Ali, *Observations*, p. 256.

[38] Michael Fisher, *The Inordinately Strange Life of Dyce Sombre: Victorian Angol-Indian MP and 'Chancery Lunatic'* (London, 2010), p. 25.

[39] Chandra Bhan Brahman, a poet in the court of Shah Jahan, notes that aside from being integral to the madrasa syllabi, an average person learned the Nasirean ethics of life as a valuable part of their moral universe; Muzaffar Alam, *The Language of Political Islam in India, c. 1200–1800* (New Delhi, 2004), pp. 50–54.

[40] Naim, afterword, *The Repentance of Nussooh*, p. 131. The commentators and writers of the nineteenth-century texts themselves relied on ethical digests, literary manuals, and books of comportment that were part of their "thinking worlds." The Hindi, Urdu and Persian sources, harking back to older literary worlds, necessitate thinking about ethical narratives that animate women subjects. There is a complex world of texts here, and the frame of intertextuality – how morals and tales are told and retold and recast in each telling – is of vital interest to me. There are many lives of a text: the time of its composition, the manner of its travels; the forms it acquires in translation,

Clearly, in the 1820s and 1830s, when Mrs. Meer Hassan Ali lived in Lucknow, and Begum Sombre was the ruler of a princely state roughly 200 miles to the west, *Gulistan* was still read by men and women, boys and girls. In the later decades why were more and more injunctions laid down against women (and girls) reading the *Gulistan*? What is it in the *Gulistan* that led to such prohibitions? The "fate" of Insha's writings might provide some hints for us, especially his bold experimentation with what Ruth Vanita calls "women's speech."[41]

Later commentators found Insha-allah Khan's *Rekhti* poetry written in women's voice "vulgar," "of the common people" and "cheap."[42] It is likely that *Rani Ketki ki Kahani* faced similar condemnation; after all, it is uncertain in its genre, playful, transgressive. It is a fate parallel to that of Sadi's chapter V, which Nasuh found inappropriate for Fahmidah to read, and that of the *Divan-i Sharar* and *Kulliyat-i Atish*, which he threw onto the burning pyre of books.[43]

The time of the composition of texts such as those of Insha-allah Khan and many of his peers was a moment of great mobility for the authors experimenting with a shifting and rich landscape of languages in different corners of northern India.[44] Thus, Shaikh Qalandar

adaptation; and the reception it gets in varied invocations. Folded into the lives of texts are the processes of their making and remaking, often a complicated and muddled business. Tusi's *Akhlaq-i Nasiri*, very different text from a very different time, was part of the inheritance of the scholarly and cultural milieu that Nazir Ahmad belonged to. So are the *Akhlaq-i Nasiri*, Sadi's *Gulistan* and *Bustan*, *Qabus-Nama*. This literature has been in circulation for numerous generations. I am concerned, therefore, to see how this ethical literature comes to be read differently in different historical contexts and of course specifically in the nineteenth century in relation to the girl and woman.

[41] Ruth Vanita, "Married Among their Companions: Female Homoerotic Relations in Nineteenth-Century Urdu Rekhti Poetry in India," *Journal of Women's History*, Vol. 16, No. 1 (2004), p. 12.

[42] Ruth Vanita, comments during the "Subalternity and Difference" Workshop, Jamia Milia Islamia, New Delhi, August 12, 2009.

[43] *Divan-i Sharar*, probably of Mirza Ibrahim Beg, a Lucknow poet of the early nineteenth century. It cannot have been Abdul Halim Sharar, who was born in 1860 and has been called "the pioneer of the historical romance in Urdu"; Ralph Russell, *The Pursuit of Urdu Literature: A Select History* (London and New Jersey, 1992), p. 99. Khwaja Haidar `Ali Atish wrote Urdu poetry in the first quarter of the nineteenth century. For details of his poetry, see, Muhammad Sadiq, *A History of Urdu Literature* (Delhi, 1984), pp. 187–193.

[44] Personal communication with Urdu literary critic Sadiq-ur-Rahman Kidwai. See also Sisir Kumar Das, *A History of Indian Literature, 1800–1910* (New Delhi, 2005, rpt.), pp.62–64.

Bakhsh Jur`at (1748–1810), an intimate friend of Insha, a poet who could be "serious and profound" at times, was at other times "light and playful." Another contemporary of Insha and Jurat, Sa`adat Yar Rangin (1755–1835), wrote several *masnavis* and at least three works of prose, including the *Imtihan-e-Rangur*. But what made him popular to his patrons was "his *Rekhti*, the themes of which embrace the life of the courtesans. The diction used in them is that of women, particularly of the lower order of society, and the spirit of these poems is that of uninhibited levity and sensuality." Rangin's follower, Mir Yar Ali Khan (1818–1897), known as Jan Sahib, "used to dress like women and read his poems with the intonation and gestures peculiar to them."[45]

This literary playfulness and boldness comes to be condemned and censored from the latter half of the nineteenth century. The constraining and disciplining tendencies lean more and more towards one literary tradition, one religious community – and on to a much more distinctly homogenized, compartmentalized, stagist view of life. One point of interest in these restrictive tendencies is the proposition of difference between Hindus and Muslims, increasingly marked in the latter half of the nineteenth century, with an accompanying reduction and erosion of shared spaces and a codification of communal attachments and commitments. An important question is to consider how the emerging Hindu/Muslim sensibility affects the gendering of roles; indeed, how Muslim and Hindu women, men, girls and boys were supposed to conduct themselves in an age of increasing urbanization, industrialization and rapid cross-cultural communication: How were marriages ordered, domestic spaces conceptualized, organized and reorganized and what was expected of the girl-child and the woman through all of this?

PLAYFULNESS

"Playfulness" is an organizing concept of this book. Let me set out what is entailed in my use of the term and explain the politics of engaging such a concept. In response to my formulation, girl-child/woman, a question that several colleagues have asked me is this: Where is the girl-child/girl/woman in your account? Are these literary fictions?

---

[45] Ibid., p. 63.

Imaginary figures? In other words, the question is: where is the "real" girl-child? Or, where are the "breathing spaces" as V. Narayana Rao put it to me in a conversation. To reformulate his question: Where do we see girls as being girls, performing girlhood, as it were?

What is being asked is a critical question, implicit in which is the tension that my formulation girl-child/woman (simultaneous infantalization and maternalization) produces. The difficulty is that of not having an obvious reference point recorded as an event or historical figure or institution in the archive. Hence the question: Which girl-child? Of what class? And so on. As the previous pages should have indicated, *Coming of Age in Nineteenth-Century India* is self-consciously not a history of anything called the real girl, or woman, or childhood or mature femininity. It is a close investigation of feminine figures, of ideas with potential that come to be restricted as certain kinds of fixed models in the course of the debates and writings of the nineteenth century. Thus, it is also a history of literary imaginations, prescriptive models and texts, which become part of the training and lives of women from the later nineteenth century to today: at the center of this history are notions that make a girl-child or woman.

Closely tied to the perplexity "where is the girl?" is the reappearance of the question that I was asked when I began research on my first book, *Domesticity and Power in the Early Mughal World*: "How are you going to do this? There are no sources for it." The matter of a concrete, officially ratified, "authoritative" archive remains an issue for historians. Despite probing, extended engagements by scholars of postcolonial studies, feminist studies and others writing about historical subjects whose histories are not automatically and obviously decipherable in what is a "classic," "authoritative," "official" record, the archive continues to haunt us.[46]

Yet, as the ongoing discussion should make clear, the archive for a history such as the one this book is concerned with, of the practices of production and erasure of girl-child and woman through much of the nineteenth century, is wide-ranging. The archival materials for this

---

[46] On the question of evidence, see Arondekar's recent compelling study, *For the Record*. For an excellent historical account via an unusual archive, see Michael Fisher's *Dyce Sombre* cited previously. Also see my review essay, "The Lure of the Archive: New Perspectives from South Asia," *Feminist Studies*, Vol. 37, No. 1 (Spring 2011): 93–110.

book include a diverse range of colonial texts in English and noncolonial texts in Persian, Hindi, Urdu and Khadi Boli (a variant of the spoken language around Delhi later standardized as Hindi); didactic and fictional accounts; tales; instruction manuals; and biographies, several of which have already been referred to.

I wish to make two other points in thinking about the questions put to me. First, the models prescribed in the texts of Hindu and Muslim educators like Nazir Ahmad, Gauridatt or Raja Shiv Prasad and the writings of other reformists and commentators that I engage in this book are still invoked. In the prelude, I detailed an extensive interpretation of the episodes of nineteenth-century texts by a *sharif* (respectable) woman, and how lived texts and spaces order everyday relations, the physical and social landscape of respectable households, the sensibilities that come with these and how these persist or have been modified. The nineteenth-century texts are still read, taught, discussed and used as mirrors, and women are chastised and disciplined in the terms of these texts even 100 years later. As Azra Kidwai's invocations should have shown, these figures and models have meaning for "real life" and "real history." Literary figures, educational institutions, texts and social practices are closely intertwined.

Second, it is important to note that neither in the figure (girl-child/woman) nor in the codified body (law, regulations to do with women) and fixed models (respectable woman of the 1870s) is there a sense of completion. As Auerbach reminds us, these are always "provisional and incomplete."[47] The vitality employed in the idea of a figure, however, allows anticipation of spaces and activities and possibilities of varied expressions that emerge for girl-child and woman – which, in fact, are about the history of *being* girls and *becoming* women. When such figures come to be recast by reformers in the late nineteenth century, as I argued earlier, a more static model appears with fixed rules, sets of prescriptions and particular tracks that a female life must follow. Domains other than those now prescribed for a good woman do not (cannot) disappear: nonetheless they are removed from view to a greater degree than ever before. I attempt to visit these lost domains and subjectivities in this book.

---

[47] "Figura" in Erich Auerbach, *Scenes from the Drama of European Literature: Six Essays* (New York, 1959), p. 58.

The concept of playfulness, it seems to me, is of extraordinary value in thinking about the production of feminine figures and how we might approach the related question of sources. At one level, this articulation, very much in keeping with a long tradition in feminist theory and feminist historiography, has sought to contest the erasure of women's experience from the record by excavating "minor" forms of agency where none were thought to have existed. And yet, specific to the South Asia scenario, my proposition of playfulness also challenges the intellectual terrain centered on delineating spaces of pain, suffering, erasure and victimization – in particular as these domains are marked out exclusively in relation to women subjects.

What happens, I ask myself, if we attempt to conceptualize playfulness as a characteristic feature of women's/girls' lives? I think of playfulness as a feminine/feminist conceptualization of enjoyment, an art that combines the social and the sexual without needing to assert authority or discipline other forms of self-expression and social interaction. In other words, I see playfulness as the domain of girl-child and woman – not the exclusive province of the male (with its attendant male pleasure and rights), but a nonpaternal practice of the feminine.[48] Girls and women as "nondominant people," to use Lauren Berlant's phrase from a different context,[49] but people nonetheless.

Playfulness allows me to blur a number of binaristic distinctions that lie at the core of my newly configured girl-child/woman: namely, the sensual and sexual, the innocent and the knowingly erotic, the juvenile and the adult, the playful and the pleasurable – girl-child and woman. In a nutshell, my attempt is to critique the centering of fields

[48] This harks back to the distinction between *jouissance* and pleasure: *Jouissance*, a French term, employed in psychoanalytic theory and in literary theory to denote unsettling experiences of enjoyment, delight and jubilation. The term comes from *jouir* and has the sense of "enjoying a right" of playfulness and is associated with sexual pleasure, which is the province and right of the father and the locus of legitimate male desire. French feminist theory sought to define a nonpaternal *jouissance* exceeding the male fantasy. Julia Kristeva sees the *jouissance* of woman as existing within the Oedipal system (woman is positioned in but not of this order), but as something that cannot be articulated in that order. For Kristeva, the figure of the mother and *jouissance* are therefore closely tied, and the *jouissance* represents "a maternal function ... beyond discourse, beyond narrative, beyond psychology ... beyond figuration." Julia Kristeva, *Desire in Language: A Semiotic Approach to Literature and Art*, Leon S. Roudiez (ed.), (New York, 1984), p. 247.

[49] Lauren Berlant, *The Female Complaint: the Unfinished Business of Sentimentality in American Culture* (Durham and London, 2008), p. viii.

of force that allow only particular subject positions to emerge. My larger question is this: How is the individual subject of desire produced and half of it (half of humanity) effaced in the same breath?

This is where playfulness comes in: an interpretive move, which is critically entangled with the literary playfulness of the authors I engage, who dwelt in milieus, hesitant, open and flexible, where the simultaneity of many genres and languages was the essence of literary life. It is in their daring ventures that we discern unsuspected areas of the lives of the girl-child and woman. Insha's tale of Rani Ketki is an excellent example of this. Increasingly, however, in the case of the later-nineteenth-century authors, we note a constraining of the avenues and the spaces of discipline such as homes and schools, given the reformist interest in casting a new woman found in several important texts of the time.[50]

In order to elaborate the historical, conceptual and archival concerns of *Coming of Age in Nineteenth-Century India*, I have organized the book into a prelude, five chapters and a retrospect. The prelude, "Opening the Door," based on the interviews with Azra Kidwai, detailed the spatial setting, the required stages and the interpretations of respectable girlhood. Chapter 1 has set out the historiographical and conceptual engagements of the book. Chapter 2, "Woman of the Forest," focuses on Insha's early-nineteenth-century writing and considers a different kind of girl-child and woman figure than the one Azra speaks about or that we find in the late-nineteenth-century didactic literature. In Chapter 3, "Woman of the School," and Chapter 4, "Woman of the Household," I turn to later texts by Inspector of Schools Raja Shiv Prasad and reformers and educators like Nazir Ahmad, Hali and

---

[50] The following articulation, taken from Judith Butler, is useful for my purposes. That the woman appears to be a "flawed copy," "the medium through which procreation becomes possible and who physicalizes and, hence, demeans that higher form of the spiritual reduplication of 'man' ..." Here, Butler calls to attention Luce Irigaray, who insists that "the homoerotic impulse toward self-duplication at work in Plato's discourse on desire and love implicates him in yet a different order of mastery ... 'spiritual desire' is that which takes place between men, not exactly a homosexuality, but *hommosexuality*, a spiritualized and desexualized desire for the form or reflection of a masculine self in another ..." This is, Butler argues, "a fantastic logic whereby men beget other men, reproducing and mirroring themselves at the expense of women and of their own reproductive origins in women/mothers." Judith Butler, "Desire," in Frank Lentricchia and Thomas McLaughlin (eds.), *Critical Terms for Literary Study* (Chicago, 1995), p. 376.

Gauridatt to suggest how their discourses aimed to produce ideal girls and women. In Chapter 5, "The Woman of the Rooftops," I invoke rooftops as an allegorical space (open and limitless and vital to women's interaction and exchanges in many premodern cities) to consider the perspectives of women interpreters, novelists and storytellers on male-inspired female figures and feminine culture.

Thus, it is the simultaneous production and erasure of the girl-child/woman – the stabilization of Indian/Hindu/Muslim tradition, and of notions of what the respectable girl and woman ought to be and to do[51] – that is the central object of investigation in this book. Let me begin with a time before this tradition was securely, and narrowly, established.

---

[51] In Zora Neale Hurston's novel, *Their Eyes were Watching God*, Janie Crawford's grandmother, Nanny, says that because she was born a slave, she never had the opportunity "to fulfill [her] dreams of whut a woman oughta be and to do." Cited in Stephanie Shaw, *What a Woman Ought to Be and to Do: Black Professional Women Workers During the Jim Crow Era* (Chicago and London, 1996), p. xi.

Map II. North Western Provinces and Awadh (later the United Provinces), circa 1860.

2

The Woman of the Forest

Azra's telling of her upbringing and training (covered in the prelude) illustrates powerfully and profoundly the significance of physical spaces and literature as complementary contexts in which the social and cultural training of a girl-child to become a respectable woman occurred. Azra's narrative is filled with vivid references to lush, heavily architected spaces in which she lived, played and learned. Yet, it is striking that her descriptions of the physical spaces such as her childhood homes, except for occasional references to leisurely activities, are filled with burdens of domestic chores, the care of younger siblings, school work and the monotony of everyday routine. As discussed in the prelude, her discussion of games, picnics, theater and the songs in her summer vacation came at the end of our five-year conversation after she heard my talk in Jamia Millia Islamia in 2009 during which I invoked the idea of playfulness, authorial vision and what a writer makes possible in creative play through a discussion of Insha's tale of Rani Ketki.

The question that I ask in this chapter follows that inquiry about playfulness. I ask about the spaces, conditions and social contexts in which men and women (for my purposes, especially women) expressed themselves, not as already formed characters conforming to an ideal (the perfect man or woman), but as boys and girls, men and women seeking to make themselves and their lives richer and less routine or duty bound.

In this chapter, I turn to a rather unusual – one might also add forgotten (and I will explain how) – text from 1803, Insha-allah Khan's

(1756–1817) tale of Rani Ketki, which allows us to consider different kinds of female figures (girl, daughter, friend, woman) in the wonderful generic possibilities that are implicit in the range of texts the story itself refers to – drama, epic, folk tale and so on. I should like to underline some striking features of this tale at the outset. As noted in the previous chapter, this text is rare in the literal sense of word, in that it is the only one of its kind available to us in written form from the early nineteenth century. Given its location in multiple Indic traditions, as well as Persian conventions of flowery imagery, including the idea of Urdu *dastans*, it stands for a form of storytelling widely in circulation at the time. We see this in the narration of the way the hero and the heroine meet and in the spatial locations of the tale – very much a part of the mode of storytelling, for instance, in the Ramayana and the Mahabharata. The point, one critic notes, is that Insha's tale was in fact a generic one, the meeting of a young man and a woman that had been told many times: it is exactly how Shakuntala meets Dushyanta in the Mahabharata, to take one example. The striking thing about this story is that in 1803 Insha decided to write it down, thus bringing the tale from an oral into a written tradition.[1]

What is eye-catching in Insha's tale, as suggested in the last chapter, is that the figures of the girl-child and woman are built up against a varied and fluid set of moral discourses. In addition, the women in his story are not fully made, confined to a disciplined, respectable, domestic world. They live within the limits of the palace; nonetheless they question the idea of fixed boundaries by speaking about their wishes, by going to the forest and playing on the swings, by being demanding of parents and even undertaking forbidden activities. Again, as I argued before, while these are not "real" figures with precise locations and dates, these are an author's ideas of potential: the characters embodying such ideas come out of and speak to the ethics of Insha's milieu.

It should be noted that Insha's tale represents a striking departure from the earlier "mirror of princes" genre of the courtly and elite circles in which he spent most of his career (at the courts of Murshidabad and Delhi before he settled in Lucknow). Insha called his narrative, originally written in the Perso-Arabic script (albeit exclusively in Hindavi,

---

[1] Personal communication with Urdu critic and scholar Sadiq-ur-Rahman Kidwai, August 2009.

without any admixture of Persian and Urdu, as the author claimed), simply "a tale."[2] This story subsequently came to be called *Rani Ketki ki Kahani* (*The Story of Rani Ketki*) or *Kahani theth Hindi mein* (*A Story in Pure Hindi*). It was picked up by scholars of Hindi, reproduced a number of times in the Devanagri script and came to be seen as the earliest example of prose in the Hindi language.

Interestingly, it is hard to find any critical reading of this text. There's an irony in all of this, especially in the story finding mention as an artifact of Hindi language, not as a tale enmeshed in the ethics of a variety of written and oral traditions. I take up the question of the "loss" of Insha's tale in the next chapter and discuss what happens to the extraordinary range of female characters and spaces in its new life in an 1867 Hindi collection, the *Gutka*, put together by Inspector of Schools Raja Shiv Prasad, who was distinguished for setting up schools and for the preparation of the first set of school textbooks in the North Western Provinces (much of today's Uttar Pradesh).

In order to fully appreciate the importance of Insha's story, especially its wonderfully varied female figures and the striking physical spaces that he envisages, which progressively get lost in the more didactic literary production of the nineteenth century, I have organized the remainder of this chapter into three sections. In section II, I detail the playful literary context of Insha's time. By looking at the debates on the inspiration for the composition of Rani Ketki and its models, as well as the depictions of gender relations and modes of sexuality that

[2] It is important to note that the Urdu version of the story, which I unearthed after searching for three years, an 1852 reproduction, also has no title. The author says at the beginning of the story: *ek din … apne dhyan mein chadi ki koi kahani aisi kahiye ki jisme Hindi ki chuut aur kisi boli ka put na mile*; the comments by L. Clint, who reproduced the Perso-Arabic version, entitled it "A tale by Insha-allah Khan." For the Perso-Arabic script of this tale, I use a version reproduced in 1852 and 1855 in the *Journal of the Asiatic Society of Bengal*: L. Clint, "Rani Ketki ki Kahani," *The Journal of the Asiatic Society of Bengal*, Issue 1, Vol. 21 (1852); S. Slater, "Rani Ketki ki Kahani," *The Journal of the Asiatic Society of Bengal*, Vol. 24 (1852). Cited as *Urdu Ketki, I* and *II*. For the Devanagari edition, I use Shyamsundar Das (ed.), *Rani Ketki ki Kahani*. The passages that I translate of this Hindi version are cited as *Hindi Ketki*. However, my translation of the discussion of the history of the production of the Ketki story taken from Shyamsundar Das's introduction is cited as Shyamsundar Das, *Rani Ketki*. For Insha's sentence cited previously, *Urdu Ketki, I*, p. 5; *Hindi Ketki*, p. 2. All translations of these texts are mine. I am especially grateful to Tim Bryson, the South Asia librarian at Emory University, for his persistent search in helping me locate the 1852 version.

Insha unfolds in his *Rekhti* (Urdu poetry in women's voices), a genre of poetry writing for which he is well known, I highlight the richly diverse character of his literary environment. Authors such as Insha readily drew on many traditions and conventions of storytelling and characterizations. Another important point about Insha's location in northern India is the distinct absence of the linguistic divide between Hindi and Urdu, or a sharp sociocultural divide between Hindus and Muslims of the kind that began to emerge in social-political contests in the later nineteenth century. In Insha's world, Hindi, Urdu, Sanskrit, Persian and other languages and dialects were very much part of a north Indian writer's heritage, and Insha was a product of this expansive sensibility. In this, what mattered was the sharing of multiple traditions, not limiting or defining creative works in terms of one language, one people or one line of descent. In fact, my argument is that even at the time of the emergence of debates on Hindi and Urdu as distinct languages, and the beginning of the attribution of these languages to Hindu and Muslim communities, a neat and sharp division along linguistic and community lines remained contested (a point I elaborate in the next chapter).

In section III, I highlight the spatial arrangements central to – and that indeed constitute the very specialness of – Insha's story. In particular, I discuss the importance of the forest and the palace as critical spatial configurations in the text. I suggest that it is in the relationship between the two that we find "breathing spaces," a space for play, and the forest as the space of freedom for the girl-child and woman. It is also in this spatial interaction that we note the constraining spaces: the palace is the site of pedagogy. As in Azra's account, Insha's invocation of physical spaces has serious implications for a history of the development of the girl-child and woman, and I argue that it is because of the foregrounding of the forest, the "peripheral" space, as it were, that we are able to detect a variety of female forms. The palace is critical too because a history and a pedagogy would not be possible without an illustration of the regulations of the palace. Nor would the magic, the meetings, the revenge, the reunions in the forest. I shall demonstrate, however, that the forest and the palace are both dynamic spaces and they both generate pedagogy and discipline in Insha's story.[3] What is

---

[3] I detail the dynamism of the forest and the palace as it unfolds in Insha's tale in the section "Forests and Outskirts." I should note that in several texts, the palace emerges

of interest to me is how in their simultaneous placement Insha is able to give life to several remarkable women figures.

In section IV, I consider the vibrant women figures of Insha's story, of the palace and of the forest: not only in the activities allowed, the prescriptions of the time, the value systems upheld, the range of contests and negotiations, but also in the rich descriptions and terms for women that become available to us (both in the story and in Rekhti). I should emphasize once more that such a discursive range for women figures is greatly dimmed in later accounts such as didactic tales or manuals of instruction, those that Azra read, for example. The grounds for the establishment of gender relations in Insha's world were very different from what follows after him, which I chart in the rest of this book. In this chapter, then, I detail a female world not yet domesticated: while it is clearly structured and has discernible rules, its boundaries are much more negotiable and much more regularly crossed than appears possible later in the nineteenth century.

A PLAYFUL CONTEXT

The ancestors of Insha (meaning "composition," which is what he adopted as his pen name) came to India from Najaf and descended from the Sayyid lineage of Kashmir. Insha's father, Masha-allah Khan (who used the pen name Masdar, or "verb root"), was a companion of Nawab Siraj-ud-daulah in Murshidabad, where Insha was born. Insha was brought up "in the style in which sons of elite families were educated in the old days ... [and] Sayyid Insha too [became] a master of all the necessary arts and sciences." As a boy, Insha was fond of singing. He memorized the Arabic grammar book *Kafiyah* and played its words on the sitar![4]

Writing of Insha in *Ab-e Hayat* (*Water of Life*), composed in 1880 – "recognized widely and immediately as the definitive history of Urdu poetry"[5] – Muhammad Husain Azad says, "few such creative and

as the place where literature and civilization subsist, and the forest is the place where the guru/hermit has his *ashram* (pedagogy): it is also the place of wildness outside civilization. The question is also what kind of forest, wild or tamed, is presented by Insha; it seems to me that Insha's forest sits in the middle of these two.
[4] Muhammad Husain Azad, *Ab-e hayat: Shaping the Canon of Urdu Poetry*, Frances Pritchett and Shamsur Rahman Faruqi (tr. and ed.), (New Delhi, 2001), pp. 222, 223 and fn. b.
[5] Ibid., p. 5.

brilliant men have been born in India." Insha "had so much liveliness that, like quicksilver, he never stayed for long in one place. Thus his Complete Works bear witness to all these matters." From Murshidabad, Insha went to Delhi during the time of Emperor Shah Alam, who was a poet himself. Insha flourished: Shah Alam "didn't wish to be separated from him for a moment." From Delhi, Insha went to Lucknow, to the court of Mirza Sulaiman Shikoh, the son of Shah Alam. Azad reminisces nostalgically: "There were gatherings of poets and judges of poetry like Mushafi, Jur'at, Mirza Qatil and so on. The gatherings adorned by such bouquets from the garden of eloquence – how colorful it must all have been!"[6]

Honored in all the courts to which he went, Insha, the "intellectual polyglot,"[7] wrote in several languages, including Persian, Arabic, Urdu, Turkish, Hindi and Punjabi. The point is not the number of languages he was skilled at, but how he managed to interlace these and how eloquently he used them. Again, to use Azad's words: "The various Indian languages are like his maidservants. Now he stands in the Punjab, now he sits holding a conversation in the East. Now he is a resident of the Braj country, now a Maratha, now a Kashmiri, now an Afghan."[8]

The range of works that Insha composed provides further testimony to his agility and experimentation: Urdu *gazals*; a volume of Rekhti; magic spells; Pushto grammar; odes in Persian; a dot-less *masnavi* in Persian; satires on complaints about wasps, bedbugs and flies; the *Murgh-namah* (about cock fighting); the *Darya-e latafat* (about Urdu grammar and rhetoric); the tale of Rani Ketki; and many other works.[9]

The matter of what literary scholars call the "aesthetics of reception" is important here and it is related to the range of sources and traditions that an author draws from. As Robert Jauss notes, when the intent of a work is undeclared and the relationship of the author to sources and models is only "indirectly accessible," then the "philosophical question

---

[6] Ibid., pp. 223, 229.
[7] Ruth Vanita, "Different Speakers, Different Loves: Urban Women in Rekhti Poetry," in Gyanendra Pandey (ed.), *Subalternity and Difference: Investigations from the North and the South* (New York and London, 2011), p. 71.
[8] Azad, *Ab-e hayat*, p. 233.
[9] For a full list and details of Insha's works, see Azad, *Ab-e hayat*, pp. 222–237.

of how the text is 'properly' ... understood can best be answered if one foregrounds it against those works that the author explicitly or implicitly presupposed his contemporary audience to know." In this way, the author creates and evokes the reader's "horizon of expectations."[10]

It is important to note that when Insha was working on the Ketki story and other writings, the structure of Hindi prose was not fixed.[11] Although Insha was part of the same context in which a very dynamic set of poets and writers, including Saadal Mishra and Lalluji Lal (1747–1824), experimented with instability (*ansthirta*) in languages, it is Insha who claimed to produce a text (his tale) without relying on any earlier source (*koi aadhar na tha*).[12]

The meeting of an aristocratic man and woman, the centerpiece of Insha's story, in fact, occurs in the texts written before 1803, such as in the story of Shakuntala and some stories in the Puranas, the *Kathasaritrasagar* and the Mahabharata. In the Mahabharata, Arjuna and Bhima, as well as the great sages, meet women or nymphs in the forests. Given his versatile use of literary and linguistic practices, Insha is certain to have been familiar with such stories. The beauty of this tale is precisely in the authorial invocations of both the Indic and non-Indic literary and linguistic conventions, including those of Hindi, Urdu and Punjabi.[13] Precisely for that reason, the claim of writing a story in the Perso-Arabic script without using a single word of Persian or Arabic becomes all the more a claim about authorial agility and playfulness.

Shyamsundar Das calls the style of Insha's story, "*nirala*," unusual, unique.[14] McGregor suggests that the subject matter of the tale is "full of romantic and the romantic and supernatural," and that its narrative

---

[10] Of course, there remains the possibility of "objectifying the horizon of expectation in works that are historically less sharply delineated [sic]." Jauss suggests bearing in mind the following factors that might help us in appreciating the "specific disposition toward a particular work that the author anticipates from the audience," namely, "familiar norms or the immanent poetics of the genre"; "the implicit relationships to works of the literary-historical surroundings" and so on. Robert Jauss, "Literary History as a Challenge to Literary Theory," in Timothy Bahti (tr.), *Toward an Aesthetic of Reception* (Minneapolis, 1982), pp. 24, 28.

[11] Shyamsundar Das, *Rani Ketki*, p. 11. The author says, "*is baat ko dhyaan mein rakhna chahiye ki ab tak Hindi gadh ka koi swarup nishchit nahi hua tha.*"

[12] Ibid., p. 11.

[13] Ibid., pp. 14–15.

[14] Ibid., p. 12.

tradition is "exemplified both in the Urdu *dastans*, [and] romance story cycles." Yet, while the Urdu Persian literary background is clear, "the use of rhyming elements, strings of verbs, and inversions and colloquialisms, with a flowery and conventionalized imagery much more Persian than Indian, marks this work as a curiosity in Hindi."[15]

Whether in terms of linguistic instability or of the varied cultural symbolic traditions that Insha's story invokes, one thing is clear: the tale is an "open" text, adhering to no single genre. In the existing cultural milieu, stories of this kind – stories built on numerous told and untold stories – were meant for entertainment. These tales were often recited and re-cited by someone who "did not have authority": like mothers, grandmothers, even grandfathers (though rarely fathers!). The stories would often be told with "a light touch, almost casually, while putting a child to sleep, during meal times" and so on.[16]

Insha, along with his famous contemporaries Rangin and Jur`at, is best known for his compositions of Urdu Rekhti poetry. A discussion of the main features of Rekhti, for which I rely on the excellent writings of Ruth Vanita and Carla Pietevich, helps illumine the openness and creative ease of Insha's milieu – and his confident play with genres, conventions and styles that allowed him to write about a fabulous array of figures, including the girl-child and woman. Such playfulness and boldness, and the lack of anxiety with which he uses Indic and non-Indic symbols, is precisely the position that would come to be critiqued and disciplined, oriented towards one literary tradition, one ethnic group – a "Hindu" and "Muslim" sensibility, "Hindu" and "Muslim" traditions – in the latter half of the nineteenth century.

Rekhta, literally "scattered," is a name for Urdu, a language known to have evolved in the Indian subcontinent from a mixture of Persian and Sanskrit-based languages. Rangin coined the term Rekhti (the feminine of *Rekhta*), written mostly by men in "women's language"

---

[15] Ronald Stuart McGregor, *Hindi Literature of the Nineteenth and Early Twentieth Centuries* (Wiesbaden, 1974), p. 64.

[16] Personal communication from V. Narayana Rao, May 1, 2009. It is important that, unlike a whole range of Hindi and Urdu texts of this time, Rani Ketki was not part of the books used by Fort William College, where, under the guidance of John Gilchrist, Hindustani books were composed, several of which were intended for school curriculum. For an extended discussion of how a variety of classics came to be catalogued and institutionalized into "vernacular" languages under Gilchrist's direction, see Rashmi Bhatnagar's monograph in progress.

with female personae. Women's language was spoken not only by women: it was the language of the non-elite and was adopted by poets to "represent an indigenous urbanity." Rekhti's "virtual disappearance" from the canon is due to its homoerotic content as well as its "nonjudgmental adoption of literary conventions and social customs drawn from non-Persianate and Hindu sources."[17] It is important to underline what it was about this linguistic and literary practice that was later thought unseemly. The "expurgation" of Rekhti was not only because of its erotic content, but also its "hybridity," the "'impure' mingling" that was, in Vanita's words, the "hallmark of their [Rekhti poets'] indigenous urbanity, distinct from the urbanity of a 'pure' Persianate provenance."[18]

Carla Petievich notes that Rekhti is "associated with the domestic sphere of socially elite, secluded women during the late eighteenth and nineteenth centuries" and that it used the aristocratic women's language (*begmati zuban*), the "particular idiom of their milieu."[19] Central to Rekhti is women's speech, told by a male narrator ("a female persona speaker") who "dwells on women's lives and concerns." What is significant in this narration of women's lives is "the [use of the] language of their private lives, of emotions, and of significant [wide-ranging] imaginative domains."[20] Thus, major Rekhti poets of the time first had to prove their skills by writing in Persian and Persianized Urdu and adhering to its literary conventions. However, these men, by birth and upbringing, were also used to "the despised 'female' terrain inhabited by the female servants who had mothered

[17] Vanita, "Married Among their Companions," pp. 1, 15, 36. Vanita has recently relocated several of Insha's manuscripts and is now translating his poetry extensively, parts of which appear in her "Different Speakers, Different Loves." I have used Vanita's available writings on Rekhti. Her book on Insha came out just as *Coming of Age in Nineteenth-Century India* went into the final stages of production. See Vanita, *Gender, Sex and the City: Urdu Rekhti Poetry in India, 1780–1870* (New York, 2012).

[18] Ibid., pp. 12, 15.

[19] Carla Petievich, "Gender Politics and the Urdu Ghazal: Exploratory Observations on Rekhta versus Rekhti," *Economic and Social History Review*, Vol. 38, No. 3 (2001), p. 229. On Begmati Zuban, see Gail Minault, "Begmati Zuban: Women's Language and Culture in Nineteenth Century Delhi," *India International Center Quarterly*, Vol. 11, No. 2 (June 1984): 155–170; and also by Minault, "Other Voices, Other Rooms: The View from the Zenana," in Nita Kumar (ed.), *Women as Subjects: South Asian Histories* (Calcutta, 1994), pp. 108–124.

[20] Vanita, "Married Among their Companions," pp. 12, 37.

them, and to different degrees, by their wives, mothers, or mistresses. If Persianized Urdu was these poets' 'father tongue,' Urdu immersed in Hindi dialects was often their 'mother tongue.'"[21] It was this combination of the "feminine narrator and its *begamati* idiom that gave *Rekhti* its generic distinctiveness."[22]

It is in the context of bold experimentation with "women's speech," the use of multiple languages, diverse genres, allusions and conventions making for a rich and layered literary landscape that Insha's story of Rani Ketki finds its place, its spirit and its figures. It is in the use of *begmati zuban* (the language or idiom of aristocratic women) and the interweaving of languages, literary allusions and metaphors that Insha engineered the kind of playfulness he demonstrates in his tale. The language – and gender play – that Insha was skilled at was in fact based upon his mastery of the rules of grammar. The great nineteenth-century literary critic, Muhammad Husain Azad, suggested in writing about Insha's grammar of Urdu, the *Darya-e Latafat*, how rules of grammar emanate from Insha's sense of play:

> Although there's the same frivolity and liveliness of manner in this book too, it is the first book that our native speakers have written about Urdu grammar... [It has] the language of various groups of Urdu speakers... Then he has set down the rules of the language and understanding of poetry. Then he has set down the rules of the language, and starting from humor and even going to obscenity, he has not omitted anything... Prosody, rhyme, speech, devices and figures of speech ... he has set out in Urdu all the branches of rhetoric... Still the truth is that whatever is there, is not devoid of pleasure.[23]

It might not be out of place to say that Insha's Ketki story (as much as his other writings) demonstrates that separate Hindu and Muslim cultural spheres, and indeed, even the proposition that Hindu and Muslim worlds were shared did not exist at this time. The question of whether a particular text or articulation bespoke of a Muslim sensibility or a Hindu sensibility, Hindi or Urdu, was not yet a major concern. All the names in the story of Ketki are Indic names. Then there are

[21] Ibid., p. 13.
[22] Petievich, "Gender Politics and the Urdu Ghazal," p. 232.
[23] Azad, *Ab-e hayat*, pp. 235–236. Azad admires this work of Insha's, but is unimpressed with several others, such as his Rekhti compositions or his Odes. Ibid, pp. 232–233.

gods and goddesses and ascetic figures that mingle with earthly characters. The tale was regarded by Insha himself as a curiosity – a sign of powerful imagination. Insha's Rani Ketki implies too that he saw language in the realm of play: he demonstrates this in the bending of rules and in the arrangements of word choice. Insha is a theorist of playfulness precisely because he was a writer who systematized Urdu grammar – creating a system of linguistic rules and regulations, putting emphasis on decorum and correctness – who was at the same time committed to linguistic and gender playfulness.

FOREST AND OUTSKIRTS

In this section, I reflect on the fulcrum of Insha's tale: its spatial setting that comes out in the distinctions he proposes between the forest and the palace. Insha's female figures are ranged along these complementary spaces guaranteeing their proliferation.[24] Let me begin with Insha's storyline, briefly summarized. His tale centers on the meeting of an aristocratic young woman, Rani Ketki, and an aristocratic youth, Udaybhan, in a forest where Ketki is playing on the swings. Udaybhan arrives having lost his way while hunting. Insha narrates the spontaneous desire that arises in Ketki and Udaybhan for each other, their secret promise of marriage, the problems encountered by both in their wish to get married and Ketki's initiative in making the marriage happen. Several other episodes are entwined with the saga of Ketki and Udaybhan's desire to marry: the involvement of the two kingdoms, ruled by the parents of Rani Ketki and Kunvar Udaybhan; the seminal role played by the guru of Ketki's parents, the ascetic Mahinder Gir, who lived in Mount Kailash, the abode of Lord Shiva; and more. The roles of the ascetic and of Ketki's close friend, Madanban – and the concurrent centering of the palace and the forest – evoke the networks and the relationships, as well as the broader social and political location in which these find meanings.

Insha's story takes place at two levels that intersect as points of distinction – the forest and its outskirts. My paradoxical inversion here, of the forest as center, and human habitation and the palace as outskirts,

---

[24] Several propositions that I make in the following pages came out of conversations with Milind Wakankar and his excellent suggestions on spatial formations and storytelling in the premodern world.

is deliberate. In Insha's telling, the forest emerges as an essential space around which and in the immediacy of which other spaces acquire meaning. The "outskirts" are the aristocratic household or the palace (not referred to directly as such in the story, but invoked in the actions of the characters), and its surrounding areas such as the villages. The possibility of freedom for both male and female characters in the tale hinges on the space of the forest.

Reference to another well-known, in fact, an epic story of the forest – that of Shakuntala – will help to set this in context. Romila Thapar says that the "bi-polarity" of the forest and the court is a running theme of the many versions of Shakuntala's story. She notes that "the hero chasing a deer during a hunt and arriving at an unexpected place is well known to folk literature." Again, hunting in the forest has many messages: hunting literally and symbolically as "romantic love in [the context of] a courtly background"; "hunt as a metaphor for pursuit, contesting emotions and ultimately submission;" hunting as an alternative to going to battle for heroic acts and so on. In the epic form, as well as in plays of early India, Thapar suggests that the duality of the dwelling and exile, settlements and forest (referred to in a range of texts as *grama* and *aranya*; or *ksetra* and *vana*; or *pura* and *janapada*) is generic and affects the characterizations of the protagonists.[25] Shakuntala of the epic version (*Mahabharata*), the woman of the forest (*aranya*), is very different from that of the play of Kalidasa, written in the context of a more established court culture, settled forms of kingship and the entrenchment of the Brahmanical order. In the former, the female protagonist is assertive and forthright; in the latter she is subdued and speaks little.[26]

What does Insha's tale do with this inheritance? The beginning of his story is set in a tamarind grove: a place of pleasure, where women sport on the swings. Udaybhan stumbles here with some insouciance. He sees forty or fifty girls, one more beautiful than the other, playing on the swings and singing songs of spring. "Who are you?" "Who are you?" the girls protest. One of them is dressed in red. They call

[25] Thapar, *Sakuntala*, pp. 36, 47, 63.
[26] For a detailed discussion of these themes, see Thapar, *Sakuntala*, chs. 2 and 3, and the next chapter of this book. Thapar suggests that the bracket 400 BCE to 400 CE would be the most appropriate time frame of the epic. Likewise, she says the date for Kalidasa varies, but he is placed in the fourth century CE. Ibid., p. 7.

her Rani Ketki. She says to Udaybhan: "What shall we say? How is this proper? You dropped upon us all at once. You know that women (*randiyan*) were playing on the swings. You have boldly walked in here." Udaybhan explains: "Don't be upset with me. Tired by a long day, I will just lie down here, making covering by a tree, protecting myself against dew. In the morning I will go away. I was in search of a deer. As long as there was light I was fine. Once it grew dark, I was greatly bewildered and wandered here, seeking shelter in trees. Without restraint, out of breath, I came here. How did I know beautiful women (*padminiyan*) were on the swings? But it was predestined." Ketki responds: "no one has yet killed a guest." A screen is then put between Udaybhan and Ketki with some clothes hung on it to separate their sleeping quarters.[27]

Note the sensual joys of transformation that take place in the forest: Ketki and Udaybhan become desirous of each other. Quite quickly after the first exchange between Ketki and Udaybhan, Insha has Ketki confiding to her confidante, Madanban: "I have lost my heart to him. You know my secrets. Whatever happens now, I'll go to him. You come with me. I beg you. No one must know. We have been brought together by his and my creator." Madanban and Ketki go to where Udaybhan is resting. Madanban explains to Udaybhan that Ketki has come to see him. "Why not?" he says: "It is a meeting of hearts (*ji ko ji se milaap hai*)." Madanban introduces Ketki, the daughter of Raja Jagat Parkash and Rani Kamlata. She explains that several kings and princes had sent proposals of marriage to Ketki, to no avail. Udaybhan introduces himself. Madanban suggests that they exchange rings. Udaybhan puts his ring on Ketki's finger; she places her ring on his finger and gives him "a little pinch" (*aur ek dhimi si chutki bhi le li*) in addition![28]

Ketki's parents, however, refuse the proposal of the marriage of their daughter to Udaybhan, whose parents are of lower status.[29] Her father, Jagat Parkash, calls out to his guru (spiritual guide), Mahinder Gir, who lives in Mount Kailash (the abode of Lord Shiva), and along with ninety *lakh* lives/histories (*ateet*, literally "pasts"), spends his time in prayers and devotion. "He could rain down gold and silver,

[27] *Urdu Ketki*, I, pp. 7–10; *Hindi Ketki*, pp. 3–5.
[28] *Urdu Ketki*, I, pp. 11–13; *Hindi Ketki*, pp. 5–6.
[29] *Urdu Ketki*, I, pp. 17–18; *Hindi Ketki*, pp. 8–9.

and transform every object as he wished. In the singing and playing
of instruments, all except Mahadeo (Shiva) confessed inferiority to
him. Even Saraswati [the goddess of learning] had learnt how to hum
and sing (*gungunana*) from him... When he chose, he could rise in
spaces between heaven and earth." Mahinder Gir orders his disciples
to change Prince Udaybhan and his parents, Raja Surajbhan and Rani
Lakshmibas, into deer. Once transformed, the three of them are let
loose in a forest, their companions torn in pieces.[30]

Via Mahinder Gir, Insha presents a palimpsest of transformations
in the forest: Mahinder Gir, the ascetic, living on Mount Kailash with
his pasts (*ateet*) thus manipulating time (past and present). Mahinder
Gir punishes Udaybhan and his parents by turning them into deer.
Udaybhan, the valorous hunting prince, becomes effeminized.

From the forest, Insha takes us to the site of culture, modesty (*laaj*)
and socialization, which is the palace, and in fact may even be seen
in the forest through Ketki's actions. At the time of the first scene of
the story in the tamarind grove, Ketki becomes deeply apprehensive
about her modesty and all at once also desirous of Udaybhan. While
this desire stays, once she returns home it must be brought to fruition
within the demands of the familial, of the accepted code of honor and
kingly decorum. It is for this reason that Ketki turns down Udaybhan's
offer of eloping when the war begins between the two kingdoms after
Ketki's parents decline Udaybhan's parents' offer of the marriage of
their son to Ketki. Later on, Madanban rebuffs Ketki's offer of looking for Udaybhan, citing the honor of the dominion (*raaj-paath*) of her
parents, the issue of modesty (*laaj*) and the peacefulness (*sukh-chayn*)
of the kingdom.[31]

In the palace we witness a negotiation around the forbidden ashes,
which Mahinder Gir has given to Ketki's parents, their purpose being
that the person who used ashes as collyrium would be able to see
everything without being seen himself and "could do whatever he
pleased."[32] Ketki tries to get the magical ashes from her mother, osten-
sibly for a game of hide and seek.[33]

[30] *Urdu Ketki, I,* pp. 20–23; *Hindi Ketki,* pp. 10–12.
[31] *Urdu Ketki, II,* pp. 86–89; *Hindi Ketki,* pp. 15–17.
[32] *Urdu Ketki, II,* p. 80; *Hindi Ketki,* p. 12.
[33] *Urdu Ketki, II,* pp. 84–85; *Hindi Ketki,* pp. 13–15.

One night Ketki says to Madanban, "I am leaving all modesty (*laaj*) behind. You help me." Ketki explains to her that all the play acting about the ashes was actually meant for a purpose: she and Madanban could put the ashes in their eyes and wander off to look for Udaybhan. Madanban refuses, explaining that such desire (*chahat*), which leads to giving up of the dominion (*raaj-paath*) of parents, modesty (*laaj*) and peacefulness (*such-chayn*) was not acceptable. Madanban says to Ketki that she is still immature (*alhad*); she has seen little of life. She advises Ketki to forget the whole affair. Ketki laughs. "There is a world of difference between saying and doing things," she says. "Do you think that times are so dark that I am going to leave my dominion, parents, modesty?" A few days later, having acquired the ashes with the intervention of her father, and without conferring with Madanban, Rani Ketki smears her eyes with ashes and leaves.[34] Ketki sets out to the forest. It is in the forest that Madanban follows her, and only then that she appreciates the depth of Ketki's feelings. It is also only after Ketki has run away to the forest in search of Udaybhan that her parents – and through them, Mahinder Gir – realize the intensity of her desire. Ketki becomes for a while the questing hero.

Conceptually, one might say, the palace is the site of pedagogy, the forest the place of literature. In Insha's tale, these intermingle but at the same time keep their distinctiveness. And it is in the distinct actions of the female in these intersecting spaces that Ketki's potential as both the girl and the woman is realized. In the extensive focus on specific physical spaces, there is a horizon of expectation that Insha builds, which animates the milieu in and for which he constructs his figures, and importantly the range of possibilities his figures inhabit. Thus, in Insha's narration, and in his precise spatial descriptions – in which a variety of women will appear – the reader may identify an unusual "aesthetics of reception" centrally concerned with the "successive unfolding of the potential for meaning that is embedded in a work."[35]

Insha's spatial invocations in Rekhti are once again critical: these enliven a variety of pleasurable experiences and with these muddy the received notions of respectability.[36] Ruth Vanita has argued that

---

[34] *Urdu Ketki, II*, pp. 86–89; *Hindi Ketki*, pp. 15–17.
[35] Jauss, "Literary History," p. 30.
[36] Vanita, "Different Speakers, Different Loves," p. 58.

Rekhti "reconfigures the city from women's perspective," bringing to life a world of meeting places: not the streets or markets that Saleem Kidwai writes about as emerging in the sixteenth- to eighteenth-century Persian and Urdu writing as sites where men met and mingled, but spaces such as gardens, rooftops, domestic neighborhoods.[37] Gardens and rooftops represented interior and exterior spaces simultaneously. In the old cities in northern India – as in the old cities of the Middle East and North Africa – many adjacent houses in a neighborhood are connected by rooftops. It is possible to pass through by stepping over the low dividing walls from one rooftop to another. There are several depictions of encounters between women set on the rooftops in the Rekhti compositions of Insha and Rangin.[38]

As in Insha's tale, there are references in a good deal of Rekhti poetry to the "green areas" outside the city, representing "temporary escape from domesticity," which is also what rooftops provide: escape from chores downstairs was one among the many possibilities that rooftops offered women (a point I detail in the last chapter, "The Woman of the Rooftops"). Women also go to the gardens on the river-banks and boat on the river. There is a celebration of women's outings in Rekhti poetry. The joys of the rainy season and spring are especially marked. "The city turns green and women dress in green to match it."[39] In the first scene of Insha's tale, Ketki sits on the swings with other women, singing songs of spring or rainy season (*sawan*), the time of expectation.

And then there is the neighborhood. In Rekhti, women forge relationships here. They borrow and lend kitchen items, watch the activities of their neighbors, invite each other for *pan* ("with its long Indic history of erotic meanings") and sweets, visit one another for slee-povers, thus building "women's networks" – as well as creating opportunities "for lovers to sleep together."[40]

---

[37] Ibid., p. 61; Ruth Vanita and Saleem Kidwai (eds.), *Same-Sex Love in India: Readings from Literature and History* (Delhi, 2000), pp. 126–127.

[38] In Chapter 5, "The Woman of the Rooftops," I take up the idea of rooftops in both the literal and metaphorical sense in order to extend this spatial metaphor and consider women's ingeniousness in the negotiation of constraining circumstances – as told in a rare autobiographical account from the NWP, as well as in other better-known women's accounts. For a brief discussion of women and rooftops in Rekhti, see Vanita, "Different Speakers, Different Loves," pp. 61–62.

[39] Vanita, "Different Speakers, Different Loves," p. 62.

[40] Ibid., pp. 63–64.

The space of pedagogy, as I have called it, is evoked in an unexpected manner in Rekhti. The respectable households of the *mohalla*, their domestic ethics and constraining demands, are the sites from which women escape to the terraces and other spaces of "freedom." In Insha's tale, the characters often leave for the forest. While Insha never neglects the pedagogic spaces (palace, respectable households), he is very effective in constantly interrupting the pedagogical and drawing out the spaces of pleasure. What is more, even with the compelling placement of the spaces of pleasure and constraint – in Ketki's case, she is married, at the end, with all the expectations of progeny and blissful succession (by means of the blessing of the mythical cow *kamdhenu*) – Insha's subjects do not seem to make a final turn to a definite, fully predictable life of responsibility and duty. The praise of the youthfulness (*joban*) of Rani Ketki and Prince Udaybhan at the time of their wedding is an excellent illustration, one among many, where beauty, youth, goodness – even anger – is marked and, unusually, celebrated at the time of the wedding.

Rani Ketki: The gentleness and beauty (*bhala lagna*) of Rani Ketki is beyond description. The arching of her eye-brows; the modesty of her eyes; her sharp eye lashes; and her frown when angry; and the way she scolds her friends; and her leaping and running after deer!

Kunvar Udaybhan: How can one describe the goodness (*achchapan*) of Kunvar Udaybhan? The beauty of his budding youth; the gracefulness of his walk; the luxuriousness of his sprouting hair; the rosiness of his cheeks like the shining of the sun's rays in the early morning of spring; the beauty of his just appearing moustache; the reflection of his shape as bright as the sun.[41]

What happens next is left open to the reader. But what happens next in the history of Insha's story is also related to the extraordinary power of this story and the figures it creates. It is because of the disruptive potential of Ketki – and the very layering and contradictoriness of her being – that *her tale will be turned into* "The Story of Ketki," forsaking the difficult wisdom of the folk for the axiomatic of instruction.[42]

---

[41] *Urdu Ketki, II*, pp. 112–113; *Hindi Ketki*, pp. 28–29.

[42] In his classic essay on the semantic development of the word *figura*, Auerbach suggests that "figures are not only tentative; they are also the tentative form of something eternal and timeless; they point not only to the concrete future, but also to something that always has been and always will be; they point to something which is in need

FEMALE FIGURES IN INSHA'S TALE

Through a variety of exchanges and statements on aspirations, prescriptions, desires in the physical spaces that he conjures up for their articulations, Insha persuasively presents many kinds of women figures.[43] Ketki, for a start, is projected as both a girl and a woman. We are not told her age at any point in the story, but in the author's marking out of Ketki's actions we trace her potential as a woman and as a girl.

Ketki is introduced to the reader playing on the swings and singing songs of spring with her girl companions in the tamarind grove. With the arrival of Udaybhan arises the issue of modesty, which Ketki speaks about. We witness Ketki who displays initiative and adventurism alongside concern about women's modesty and the importance of honorable comportment. Insha shows her to be concerned about appropriate conduct right from the beginning of the story – as soon as Udaybhan appears in the tamarind grove. Quite quickly after the first exchange between Ketki and Udaybhan, Insha has Ketki confiding her desire to her close friend, Madanban. Madanban introduces them and they exchange rings.

of interpretation, which will indeed be fulfilled in the concrete future." Auerbach, *Scenes From the Drama of European Literature*, p. 59. Throughout this meditation on *figura*, Auerback seeks to establish its vitality: a word that in its earlier manifestation meant "plastic form" in fact "becomes quite unplastic." How the word impinged on the domain of other words – form, image, portrait, model, species, simulacrum, schema, history, allegory, – but somehow managed to keep its "identity" and "specialness." That specialness lies in both the present and the future implied in "figura": the presentness of abstraction, idea, "dynamic, outline and body," but also a word that "foreshowed something in the future." (Ibid., pp. 35, 37). In other words, "the interpretation of one worldly event through another; the first signifies the second, the second fulfills the first. Both remain historical events; yet, both, looked at in this way, have something provisional and incomplete about them; they point to one another and both point to something in the future, something still to come, which will be actual, real, and definitive event." Ibid., p. 58. Of course, Auerbach in the play between present and future is thinking about the Old and New Testament in medieval exegesis, or to put it more succinctly, "The Old Testament is a promise in figure, the New is a promise understood after the spirit." Ibid., p. 41. It is this potential, "future," implicit in "figure," that I wish to build upon in this chapter and the next. In particular, I consider the play between figure and model – a variant (of figure) that had a "great vitality, and [was] to enjoy a significant career." Ibid., p. 17.

[43] I am especially grateful to Wendy Doniger for an afternoon of thought-provoking discussion on how authors direct reading.

The expectation of the reader is immediately redirected to more than one woman: a concerned, desirous *and* playful Ketki. A teasing, and concerned, Madanban too, as we shall see a little later on. Insha plays with such contradictory emotions and practices throughout the text. Udaybhan is introduced as a fifteen-year-old arrogant aristocrat (*kunvar*) – son of Raja Surajbhan and Rani Lakshmibas – who did not think much of anyone (*kisi ko kuch na samajhta tha*).[44] One day, Insha says, he mounted a horse and went away to see the country along with friends. At this point, he met Ketki. On his return, Insha tells us, Udaybhan "neither spoke nor listened, [and he] remained immersed in his thoughts." He would not step out of doors. The women (*ghar-waliyan*) could not distract him. And if someone teased him too much, he would "go to his bed, hide his face, and cry."[45] No longer quite the same kind of brash, aristocratic, young man.

Seeing how disconsolate he is, Udaybhan's parents go to him and ask him to open his heart to them. If he finds that difficult, they suggest, he should write and tell them what has caused him so much grief. He writes and explains all that transpired in the tamarind grove, how he and Rani Ketki had exchanged rings and pledged an agreement in writing (*likhot bhi likh di*).[46] They write back: "we honor the ring and the agreement. If Rani Ketki's parents agree, they will become our *samdhi* and *samdhin*. Both kingdoms will become one. If not, then on the basis of the sword, we'll unite your bride with you. From today, stop being upset. Go: play, mingle, enjoy (*khelo-kudo; bolo-chalo; ananden karo*)."[47]

Udaybhan is cast as a spoilt young aristocrat, albeit a person of various dimensions. He is sensitive to the issue of comportment in his unannounced arrival in the grove, after Ketki points it out. On his return to his parents' home, he is presented as an emotional youth, lost in grief, parted from his beloved. His boyhood is marked in his parents' advice to him: "play, mingle, enjoy." It is they who will take on the encumbrances; he must remain happy and carefree. Thus, Udaybhan appears in a variety of forms: in Insha's introduction of him (when he seems arrogant and spoilt), in his being teased by the

---

[44] *Urdu Ketki, I*, p. 7; *Hindi Ketki*, p. 3.
[45] *Urdu Ketki, I*, pp. 14–15; *Hindi Ketki*, pp. 6–7.
[46] *Urdu Ketki, I*, pp. 15–16; *Hindi Ketki*, pp. 7–8.
[47] *Urdu Ketki, I*, pp. 16–17; *Hindi Ketki*, p. 8.

women of the household who could not distract him after his meeting with Ketki (when he appears gentler and vulnerable), and again, from the standpoint of his parents (in whose view he must enjoy the pleasures of boyhood).

The author's Ketki is similarly complex and richly multidimensional. Ketki, the girl-child, finds life in the descriptions of the games and of the women playing, in the talk of swings, of hide and seek and more generally in a sense of mischievousness that the reader repeatedly detects in the narrative. But she is also a figure that has built into her an awareness of appropriate directions for respectable life and the accompanying responsibilities and duties. She takes the initiative in expressing her desire for Udaybhan, in going out to search for him, in leaving her home because she desires him. But she is not willing to deny propriety simply by eloping with Udaybhan.

When Ketki's parents decline the offer of the marriage of their daughter to Udaybhan, Udaybhan sends a letter to Ketki, saying: "My heart is breaking. Let the Rajas fight against one another. By whatever means, call me to your side. Together, we will go to another country. Whatever will be, will be." Phulkali, a gardener's wife, delivers the letter. Ketki sends the following reply: "this matter of running away is not good. It would be an insult to our forefathers."[48]

Meanwhile, Udaybhan and his parents are turned into deer. Distressed by the events that have transformed Udaybhan and his parents into deer, Ketki confides in Madanban that her heart is broken thinking of Udaybhan as a deer. She also urges her mother to give her the ashes to play hide and seek (*aankh micholi*). Rani Kamlata refuses, saying they are not meant for children's play, and adding, "Daughter, these ways of girlhood (*ladakpan*) are not good." Ketki is upset with her mother. The mother tries to fuss over her daughter, but nothing works. In the end, Kamlata gives a little ash to Ketki, who wears it, and hiding on its strength, plays about.[49]

It is at this time Ketki attempts to confide in Madanban, asking for her help in looking for Udaybhan, explaining that in her view the ashes were meant for a purpose. Madanban underscores Ketki's immaturity. However, as we know, a few days later,

[48] *Urdu Ketki*, I, p. 19; *Hindi Ketki*, p. 9.
[49] *Urdu Ketki*, II, pp. 84–85; *Hindi Ketki*, pp. 13–15.

without conferring with Madanban, Ketki smears her eyes with ashes and leaves.[50]

There is in these discussions – as in the rest of the story – a simultaneous depiction of Ketki's considered agency as well as the impulsive ways of girlhood. Rani Kamlata and Madaban's points of view help the reader follow the author's conception of the female. Through Ketki's exchanges with her mother and Madanban, Insha provides a palpable sense of women living lives: arguing, disagreeing and negotiating. There is craziness here, and cheating, if one might use that word for Ketki's secretive departure with the ashes in search of Udaybhan. The exchanges in themselves are essential in showing human frailty and emotion, living female figures that Insha so brilliantly brings to life. Ketki gets upset with her mother, the mother fusses over her daughter, the father indulges Ketki in asking his wife to give a little bit of the magical ashes for her to play with, and so on.

In other words, there is considerable room for play, for maneuvering, even within the confines of the palace: in the conversation between women, in the negotiation between mother and daughter, in the disagreement between friends. Insha marks Ketki's innocence and inexperience in her mother's use of the term *ladakpan*, the naïveté of girlhood, and in Madanban's discussion of her inexperience (*alhadpan*) as well as in her need to stress to Ketki the serious importance of modesty and decorum. Ketki confers with Madanban, disagrees and exercises her agency in a creative way by using the magical ashes given by the guru of the family. The coexistence of girlhood and womanhood and the desire of girl-child and woman is a distinctive feature of the tale.

After Ketki leaves, her parents realize that if anyone knew where she went, it will be Madanban. Madanban reports her conversation with Ketki to them. Next Madanban puts ashes in her eyes, becomes invisible and goes out in search of Ketki. They finally meet.[51] Ketki gives her consent to Madanban to bring her parents, along with Mahinder Gir, to the forest. Madanban returns to Raja Jagat Parkash and Rani Kamlata. The raja burns a hair from the skin, a means of making Mahinder Gir appear. After Jagat Parkash tells his guru everything

[50] *Urdu Ketki, II*, pp. 86–89; *Hindi Ketki*, pp. 15–17.
[51] *Urdu Ketki, II*, pp. 89–91; *Hindi Ketki*, pp. 17–18.

that had happened, Mahinder Gir asks why they gave the ashes to the girl. He adds, that as far as Udaybhan and his parents are concerned, it will be easy to turn them back into humans. He then advises the king and queen to go back to their kingdom and make preparations for the wedding. Mahinder Gir, along with Raja Jagat Parkash and Rani Kamlata, goes to the forest to meet Ketki. Mahinder Gir takes Ketki in his lap and gives her as an offering in marriage to Udaybhan (*apni goad mein lekar Kunvar Udaybhan ka chadhava chadha diya*).[52]

Once more, both tendencies – girlish and womanish – are underscored. Mahinder Gir putting Ketki on his lap when he meets her in the forest is yet another demonstration of the indulgences given in girlhood[53] – at the very moment that her marriage is being arranged. Insha's play with girlhood and womanhood continues in his characterization of Madanban, Ketki's close friend. It is not clear to the reader how old Madanban is. Like Ketki, she emerges in various feminine roles: in her teasing of Ketki, in her advice to her, in their discussions and disagreements and in the demonstration of their affection.

Critical in the depiction of these women is the vocabulary through which Insha calls them into being.[54] He resorts to the vocabulary of mothers, wives, mistresses, servants – the language of his infancy and youth. The range of terms Insha uses in his tale is significant. It is precisely such multidimensional, complex, historical women figures that taper off in the later nineteenth century, and with the shrinking vocabulary, the reader has increasingly less access to the richness and range of women figures.

In the beginning of Insha's tale, in the midst of a grove of tamarind trees, Udaybhan sees forty or fifty girls, *randiyan*; when Ketki brings up the matter of comportment, saying that he knew that the girls were playing at the swings, she still uses the term *randiyan* for

---

[52] *Urdu Ketki*, II, pp. 91–98; *Hindi Ketki*, pp. 18–21.

[53] However, one might suggest another reading of this moment in the tale. The wandering ascetic, Vanita tells us, is an erotic figure in Riti poetry, an inspiration for Rekhti. "This [ascetic] figure has mystical significance in Hindu devotion, but in later medieval poetry, his erotic aspects tend to displace his mystical ones." See "Married Among their Companions," p. 42.

[54] I am grateful to Michael Fisher for reminding me of the incredible range of terms for women in Insha's writings that I glossed over in the early stages of writing this book, and for his probing question on linguistic terms and the construction of social history.

girls. In many Rekhti poems too, women speakers (via the male narrator, of course) call other women *randi*. At the time of Insha's composition, the meaning of the term was not fixed: *randi*, in particular, we are told, "may refer to women who actually work as prostitutes or it may be a term of abuse for any woman the speaker likes. In some poems, the context seems to be a courtesan's house, where the speaker and her *dogana* adorn and display themselves not only for each others' but for a man's, sometimes the poet-persona's, pleasure."[55] In Rekhti, in particular, what is striking is that it "tends to undo the conventional distinction between respectable women and courtesans, both in its use of language and in its representation of women in love, experiencing emotions not peculiar to any particular marital or social status."[56]

But none of these – prostitute, a woman or her *dogana* in a courtesan's house – applies to the women in Insha's story. The *randiyan* are Ketki's companions. The specific meaning of *randi* emerges in Insha's narration itself. Immediately after Ketki's question, Udaybhan responds: "How did I know beautiful women (*padminiyan*) were on the swings?" The same characters, *randiyan*, are now described as *padminiyan* (multitude of lotuses). Thus, *randi* and *padmini* are used interchangeably to describe girl/women, the playmates of Ketki. This is perhaps what Shyamsundar Das calls the "instability" of Insha's language. It is the sort of language that is open and that draws on an assorted set of linguistic conventions. In Insha's use of *randi* in his tale a variety of meanings is visible. Of course, *randi* today has completely moved from woman to prostitute.

Consider another term: when Ketki and Madanban come out to meet Udaybhan, Insha describes Madanban as Ketki's "friend of girlhood," *ladakpan ki guiyan*. As a feminine noun, *guiyan* means "a (woman's) female friend or companion" and as a masculine noun, "partner (in a game; fellow team member)." It also means "friend."[57] In Rekhti, the poet Rangin defined *guiyan* "as a type of Dogana."[58] In Insha's

---

[55] Vanita, "Married Among their Companions," p. 35. In Rekhti, *dogana* is used to refer to and address a woman's intimate companion, and also to sexual intimacy between them. Ibid., p. 18.

[56] Ibid., p. 35.

[57] R. S. McGregor, *The Oxford Hindi-English Dictionary* (New Delhi, 1993), s.v. guiyan.

[58] Vanita, "Married Among their Companions," p. 19.

tale, Madanban is Ketki's *ladakpan ki guiyan*; the author's emphasis on *ladakpan* (girlhood) is significant. It suggests a long-term friend and the specific dimensions of that friendship emerge in the various episodes of the tale. Nevertheless, the use of the same term – *randi, gui-yan* – for both friendship (in the Ketki story) and same-sex love among women (in his Rekhti compositions) is suggestive of Insha's range.

Then there is the reference to *gharwaliyan*, literally "women of the house," who could not distract Udaybhan from his sorrow when he returns to the palace. Here the women referred to are the women in the palace quarters of Udaybhan, perhaps attendants, helpers, companions of his mother; not a householder or a wife, the more contemporary meaning of *gharwali*. At the time of the wedding of Ketki and Udaybhan following their return from the forest, we get many other terms for many kinds of women. When Jagat Parkash (Ketki's father) returns to his throne, he issues a proclamation about wedding celebrations: in every village, at every entrance, people are to build a three-arched house, covering it with red cloth, and to sew upon the cloth embroidered fringes, bells, lace and tinsels; and on banyan and pipal trees, they are to hang garlands covered with flowers made of laces. Wherever the newly married brides put on bracelets of small pods and the wives bracelets of new buds, writes Insha, they (*naval byahi dulhane aur suhagine*) fill their bosoms with flowers of favor and love.[59] Thus the newly married, the new brides (*dulhane*), older wives (*suhagine*) are brought together in Insha's narration. Insha also notes the joy of the queens, *raniyan*, in the palace.

Along with the aristocratic men and women, there are godly beings at the wedding, Insha tells us. Mahinder Gir and Lord Indra, who helped him bring the three deer back to human life, arrive on the famed elephant Eravat. In addition, all the ninety *lakh* pasts of Mahinder Gir, now turned into ascetics wearing garlands, appear and rejoice. Mahadev and Parvati also arrive; and so do the ascetics, Gorakh Nath, Machinder Nath. The great heroes of the epics, Parsuram and Narsingh, join the crowd; as do the popular gods and goddesses, Ram, Lakshman, Sita; you could see Ravan and the battle in Lanka; Krishna and the celebration of his birth, Janamashtmi; Vasudev's departure to Gokul; Radhika's arguments; the milkmaids; and the making of the

[59] *Urdu Ketki, II*, pp. 91–98; *Hindi Ketki*, pp. 18–21.

golden Dwarka. All these as marks of the auspiciousness of Ketki and Udaybhan's wedding.[60]

Beyond those named directly in the Ketki story, Insha depicts other kinds of female figures, including those of female intimates as in Rekhti. Vanita notes that "Rekhti develops a taxonomy of specific names for a woman's intimate female companion who is often a lover, such as Dogana, Zanakhi, Ilaichi."[61] Petievich says that "while there is little explicit lesbian content in *Rekhti*, erotic relationships between the narrator and her beloved 'other' are overwhelmingly alluded to by employing these terms [such as *dogana, zanakhi* and so on]."[62] For my purposes, that Insha calls these women into being in various ways is in itself highly significant. These terms suggest a variety of women as part of a wider, fuller, richer universe – thinking about relationships, telling stories, composing poetry – and to share Petievich's sentiment, "it does seem remarkable that two centuries ago, during an expansive period in Urdu culture, men were open to exploring the notion of a distinct female experience."[63]

The Rekhti of Insha and Rangin was extensively peopled by servants and other subordinates, who sometimes play a more important role than relatives (with the possible exception of *baji* or older sister, a term also used to refer to any older woman friend or lover). Older female servants, *dai, dadda* or *anna*, find a constant mention: a confidante, go-between, messenger and advisor. The son or daughter of such an elderly servant is termed *koka*. Then there are references to the caste names, *Kahars* (palanquin-bearers), *Domni* (low-caste woman singer), *Asil* (young maidservant), *Ronna* (boy servant) and *Mughlani* (she appears as a seamstress in Rekhti).[64]

In the tale of Ketki, Phulkali, the gardener's wife, carries Udaybhan's letter to Ketki; women console the lovelorn Udaybhan and the newly wedded village women celebrate Ketki and Udaybhan's wedding along with the gods and goddesses who also attend the celebration. Even in the domain of the earthly, Insha builds the prospect of the direct

[60] *Urdu Ketki, II*, pp. 101–107; *Hindi Ketki*, pp. 25–26.
[61] Vanita, "Different Speakers," p. 9.
[62] Petievich, "Gender Politics and the Urdu Ghazal," p. 244.
[63] Ibid., p. 241.
[64] For an extensive discussion of the terms for women and for female–female sexual relations, see the writings of Vanita and Petievich, cited here.

involvement of the "extraterrestrials." Thus Indra gives to Ketki a bed made of a single diamond and a box of topaz, a calf of the famed cow Kamdhenu tied beneath it, and twenty-one women (*laundiyan*) who are clean, who sing and play and knit and sew. The bed, the tree that gives whatever "fruit" one desires and the calf of the Kamdhenu cow signify fertility and progeny. The figural possibilities are immense here. To say nothing about the beautiful women enjoined not to "converse" with Udaybhan (*baat cheet na rakhna*, used literally for having sex or physical association!).[65]

THE FUTURE OF INSHA'S TALE

Insha narrates a full, lived and living life in his tale of Rani Ketki. Implicit in the story is the appreciation of the time of *shaishava* (child-hood) and *yauvana* (youth), part of the four (biological) states of a Hindu life cycle: *shaishava* (childhood), *yauvana* (youth), *kaumara* (adulthood) and *vaarthakya* (old age). These are not the more perva-sive ideological reconstruction of the four spiritual stages that becomes central to many colonial and noncolonial writings on Indian life and its progress later on[66]: *brahmacharya* (period of learning), *grhastha* (period of domestic life), *vanaprastha* (period of retirement to the for-est in preparation for gradual detachment from the world), *sanyasa* (period of renunciation). The important point is that the *ashrama* stages demand specific duties of persons, that is, social and spiritual practices are prescribed for each of these stages and must be undertaken to make human life fulfilling. The states of a Hindu life cycle involve, on the other hand, the practices, the joys, the challenges, frustrations and pleasures of these states.[67] In other words, what a girl or boy does

---

[65] *Urdu Ketki, II,* pp. 113–117; *Hindi Ketki,* pp. 29–31.

[66] For an elaboration of this point, see Chapter 1.

[67] In the Telugu texts written before the nineteenth century, there is talk of exclusive games for girls such as using cooking utensils, hopscotch, creating doll weddings, and so on, in which boys do not participate. Outside the textual tradition, as in northern India, there is a discourse on child-gods via Rama Lila, Krishna Lila and so on. In Tamil Nadu, the girl-goddess, Andal, also known as Goda Devi, is very popular. In the nineteenth century and after, when men begin writing books for women, the ear-lier space for women's activities becomes constricted. Examples of such later texts in Telugu include, among others: *Bandaru Accaamamba,* "*Abala Satcaritra Ratnamala*" or "Biographies of Good Women." Texts such as the *Bandaru Accaamamba* were read by adult educated women. Texts like *Kumari Sataka* were meant for girls before

in her or his *shaishava*: the adventures of boys and girls; their songs, the teasing, the companionships; what they look like in their *yauvana* (youth); what gestures typify them; what desires they inhabit.

Insha composes Ketki as two figures, at once separate, but in which a potential to be one or the other (or both and more) is always there. Ketki is agential, wise and thinking. All through the text, the author highlights the choices she makes, the initiatives she takes. And simultaneously, he wants us to know Ketki, the girl-child, playful, shy, demanding in front of her mother and father, yet aware of inner desires and the means by which she might attain her wishes. The important point here is not a literal one about Ketki's agency and deliberation, but the vision that the author builds in a figure, whereby such a figure is shown as able to enjoy living in various domains.

In all this, Ketki is a figure with a present and a future. That future was to be recast in a new "reality" in the later nineteenth century. In 1867, Ketki came to sit in Raja Shiv Prasad's *Gutka* alongside exemplary (ideal) women, such as Damyanti, Ahilya Bai, Rani Bhavani and Shakuntala, among others. In this new placement, certain physical spaces were reduced and disprivileged, and alongside these erased spaces, certain female modes were also seriously diminished.

In the *Gutka*, claimed to be the first collection of prose in Hindi from different kinds of genres and the "most important contribution to the moulding of the emergent Hindi style,"[68] as we shall see in the next chapter, Shiv Prasad was interested in documenting the emergence of the Hindi language and marking the contours of a respectable Indian history. Several stories of exemplary and historical ideal women

their marriage. I am grateful to V. Narayana Rao for making these suggestions. For a similar criticism of the *ashramadharma*, and a proposition about childhood *samskara* with detailed descriptions of rituals and ceremonies, see Sudhir Kakar, *Indian Childhood: Cultural Ideals and Social Realities* (R.V. Parulekar Lecture; Delhi, 1979). Doniger notes that in chapter II of the Kamasutra women were told to read; in chapter IV, women were encouraged to learn the arts from a sister. There is no mention of the *varna* even once; anyone with money could learn the arts; see Wendy Doniger and Sudhir Kakar (trs.) *The Kamasutra* (New York, 2009).

[68] McGregor, *Hindi Literature*, p. 72. As we know, Insha wrote the story in Perso-Arabic script claiming no Persian or Arabic word (all languages the author was proficient in): the script is one reason why McGregor thinks it faced "comparative neglect ... and thus was not fully accessible at first to those who might have been most receptive to it." It was printed in Devanagri script twice by the mid-nineteenth century, enjoying "continuing circulation" only after it was incorporated in Raja Shiv Prasad's *Gutka*. Ibid., pp. 64–65.

(in some cases, their life histories were well known; in the case of others, their stories had been told repeatedly) were put together in this collection as materials for the Hindi syllabus for the junior civil servants and army officers of the British Empire. Shiv Prasad reproduced Insha's tale in this collection in the Devanagiri script. Additionally, he also gave the story a title, *Kahani theth Hindi mein* (*A Story in Pure Hindi*). Thus, the ground for the inclusion of Rani Ketki's tale in the *Gutka* became a newly elevating linguistic tradition (hence a story in "pure" Hindi), told through the accounts of courageous women.

We have two physical presentations of the Ketki story: Insha's 1803 version and Shiv Prasad's 1867 *Gutka*. *Although retelling exactly the same tale*, Rani Ketki acquires a very different emphasis for its readers in these two placements. In Insha, we notice the vibrant, bubbling, overflowing language (and unrestrained, adventurous and experimental figures even within the parameters of respectability and duty); in the other, markedly more disciplined languages and standardized models with elevated characters become discernible. The story is the same: it is Insha's, word for word. But by restricting it as a story in "pure Hindi" and by making it part of a historical anthology of great women, Shiv Prasad invites us to read it very differently: it is the exemplary-ness of the figures towards which our eyes will be directed in the latter half of the nineteenth century, as the next chapter shows.

3

The Woman of the School

Education – as cultivation of language, manners and values, and as training in skills necessary to fulfill one's duties in life – was radically transformed in nineteenth-century India. Except for a handful of boys and young men requiring concentrated training in particular vocations (music, priesthood and some highly specialized crafts), and even more infrequently for girls and women, there had been no need for education outside the home or familial circle. In colonial India, a new kind of general education came to be privileged. The site of this education was to be the school. Not only young boys, but little girls and young women, and in time if the modernist discourse was accepted, large numbers of youth (the masses), would receive this general education, collectively, in new locations called schools – with their own rules, boundaries, experts and expectations.

Girls and women, along with boys and men, were to come out of their homes, their familiar localities, and wend their way – across unknown territories – to these schools (albeit there would be separate schools for boys and girls). They would come out along with others from the neighborhood, even from other neighborhoods! What opportunities did this new thinking about general education open up? What dangers did it create? These were questions that Indian (and colonial) reformers had to confront in the context of their efforts to improve India.

In 1859, Raja Shiv Prasad (1823–1895) – then a joint inspector of schools in the Banaras Circle, deeply involved in the setting up of

schools in urban and rural areas of the NWP and designing of school
curriculum, who was to become a controversial figure in the debate
on the Hindi and Urdu languages, and of India's history – wrote the
Vamamanranjan, also titled *Tales for Women*. This was a vernacular textbook, designed for the education of the schoolgirl, written in
the "hortatory genre" that became widespread in northern India and
Bengal.[1] Scholars have suggested that it was the first widely used Hindi
reader for girls in north India, and served as the standard textbook for
generations of girls in Hindi-medium schools. Although these were
texts in different genres, the *Vamamanranjan* was listed on the official
syllabus as the Hindi counterpart to Nazir Ahmad's *Mirat al-'Arus*.[2]

In 1867, Raja Shiv Prasad, now inspector of schools (after Banaras
and Allahabad in the Agra and Jhansi circles), edited what has been
claimed as the first collection of prose in Hindi from different kinds
of genres: the *Gutka*, or *Hindi Selections*, another title by which it
is known, published by Banaras Medical Hall Press. This book was
designed for the Hindi examination syllabus for junior civil servants
and army officers of the British government.[3] In the *Gutka*, Shiv

[1] C. A. Bayly suggests that the book was first issued in 1849: C. A. Bayly, *Empire and
Information. Intelligence Gathering and Social Communication in India, 1780–1870*
(Cambridge, 1996), p. 236. Ulrike Starks contends that the date of its composition is
1856. She also suggests that the second edition of 1859 lists 1856 as the date of the
first edition. Ulrike Stark, "Towards a New Hindu Woman: Educational Ideals and
Female Role Models in Shivprasad's *Vamamanranjan* (1856)," in Ulrike Roesler and
Jayandra Soni (eds.), *Aspects of the Female in Indian Culture* (Marburg, 2004), p. 172
and fn. 11.Veer Bharat Talwar maintains that the date of the composition of this text
is 1859. [Veer Bharat Talwar, *Bhartiya Sahitya ke Nirmata: Raja Shivprasad 'Sitara-e
Hind'* (New Delhi, 2005), p. 31]. The first edition I was able to acquire is dated 1860:
Raja Sivaprasada, *Vamamanaranjana or Tales for Women* (Ilahabad, 1860). India
Institute, Oxford, Hindi Shiv P1. Cited as *Vamamanranjan*. I have also consulted several subsequent editions. For an excellent and concise biography of Raja Shiv Prasad,
see Talwar, *Bhartiya Sahitya* (New Delhi, 2005). A good biographical sketch and list
of Shiv Prasad's publications is also available in George A. Grierson, "The Modern
Vernacular Literature of Hindustan," *Journal of the Asiatic Society of Bengal*, Part I
for 1888. Special number of the Calcutta Asiatic Society.
[2] Stark, "Towards a New Hindu Woman," p. 172. As indicated in the prelude and Chapter
1, the *Mirat al-'Arus* or *The Bride's Mirror*, is a very important and popular didactic tale
that remains in circulation even today. It won a prize and was translated into several
Indian languages. I discuss this text extensively in the next chapter. It was written by
Nazir Ahmad, an inspector of schools in the NWP and a contemporary of Raja Shiv
Prasad, well known as a major proponent of women's education and social reform.
[3] Although she does not give the date, Vasudha Dalmia points out that the *Hindi
Selections* was also prescribed as a textbook by the Education Department in

Prasad included Lalluji Lal's *Premsagar* and his *Sabhavilas*; parts of *Shakuntala* composed by Laxman Singh; Insha's tale of Rani Ketki, now entitled *Kahani Theth Hindi Mein (A Story in Pure Hindi)*; *Balkhand* by Tulsidas; Kabir's *Sakhi* (selected parts); *Mahabharata* (Hindi translation); and *Satsai* by Bihari (selected *dohas*). In addition, the author incorporated three of his own compositions: *Veer Singh ka Vrittant* (concerned with female infanticide among the Rajputs); *Raja Bhoj ka Sapna* (written against extravagant display and superstition in religion); and the first three stories – *Damyanti, Ahilya Bai* and *Rani Bhavani* – from the *Vamamanranjan*.[4]

The stories of the *Vamamanranjan* and those of the *Gutka* (especially those reproduced here from the *Vamamanranjan*) – although written in fairly different social and political contexts and for very different kinds of audiences – are excellent sources to consider what happens when a school inspector selects and uses stories and writes new ones himself as part of a new school curriculum for girls.[5] Wrapped in the morals of the stories of the *Vamamanranjan* (and the *Gutka*) is a very specific girl-child/woman figure, which is produced in and illustrates the hesitant sociopolitical context of Shiv Prasad's time.

Insha's tale of Rani Ketki (the focus of the preceding chapter) was reproduced in the *Gutka*, but not in the *Vamamanranjan*. Alongside its new physical location in the *Gutka*, Shiv Prasad also gave it a title: *Kahani Theth Hindi Mein (A Story in Pure Hindi)*. The physical relocation of Insha's tale tells us a lot about what it was, in Shiv Prasad's view, that girls must – *and must not* – read, who their models should be, indeed, how they should read a story. It is not an accident that

---

Allahabad. Vasudha Dalmia, *The Nationalization of Hindu Traditions: Bhartendu Harischandra and Nineteenth-Century Banaras* (New Delhi, 1997), p. 159, fn. 18. I use an 1882 edition of the *Gutka*. *Gutka or Selections, Part I, II, and III* (Allahabad: Printed at the N.W. Provinces and Oudh Press, 1882); India Institute Library, Oxford, Hindi Misc. B 17/1–3. Cited as *Gutka*.

4 Talwar, *Bhartiya Sahitya*, p. 31. In the citations that follow in this chapter from Talwar's book, all translations from Hindi to English are mine.

5 Author of forty-five books, translations and original compositions in Hindi and Urdu, Shiv Prasad has been most widely discussed for the controversial historical views expressed in his three-volume history, *Itihastimirnashak* (1864–1873), claimed to have been the second most read book of the nineteenth century in Hindi after *Chandrakanta* (Talwar, *Bhartiya Sahitya*, p. 29). Although the *Vamamanranjan* and the *Gutka* are central to my concerns in this chapter, I also look at several other texts of Shiv Prasad, especially his stories for children, copies of which are in the British Library.

Insha's tale, a highly playful story suggestive of many different kinds of female spaces, activities, forms of conduct for the girl-child and woman, does not appear in the *Vamamanranjan*. Nor is the new title to the story irrelevant.

In Shiv Prasad's time, writing textbooks, especially for girls, was no routine matter. His was a new, even unprecedented endeavor, one fraught with formidable social, cultural and financial difficulties. In 1855–1856, writes Shiv Prasad, when he began the project of opening up of schools (this is after he had composed the *Vamamanranjan*), it was extremely hard to promote a modern, general education, even in urban areas, let alone in the rural countryside. Shiv Prasad gave poverty and caste sensibilities as the two gravest impediments in the implementation of general education. Speaking in front of the Hunter Commission, appointed to review the progress of education in India, in 1882, he noted the difficulty posed by the caste system. He cited a proverb: "Nine easterners, ten kitchens (*nau purabi, das chulhe*)." How would little boys staying in boarding schools cook for themselves? Every parent could not send a cook with their children. Then there were Christian children in the boarding schools. How would Hindu children stay with them? For the poor, the problem was the work that children had to do along with their parents: this prevented their going to school.[6]

In the preparation of school textbooks, Shiv Prasad also faced the question of the appropriate script for school texts. As it happened, Hindu students read in the Devanagri script in several schools and Muslim students in the Persian. However, Shiv Prasad never conceded, throughout his career, that if the scripts for Hindi and Urdu were now different, and if Hindus and Muslims tended to favor different scripts, the languages and cultures had to be separate too. It was Shiv Prasad's unfailing endeavor, as Veer Bharat Talwar's eloquent biography reminds us, to "create a vision in his books in which Hindi and Urdu would lose their separateness (*algaav*) and become one (*ek ho jaati hain*),"[7] something for which he has not been recognized adequately. In his own time, Shiv Prasad often got chastised both by Hindus and Muslims for his anti-Hindu and anti-Muslim sentiments, which he

---

[6] Talwar, *Bhartiya Sahitya*, p. 22.
[7] Ibid., p. 59.

certainly articulated on numerous occasions and in several of his writings, most notably in the *Itihastimirnashak*.[8]

In connection with the history of the girl-child and woman in nineteenth-century northern India, this chapter investigates how Shiv Prasad approached the subject of textbooks for girls in a context in which it was hard enough for boys to get an education, and in a political environment which had already begun to encounter sharpening contests over Hindi and Urdu and Hindu-Muslim sensibilities. How would any reformer create a "textbook" in Shiv Prasad's time? Why did he choose the particular female models for the *Vamamanranjan*? And how did he tell their stories? What were the ways in which he recast older tales and wrote his own? How would the female readership of the time respond to his stories and models, especially girls who were first-generation pupils, crossing the domestic threshold and going to an institutionalized setting for purposes of education as none of their women elders had done before? Along with caste and poverty, surely the very matter of physical settings – the shift from home to school – would be one that girls and women had to negotiate in unprecedented ways.[9] Let me begin my investigation of these questions with an examination of the political and cultural milieu in which they arose.

THE TIMES THEY ARE A-CHANGING

A scholar of nineteenth-century Hindi literature seeks to indicate the flavor of Shiv Prasad's world in comments regarding the distinctiveness of *Vamamanranjan* as the first "vernacular textbook" for schoolgirls. The *Vamamanranjan*, writes Ulrike Stark, provides an "interesting" example of "a cultural synthesis in which traditional Indian values, on the one hand, and indigenous social reform on the other, mingled with prevalent British-Victorian notions of feminity [*sic*] in an educational as much as ideological quest to modernize Indian women though a redefinition of gender roles." She characterizes the text as a "vernacular textbook," and goes on to say that it "served as an

---

[8] "In the history of Hindi language and literature, his image has come to be rendered almost like that of a villain (*unki chavi ek khalnayak jaisi bana di gayi*)." Ibid., p. 40.
[9] See also Nita Kumar, *Lessons from Schools: The History of Education in Banaras* (New Delhi and London, 2000), ch. VI, especially pp. 151–160.

ideological tool in the construction and propagation of a new ideal Hindu woman."[10]

Such an inference is, however, perhaps a little too hasty. It seems almost to suggest that a nationalist (or proto-nationalist) strain in Shiv Prasad's thinking automatically led to a pedagogy that had to reimagine the heroines of *Vamamanranjan* in a "modern," "reformist" mold. I would argue that the time of the writing of *Vamamanranjan* and of the compilation of the *Gutka* was not one when the so-called Hindu context or Hindu culture or readership – or for that matter, the "new ideal Hindu woman" – was already demarcated. We need to consider much more carefully the particular concerns that marked the loyalist politics of Shiv Prasad's generation.

Stark's argument that Shiv Prasad "took great care to assimilate the religious experience of his Christian role models into a Hindu context by using a terminology familiar to his Hindu readers"[11] takes away the ambiguity that Shiv Prasad reflected in several of his compositions.

Shiv Prasad certainly expressed strong anti-Muslim sentiments in several of his writings. *Vamamanranjan* and *Gutka* are not exceptions to such rants. The important point, however, is that Shiv Prasad's writings and politics remained very mixed in character – praising the colonial masters, condemning Muslim depredations, yet passionate about the unity of the Urdu and Devanagri scripts and devoted to a vernacular school education. In these various endeavors, Shiv Prasad made selections, highlighted specific points in historical traditions and, as an inspector of schools, showed concern about the demands of the schools to do with enhancing character, cultivating manners and producing disciplined students. Learning to write letters, which stories to read and how to behave were all part of Shiv Prasad's inquiries, as we shall see in the pamphlets he wrote for children.

Some fifty years before Shiv Prasad, Insha, whose story he reproduced in his *Gutka*, had different questions. I elaborated the point about the sheer joy displayed by Insha in his hybrid compositions, in the last chapter, but let me reiterate a few examples of his play with Indic traditions from his tale of Ketki. Note the first scene of the story when Udaybhan arrives in the forest and encounters Rani Ketki and

[10] Stark, "Towards a New Hindu Woman," pp. 168, 172.
[11] Ibid., p. 174.

many of her friends. Romila Thapar notes that "the hero chasing a deer during a hunt and arriving at an unexpected place is well known to folk literature, and in the Indian context the deer enticing the *ksatriya* [warrior] is familiar from other sources as well, not least the *Ramayana*."[12] The scene is also remindful of Krishna's play with *gopis* in the *Bhagvatpurana*. *Gopis* were meant to express desire as women (in this respect the *gopi* perhaps sits between the respectable woman and that of the courtesan).[13] The place of a woman's desire is critical to Insha's story: we see this in his inversion of the story of deer hunting (usually it is man who is the hunter, but here Udaybhan is turned into a deer, effeminized: it is Ketki who goes in search of him), as well as in his charting of the space of the forest as that of disguise, magic and freedom for the girl-child and woman. Would Shiv Prasad be able to replicate the desiring, agential, even contestatory Ketki when he reproduces that story in the *Gutka*? Some examples from his writings and debates around these writings should begin to provide a context for an answer.

The first part of Shiv Prasad's *Itihastimirnashak* (*History as the Dispeller of Darkness*), his most discussed work, was published in Allahabad in 1864. In the preface to this book, Shiv Prasad wrote about the English and Persian sources he had used, Marshman and Elphinstone's histories, drawing more heavily from the latter. Avril Powell has shown that while Part I, "Hindu and Mohammedan Periods," and Part II, "Rise and Growth of the British Empire to 1858," of the *Itihastimirnashak* "were similar in format to previous periodised dynastic histories," the focus in Part III on "changes in the manners and customs from Vedic times to today" "was innovative in vernacular school text-books," though pioneered in Elphinstone's history.[14]

Veer Bharat Talwar highlights two qualities of the *Itihastimirnashak* that "join this book to [the tradition of] modern history writing." One was that this book attempted to separate history writing from

---

[12] Thapar, *Sakuntala*, pp. 36–37.

[13] Thanks to Laurie Patton for the reference to the *Bhagvatpurana* and a discussion of the *gopis*.

[14] Avril A. Powell, "History Textbooks and the Transmission of the Pre-colonial Past in North-western India in the 1860s and 1870s," in Daud Ali (ed.), *Invoking the Past: The Uses of History in South Asia* (New Delhi, 1999), p. 112.

religious beliefs and Puranic tales and grounded it on the evidence of historical and archaeological documents. Second, this was the first "historical text" in Hindi that did not claim a foundational character; nonetheless, it highlighted and corrected some of the errors of European history writers, including Marshman and Elphinstone. Shiv Prasad's *Itihastimirnashak* was highly influenced by Henry Elliot's collected and edited volume, *The Bibliographical Index to the Historians of Muhammadan India*, published in 1849. The way the materials of the Indian past were organized in this book immediately put the Muslim rule in a negative light. "Shiv Prasad was clearly anti-Muslim [*muslim virodhi*], and so was the Director of Education of North-West Province, Thomas Kempson. Both agreed with Elliot's historical perspective."[15] Shiv Prasad's anti-Muslim attitude emerged strongly in the *Itihastimirnashak*: he depicted the Turk, Afghan and Mughal rule in India as a period of decline, making claims such as this: "wherever Muslims went, exactly such conditions [of decline] followed. During their rule, no country could move towards progress." These kinds of assertions by Shiv Prasad led Sir Sayyid Ahmad Khan, among others in the NWP, to come out in strong opposition to him.[16] While the first part of the *Itihastimirnashak* was published "without any public comment," later renditions in Urdu (by Siva Prasad himself) and in English (by Kempson) resulted in objections from Muslim spokesmen, led by Sayyid Ahmad Khan (this led to the removal of the "most objectionable" pages on the 1857 rebellion).[17]

Talwar tells us of another strand of antagonism against Shiv Prasad: that he wrote "refined Urdu in the Nagri script [*nagri aksharon main khalis Urdu*]." One of the reasons for this was that Shiv Prasad never supported the anti-Urdu Hindi revolution that began in his time. Because the colonial government favored Urdu at the time, Shiv Prasad (a government employee) came to be seen as an enemy of Hindi. This was a man who made Hindi a medium of education, wrote textbooks in Hindi and wrote influential Hindi prose. What he did not do was join the so-called anti-Urdu movement, for he

---

[15] Talwar, *Bhartiya Sahitya*, pp. 29–30.
[16] Ibid., pp. 33–34. For more details, see chapter IV of Talwar, "Muslim Virodh aur Angrezbhakti"; Powell, "History Textbooks," pp. 113–118; and Dalmia, *Nationalization of Hindu Traditions*, pp. 330–332.
[17] Powell, "History Textbooks," pp. 114, 121.

never believed in the separateness of Urdu and Hindi.[18] In August 1868, however, Shiv Prasad gave a memorandum to the government: *Court Character in the Upper Provinces of India*. In this document, he urged that the language of the court be written in Nagri (since 1837 the language of the court in the North Western Provinces had been Hindustani, written in the Perso-Arabic script). In fact, sometime before 1868, Shiv Prasad had argued in another memorandum that the script of the courts should be one, either Persian or Nagri. In 1868, he preferred the Devanagri. Talwar suggests that there was confusion in Shiv Prasad's mind on this issue. Although he was against the difficult Perso-Arabic vocabulary of the courts, he never considered Urdu and Hindi as separate languages, insisting only on a change of script.[19]

S. K. Das notes that Shiv Prasad was a "much misunderstood man in both Hindi and Urdu circles," representing the vacillation of the time.[20] Shiv Prasad's ambivalent choices are indicative of the difficulty of the selections he had to make. As several scholars have argued, he was a loyalist of the colonial regime, like so many other thinkers and publicists of the time, including his critic Sayyid Ahmad Khan.[21] In his history writing, Raja Shiv Prasad wrote about the idea of "dark ages" that was set by the rule of various Muslim dynasties in India – a point highlighted in the colonial historians he read. Alongside such persuasion was also Shiv Prasad's deep sympathy for the common culture of northern India (or at least the NWP), for shared languages even though the Hindi and Urdu scripts were different. Still, he submitted a memorandum to the government, and it is significant that "the terms in which he couched his argument foreshadow[ed] clearly

---

[18] Talwar, *Bhartiya Sahitya*, p. 38.
[19] Ibid., p. 52; cf. Alok Rai, *Hindi Nationalism* (New Delhi, 2000), p. 39.
[20] Das, *Indian Literature*, p. 142; See also McGregor, *Hindi Literature*, pp. 71–72; More recently Ulrike Stark has begun to note similar uncertainties and mixed aspirations in Shiv Prasad. I am grateful to Stark for giving me chapter 6, "At the Grassroots" of her biography of Raja Shiv Prasad (in progress), *In Times of Transition: Raja Shivpraasad 'Sitara-e Hind' (1824–1895)*.
[21] For a discussion of the loyalist leaders and the politics of the time, see Gyanendra Pandey, *The Construction of Communalism in Colonial North India* (New Delhi, 2006, 2nd edn.); pp. 158–163. Alongside his anti-Muslim sentiments, Shiv Prasad's devotion to the British – and his well-known opposition to the Mutiny of 1857 – has been discussed extensively by scholars. Talwar, *Bhartiya Sahitya*, p. 35; and Powell, "History Textbooks"; among others.

the more radical communalising developments which were soon to follow."[22] In his memorandum, nevertheless, "he connected the Nagri script and the Hindi language with the Hindu community [*Hindu jati-yata*], thus giving it a sectarian or communal character [*sampradayik charitra*]."[23]

We note a similar ambivalence in Shiv Prasad on matters more directly concerned with religion. He never supported any religious movement. Strikingly, he thought of the *Manusmriti* not only as the main religious text of Hindus, but also as a very useful text for humankind.[24] He pointed to America, the country of Colonel Henry Olcott, to whose Theosophical Society, young, educated Hindu men were turning to learn about the Hindu religion. Critiquing the ten rupee fee with which people could become members of the Theosophical Society and learn about Hindu religion, Shiv Prasad argued: "What kind of a theatre [*tamasha*] is this that our youth, newly educated, university graduates ... on the one hand struggle to be Collectors and Commissioners, and then want to go acquire scriptural learning [*Brahman Vidya*] from Colonel Olcott for ten rupees!" And further: "Hindus! Don't go to hell [*paataal*, America] to search for ways of being and religion [*karm-dharm*]. Look to the sky! *Manusmriti* came from there... Follow it."[25] He thought of religious sensibility as an inner human affair and critiqued superstitious behavior and the para-phernalia associated with religious practices, for example, in his influ-ential story, *Raja Bhoj Ka Sapna*, included in the *Gutka* in 1867. Yet, as Talwar observes, "he was never able to understand that in many

[22] Rai, *Hindi Nationalism*, p. 39.

[23] Talwar, *Bhartiya Sahitya*, p. 52; Rai, *Hindi Nationalism*, p. 39.

[24] Scholars contend that the Law Code of Manu probably became visible around the first century CE; and Manu had nine different "authoritative" commentators by the seventeenth century. How authoritative was Manu? It is hard to know whether this text was used in the ancient legal decision-making process; it was probably more used as an ideal resource than a pragmatic one. In their concern with the textual basis of Indian/Hindu life, the colonial observers pick on a number of authors and texts who they think are quintessential. Mill's obsessive writing with "Menu" is a case in point. It is also important to note that several Indian commentators picked up read-ings on texts such as Manu from the writings of colonial observers. What happens in transference of knowledge is a rich area for investigation. For Manu, see Doniger, *The Laws of Manu* (cited previously); and for a good discussion of the circulation of Manu, see also Doniger, *The Hindus: An Alternative History* (New York, 2009), especially pp. 378, 616, 619, 633.

[25] Talwar, *Bhartiya Sahitya*, pp. 43, 46–47.

instances the *Dharmshastras* themselves were responsible for the propagation of superstitious views and beliefs. He never challenged such texts."[26]

Making clear-cut choices out of the rich variation of linguistic and cultural practices in the north Indian world that Shiv Prasad inhabited was clearly not an easy task. Alok Rai evokes the character of this rich milieu:

> [T]his people's Hindi is truly a middle language, the easy going vernacular of north India, born out of the necessities of intercourse between different people, communities and cultures, which were forced to rub together [*sic*] in the daily business of living, over centuries. Like all real languages, it is a complex system of overlapping registers and dialects. This is a genuinely secular creation, not only in the sense that it is mundane in its origins and purposes but also in the sense of its being poly-communal as well as multilingual in its sources. For such a shared linguistic domain and inheritance to become a site of communal differentiation and identity politics produces surprising kinds of violence, even linguistic violence.[27]

Such "violence" was likely to produce anxiety in an author like Shiv Prasad, and thus in his books, which may be noted in his interpretation of historical phenomenon, in his selections of what he highlighted in his writings and in what he left out. Making clear choices, putting things in a neat way – one way or another – was hardly feasible for Shiv Prasad, given the "shared" traditions he inherited. In keeping with his cultural, political context, therefore, one appreciates the enormous difficulty he faced in the project of general education for girls and in the writing of textbooks for them. The question for us is what expectations would he have for the girl he wished to send to school? What kind of woman would he expect her to become? What models would he deem appropriate for her? And why these? In order to reflect

[26] Ibid., p. 47. The Arya Samaj was a Hindu social reform movement "committed somewhat quixotically to the recovery of 'Vedic excellence' in all spheres." The major area of the work of Arya Samaj was in Punjab and hence the work there was done in Urdu, despite Dayanand's commitment to "and apparently formidable competence in Sanskrit." Dayanand was persuaded to adopt Hindi instead of Sanskrit, and the Hindi that "developed under this complex of influences grew progressively distant from Urdu, and became more and more Sanskritized 'Hindi.'" Rai, *Hindi Nationalism*, p. 67.

[27] Ibid., p. 103. The question of communal differentiation and identity politics is extensively discussed by Pandey in his *The Construction of Communalism*.

more directly on these questions, let us turn next to the space of the school for the schoolgirl.

SCHOOLGIRL

It has been noted that there were no public schools for girls when Shiv Prasad started out as a school inspector in 1856. "Over the next decade the Education Department would enroll no more than 12,000 girls in its various aided and supported schools." Citing these statistics from William Hunter's review of the progress of education in 1882, Stark says the "report spoke a different language: the percentage of girls under instruction to the female population of school going age remained at a dismal 0.27 percent, putting the NWP at the bottom of the league." It was only in 1864 that the first girls' schools opened in the Banaras Circle, and in the following year the number of girls went up from seven to eighty-nine. The aim of girls' education "had not changed much since W. Adams had outlined it in 1836: they would receive 'a good plain education both in their own and in the English language, be trained to the habits of industry and usefulness, and remain in the institution until they marry.'" Shiv Prasad, Stark writes, was "blissfully unaware of the disappointment" that awaited him when he started the project of girls' schools in the 1860s.[28]

This statement would seem to imply that Shiv Prasad was unaware of the traditional situation of girls, including the social constraints in their training and literacy, before he proposed his new schools for girls. Yet, everything in Shiv Prasad's work suggests the opposite. My argument therefore is this: Shiv Prasad's reflection on the challenge of moving girls to the formal setting of the school may be seen in his careful construction of the *Vamamanranjan*. In this book, he takes the tales of the old world, often told in the domestic sphere by older women, to a new physical space of learning for girls. This is an extremely sensitive move (suggesting a keen awareness of the problem of changing spaces for the education of girls). Along with stories told in the

---

[28] Stark, "At the Grassroots," pp. 32, 33. In the case of Banaras, Nita Kumar notes that "there is little evidence to suggest that, in the second half of the nineteenth century, women received any kind of formal schooling in Banaras at all. The institutions where education was imparted – *tols, pathshalas, vidyalayas, madrasas* and *maktabs* – were exclusively for boys." Kumar, *Lessons from Schools*, pp. 152–153.

domestic world, he included new tales, as well as his own, to address the changing needs of the time. An interesting universe is created in the bringing together of tales and morals from the world that he grew up in – and several others from Europe. What we have in a text like the *Vamamanranjan* is hardly a final setting of the qualities of the "new Hindu woman," to use Stark's formulation.[29] The contest over the *new*, the *Hindu* (or *Muslim*) and the *woman* would continue for a long time yet!

Writing about the character of Sanskrit education in late-nineteenth-century Banaras, Nita Kumar says, "The guru was part of a larger system which can be understood in two familiar ways. It was an unveiling of the truth of the *shastras* and of the Self, for one. But the more interesting facet of Sanskrit education is its 'hidden curriculum' ... for the sake of learning itself."[30] She writes about precolonial schooling, before the institutionalization of schools in the NWP, by reading "more 'uncontaminated'" noncolonial sources such as "the corpus of anecdotes about pundits, both oral and written." Kumar argues that as far as the space of education was concerned, there was no "indigenous institutions of the kind [that were] becoming the norm in England... There was no Sanskrit or Hindustani term equivalent to 'school.' The closest equivalent is *shiksha-diksha*, or the giving and receipt of education."[31] As far as the subjects of such training were concerned, these included grammar, literature, logic, astrology, philosophy

---

[29] In her discussion of the *Vamamanranjan*, Stark suggests that "there are numerous examples in the VMR [*Vamamanranjan*] that indicate an attempt to reconcile the great dichotomy of female existence between the domestic and public spheres, the home and the world." And further, that the *Vamamanranjan* "invested the concept of *seva* [service] with a *brand-new meaning*, in a way that preempted future nationalistic interpretations of women's role in society [emphasis mine]." Thus, this text "presents new role models which, while drawing on traditional Hindu notions of female virtue, transcend the same, according the woman a more active role in society... The envisaged ideal of the new educated Hindu woman, combining traditional and 'modern' features." Stark, "Towards a New Hindu Woman," pp. 175–176. As this chapter will clarify, while the *Vamamanranjan* was designed for schoolgirls, it was neither designed for a "new" female figure, nor were its models recast as "new role models" – let alone the production of what Stark calls "the new educated Hindu woman." The question of the so-called new woman and its relevance to the nineteenth-century northern Indian milieu is a point of great debate among scholars, which I have discussed extensively in Chapter 1.
[30] Kumar, *Lessons from Schools*, p. 43.
[31] Ibid., pp. 45–46.

and the Vedas. Service, responsibility and discipline were highly valued, and "underlying these principles of space, time and curricula ran some basic presumptions of hierarchy. The patron of learning was a goddess, Saraswati, one of the forms of the goddess of many names and forms in the Hindu iconical system... [Yet] no females were taught the Vedas or any other branch of the sastras. No girls went to pundits to study, and if any of them did acquire Sanskrit it was within the family, as daughter or sister or, more rarely, wife, of a pandit."[32]

Hence for the girl-child or woman, literacy was restricted to the home, sometimes with boys, but mostly separately, and for girls, occasionally by semitrained teachers such as the *panditayani* or *ustani* (Sanskrit and Urdu terms). Singing, dancing, crafts, midwifery, housework, knowledge of scriptures were given "orally and informally." Other areas of learning were the rituals, festivals, performances and storytelling. "But primarily it was the *Ramacharitramanas* and the Mahabharata, and popular stories and sayings extemporizing within the corpus of their mythologies, which educated women into their wifely roles."[33]

In Shiv Prasad's time, and indeed later into the nineteenth century, such home-based training for the girl-child continued. Even in Bengal, where school education for girls was introduced earlier than in the NWP, and Bethune College was established in Calcutta in May 1849 (with its emphasis on a decidedly "secular" education), this experiment had apparently failed and for some time educators had to turn their attention back to a more traditional education in the *zenana*.[34]

In the following pages, I detail the approach to educating girls and boys before the idea of the modern school came to be elaborated in the NWP. I point to the domestic space as the space of training for girls in Hindu as well as Muslim families in northern India. The examples I provide underline the importance of specific morals critical in the

---

[32] Ibid., pp. 47–49.
[33] Ibid., pp. 153, 155. A similar kind of training of women in Bengal in the mid-nineteenth century, which is in the home and the *zenana* (women's quarters), is detailed beautifully by Meredith Borthwick in her book entitled *The Changing Role of Women in Bengal: 1849–1905* (Princeton, 1984), see especially chapter III, "Expanding Horizons: The Education of the Bhadramahila."
[34] Borthwick, *The Changing Role of Women in Bengal*, pp. 73, 75, 79.

training and literacy of boys and girls. Shiv Prasad's books, such as the *Vamamanranjan*, reflect a continuing concern with these values and with the principles he was brought up with.

In the late 1820s, Shiv Prasad was raised by his grandmother (not mother, but rather the aunt of his father), Bibi Ratan Kunvari. Ratan Kunvari was a poet, and also wrote a prose composition about devotion to Lord Krishna entitled *Prem Ratna*. She knew Sanskrit and Persian well and was highly accomplished in music. Shiv Prasad's two sisters also grew up in the care of Bibi Ratan Kunvari. Women would recite the *Ramacharitramanas* and the *Sursagar* and the "boy Shiv Prasad would hear them." Shiv Prasad's training in his boyhood included learning about *Shastras* from Bibi Ratan Kunvari and an emphasis on ideals such as discipline (*anushasanpriyata*), timeliness (*vaqt ki paabandi*), accomplishing the work allotted to oneself (*kaam karne ke saliqe*), as well as inculcating civil ways (*sabhyata ke taur-tariqe*).[35] We find detailed descriptions of these qualities in several booklets that Shiv Prasad composed for children.

These booklets provide glimpses into the kinds of instruction that Shiv Prasad received, treasured and replicated in his writings several times. We see this, for example, in his *Ladkon ki Kahani*, literally *Story of Boys*, or as the official subtitle has it, "Anecdotes on the Duties and Moral Training of Children," written in Banaras in 1861.[36] The subtitle clarifies that the book is for children; in the title we have *ladke*, boys, but we should remember that then as now *ladke* was also used to refer to children of both sexes. In this booklet, Shiv Prasad gives general instructions followed by a story out of which precise morals are made evident. A few examples of the morals of the stories are: not to touch things that do not belong to you; follow manners about sitting, getting up and walking; do not tease animals; do not be lazy; cultivate alertness; fight against jealousy and greed; and how to acquire comfort.[37] The protagonists that live out these lessons range from the Muslim kings Mahmud Ghaznavi and Aurangzeb (who are condemned); to Alexander the Great; Prithvi Raj, a Hindu king of India; and two sons

---

[35] Talwar, *Bhartiya Sahitya*, p. 11.

[36] Babu Shivaprasad, *Ladkon ki Kahani*, Banaras 1861. British Library, OIOC 14156.h.10. According to the title page, this was a second edition. Translations mine. Cited as *Ladkon ki Kahani*.

[37] *Ladkon ki Kahani*, pp. 7, 9, 15, 19, 26, 28, 33, 40.

trained by a talented woman called Alice, who lived during the time of
Queen Victoria (who is also admired).

In his *Balabodh* (published in Allahabad in the same year as the
Gutka, 1867), Shiv Prasad translated a variety of parables and morals
from English to Hindi. The front page of the copy I consulted notes
that this was the tenth edition and thirty thousand copies of it had
been printed.[38] Shiv Prasad's line of thought here is similar to that followed in *Ladkon ki Kahani*. The author emphasizes the importance
of reading, of sentence construction, punctuation marks and so forth.
Then he speaks directly to *chote ladke* (small boys), saying that if they
are shy of reading and writing (*padhna-likhna*), playing a lot more,
then it would be harmful for them (*haani hai*).[39] He writes about the
creation of the world, of flora and fauna, of different kinds of animals, trees, insects, of marveling in the creations of God (*Ishvar ki
shrishti*). And of the amazing things that ears, eyes, nose, mouth, teeth,
feet can do, further proof of God's wondrous work. Shiv Prasad says,
"Although no one can see him [God], but he can always see good
and bad deeds (*bhale, bure kamon ko sada dekhta hai*). Therefore it
is right (*uchit hai*) that human beings should be alert and do good
works (*saavdhan rehkar uttam uttam kaam karain*)."[40] The booklet
teaches its young readers parables of animals, trees, earth and nature.
Qualities such as restrain and hard work are emphasized repeatedly.[41]
In the qualities that Shiv Prasad spells out, he depicts a moral space
for boys and girls in which there is a great emphasis on a cultivation
of the self that includes an awareness of nature and its relationship to
the human world, as well as good bearing towards nature, the divine
and the worldly – all of which are interlinked.

Even after Shiv Prasad's textbooks and collections had been produced and widely distributed, the practice of traditional learning and
home-based education of girls largely continued. In Gauridatt's 1870
Devrani Jethani ki Kahani, set among the trading Baniya community
of Meerut (in the context of the active debate on women's education), Anandi's (the heroine's) literacy (*padhi-likhi*) and intelligence

---

[38] Raja Shiv Prasad, *Balabodh* (Allahabad, 1867), British Library, OIOC 14160.a.3 (3.).
   All translations are mine. Cited as *Balabodh*.
[39] *Balabodh*, pp. 1–6, 7.
[40] Ibid., pp. 8–11.
[41] *Ibid.*, pp. 12, 16, and the conclusion on page 27.

are marked repeatedly, as are her cooking skills and efficient management of the house. The author refers to her reading Nagri alongside
cooking twice a day, stitching, knitting and doing embroidery. She also
teaches girls of the extended kinship networks and the neighborhood.
She recites couplets from the *Bhagvad-Gita*, and on days of festivals
(when the women are excused from stitching and other such chores)
she sings devotional songs from poets Tulsidas and Surdas.[42]

And a similar, yet subtly changed, emphasis is found in Nazir
Ahmad's 1868–1869 *Mirat* and in the 1872 *Banat-an-Na`sh*, as well
as Hali's 1874 *Majalis-un-Nissa*. Again, the *sharif* Asghari in the *Mirat*
is educated (*padhi-likhi*), but she teaches the girls of the neighborhood only in her own house and without any monetary returns. For
Nazir Ahmad, literate women who cultivate their talents (*hunar*) for
the business of the world and who are aware of the need for good
comportment (*adab*) and right ways (*qa`ida, tariqa*) are the guardians
of respectability. Reading, writing, sewing, making up beds, arranging
jewels, learning to make specific dishes – all these were things to be
proud of.[43] For the author, *khanadari* (housekeeping) and *duniyadari*
(matters of the world) were the same thing.[44] Teaching ethics (*akhlaq*)
and good housekeeping (*khanadari*) was a point that Nazir Ahmad
elaborated forcefully in his *Banat-an-Na`sh*, where Asghari, the *ustan-
iji*, teaches the girls of the *mohalla*. Husnara, a young, ill-behaved *sharif* girl is put in the hands of Asghari for training and cultivation.

Altaf Hussain Hali's *Majalis-un-Nissa* (1874) gives unusual detail
about the education of a girl. Hali's heroine, Zubaida Khatun, lists the
vital tasks she learned as a girl-child: saying prayers properly; correct
behavior in eating, drinking, getting up, sitting down, listening; respecting the elders; avoiding "fraternizing with servants," not talking or
laughing too loudly, no running around or looking someone boldly in
the eye while talking; no going about without head covered. Zubaida
Khatun studied the Quran with her *ustani* and learned the injunctions
concerning prayer, fasting, bathing and cleanliness. A Mughlani taught
her stitching. Her father taught her *naskh* and *nasta`liq* calligraphy, as
well as Persian and arithmetic. Zubaida Khatun's father also advised

[42] Pandit Gauridatt, *Devrani Jethani ki Kahani* (Patna, 1870; rpt. 1966), p. 12.
Translations mine.
[43] *Mirat* Urdu edn., p. 34.
[44] Ibid., pp. 50–51.

her to read the *Tales of the Four Darvishes* (*Bagh-o-Bahar*). With all this, Zubaida Khatun explained to her son, "mother had drilled into me from the beginning that work was so important that, even in childhood, I didn't enjoy playing much."[45]

This was the shared world of Hindu and Muslim respectability that Shiv Prasad knew well. His translation of the ethics of this female world into a textbook for schoolgirls was no small achievement. The time of the composition of the *Vamamanranjan* was one when the canon for schools was of course still being put together. Hence, the models that would be helpful in these challenging times, when girls had to cross the domestic threshold and go into modern schools, were not already known, available, ready-made for the authors. In books produced by modern reformers and educationists, didacticism and tales would intermingle, as would locations and times. It was only much later that readers, officials and scholars classified these as "the first textbook," as a "textbook," as a "classic" and so on. The central issue for my purposes, then, is to consider how Shiv Prasad struck a balance between the old texts and traditions and the new curriculum that had to speak to the demand of colonial modernity.

TEXTBOOK FOR GIRLS

Shiv Prasad never wrote anything exclusively on the subjects of child marriage, widow remarriage, inter-caste marriage or the education of women (issues central to the writings of his contemporary, Nazir Ahmad). Yet, it is evident that several of his books and stories, including the *Vamamanranjan* and the *Gutka*, are concerned with these questions.[46] Let us begin by examining the first of these.

The *Vamamanranjan* is a cartographic compilation of seventeen stories that derive from Indic as well as European sources. Each story,

---

[45] Gail Minault (tr.), *Voices of Silence* (Delhi, 1986), pp. 50–51. Shah Abdul Qadir was the son of the eighteenth-century reformer, Shah Waliullah of Delhi, and he translated the Quran into Urdu. Gail Minault notes that Zubaida Khatun first read the Quran in Arabic and then read the translation (Ibid., p. 157, fn. 8). *Bagh-o-Bahar* by Mir Amman Dehlavi was originally written in 1801 for training European students of Fort William College in Urdu.
[46] It should also be noted that Shiv Prasad selected several stories of Thomas Day, an eighteenth-century English social reformer who wrote against slavery and the social differences between the rich and the poor, and collected these in a volume entitled *Sandford and Merton*.

selected by Raja Shiv Prasad, serves as a mnemonic device in that it demonstrates a specific virtue that girls would memorize. The special-ness of the morals of each of these stories lies in the fact that they are remindful of the parables that Shiv Prasad wrote in his conduct manuals for boys – principles of good life that were clearly important to him.

Briefly, the first five tales are: *Damyanti* (*Nal-Damyanti* is the more readily recognized and used title from the *Mahabharata*), *Ahilya Bai* (*Rani of Indore*), *Rani Bhavani* (*Rani of Nathaur, Bengal*), *Kalidas ki Stri* (*Wife of Kalidasa, the bard, Vidyottma*) and *Draupadi* (again from the *Mahabharata*). Placed between *Kalidas ki Stri* and *Draupadi* is a story entitled *Ma Baap ki Seva* (*The Care of Parents*), set in 1783 New York, relating the familial devotion of an American girl. Other stories include: *Bibi Ambos*, about a German woman, told by a Bibi Jamieson; `*Auraton ki Himmat* (*Courage of Women*), about two women Christian martyrs who lived in the second century CE in Carthage; *Pulcheria* (399–453 CE, the daughter of the East Roman emperor Arcadius); *Elizabeth Hungary Vali* (Elizabeth of Hungary, 1207–1231); *Chilonis* (the daughter of King Leonidas II of Sparta who ruled from 254 to 235 BCE); *Sybilla* (daughter-in-law of William the Conqueror); *Gambar Karodhring* (a Danish heroine); *Caroline* (also known as Caroline of Brandenburg-Ansbach, 1683–1737), who was the wife of George II of England); *Bhai ka Moh* (*Affection for a Brother*), about the wife of Entopharnis (?) of Persia; *Pita ka Moh* (*Affection for a Father*), about a woman in Nero's Rome; and another work entitled *Pita Ka Moh*, about the service of the daughter of the Duc de La Roche-Foucauld of France.[47]

I wish to underline an important point about Shiv Prasad's repro-duction of these tales in the *Vamamanranjan*. In reflecting on the Eurocentric and statist limit of world history, arguing that historians

---

[47] The basic introductory detail to the characters of these stories that I provide in the brackets is not mentioned by Shiv Prasad. In several cases, such as that of the Danish heroine, Gambar Karodhring, I have found it hard to find out any details. Similarly, there are two men named Francois de La Rochefoucauld that I came across in my searches: Francois VI, Duc de La Rochefoucauld (1613–1680), a noted French author of maxims and morals, and Francois de La Rochefoucauld (1558–1645), a French cardinal and an important figure in the French counter-Reformation Church. Given the cryptic character of Shiv Prasad's retelling, it is hard to establish which of these historical characters he refers to.

should learn from literature to think about history and historicality, Guha makes the following propositions about the place of story, history and novel. He says story, history and novel during the Hellenic era fell centrally under the "storyteller's initiative." In India, on the other hand, "the story, or *katha*, owed its inauguration primarily to the listener's demand." In elaborating this point with the help of the tales of the Mahabharata, "the greatest of the *itihasa* genre of narratives," Guha speaks about the different kinds of relays, digressions and tales within tales. He explains that "in all this it is the story teller who has pride of place. It is generally assumed, without too many questions asked, that the story flows directly from his initiative." He then gives examples from the Mahabharata to bring out the critical place of the interlocutor. So each "principal narrator of the Mahabharata has an interlocutor": Ugrasrava has Saunaka, Vaisampayana has Janamejaya, and Sanjaya has Dhrtrashtra. The interlocutors, says Guha, are the initiators. They are more than "decorative" figures: "they have a strategic function in gathering the listeners' will in the development of the narrative cycle and presenting it at the inauguration of each of its episodes."[48]

Likewise, in reflecting on the multiple adaptations of *Nala-Damyanti*, David Shulman and V. Narayana Rao make an important point about the "life of a story," also relevant for my analysis of the *Vamamanranjan*, in which a version of *Nala-Damyanti* is included as well. Shulman and Rao observe that the Mahabharata has the oldest attested version of *Nala-Damyanti* and then there are hundreds of "recorded versions" – variations or transformations – of that text.[49] What is important, the authors note, is not to look to the original story in order to analyze how a variation of a core tale is produced in a new rendering. Rather, each retelling is significant in itself because it is "rearranged according

---

[48] Ranajit Guha, *History at the Limit of World-History* (New Delhi, 2002), pp. 56, 58, 59.

[49] David Shulman and Narayana Rao, "Nala: The Life of a Story," p. 1. This is an introductory chapter to Susan Wadley (ed.), *Damayanti and Nala: The Many Lives of a Story* (New Delhi, 2011). I have used the draft version of this chapter shared generously by Narayana Rao. For an excellent discussion on the continuous transformation of the *Ramayana* materials, see Paula Richman (ed.), *Many Ramayanas: The Diversity of Narrative Tradition in South Asia* (Berkeley, 1991); and more recently, Robert Philips, *Garden of Endless Blossoms: Urdu Ramayans of the 19th and Early 20th Century* (PhD Dissertation, University of Wisconsin-Madison, 2010).

to the individual perception and experience [of the author]... Each Nala has an independent existence."[50] Shulman and Rao are pointing to the versatility of this tale: "a vast range of contexts and intentions – to such an extent that we cannot even determine what the narrative skeleton might be, outside context and intention... You need an audience to recognize the story just as Nala needs Damyanti to recognize him."[51]

In reading tales from the *Vamamanranjan*, which the didactic impulse would urge them to memorize, what would schoolgirls recognize and idealize in the stories? The issue that requires probing is what is meant to draw the girls' attention in Shiv Prasad's rendering. For a start, the answers are implicit in the titles, which in turn are tied to the morals of the tales. The title of the story of Nal-Damyanti is given by Shiv Prasad as *Damyanti*, to take one example. This fits the tradition of the other exemplary women heroines he selects from India. The focus in the first part of the *Vamamanranjan* is on the women from the epics and other classics, and more recent examples such as Ahilya Bai or Rani Bhavani, many of whom are likely to have been fairly well known among girls of respectable families who made up the first generation of girls sent to school.[52] The precise qualities emphasized in the case of such praiseworthy women are of special interest.

In Shiv Prasad's *Damyanti*, it is the heroine's virtuousness that is recognized. At the beginning of this tale, Nala leaves Damyanti in the jungle after he had lost his kingdom where they wandered homeless. He worries about her ability to cope with such hardship, but also knows that she would never leave him during this time of suffering. So he leaves her while she sleeps under a tree. When Damyanti finds Nala gone, she wanders desolate in the forest. She is threatened by a serpent at one point. A hunter (*vyadha*) tries to help her, but in turn he wants

---

[50] Shulman and Rao, "Nala," p. 3.

[51] Ibid., pp. 6–7.

[52] To use Shiv Prasad's words; there is "no body in the whole of India from the Himalayas to Rameshwaram [who] has not heard of Ahilya Bai." Cited in Bayly, *Empire and Information*, p. 236. Bayly says in the context of Ahilya Bai: "The citizens of Banaras and its regions would indeed have known her well as someone who constructed a bathing platform during the great Maratha renovation of Banaras in the eighteenth century." Bayly, *Empire and Information*, pp. 236–237. I would add that Ahilya Bai would also be recognized, significantly, because she was a female patron. This would be in line with remembering female saints and rulers, which, in fact, Shiv Prasad discusses.

to destroy Damyanti's honor (*satya dharma naash karna chaha*). So she invokes the gods and the spirits and prays that if she was a pure and virtuous (*sati*) woman, the hunter should be turned into ashes. And he does.[53] Eventually Damyanti returns to her father's kingdom and continues looking after her two children. Meanwhile, Nala reaches Ayodhya and becomes the charioteer (an art he is skilled at) of Raja Rituparna, and takes a new name, Bahuk. Damyanti's father's messenger finds out about Nala, but despite the king's efforts Nala does not return. Damyanti, with her father's approval, has a letter written to King Rituparna saying that since the whereabouts of Nala could not be established, there was going to be a *swayamvara* (an early Indian tradition in which the woman chooses a groom for herself) for her to find a new groom. Rituparna was requested to attend and the day of the *swayamvara* was set fairly close.[54] Damyanti knew that only a great charioteer like Nala could bring Rituparna in time, which he does. With the help of her friend Keshini, Damyanti establishes that Bahuk was her lost Nala. The story ends with Damyanti meeting Nala, their reunion and Nala's recovery of his lost kingdom.

Damyanti sends Keshini to meet Nala in order to establish who he really is. Nala introduces himself and says he is the charioteer, Bahuk, and that he has brought his king Rituparna for the *swayamvara*. He then says, "It is surprising that King Nala's *pativrata* queen Damyanti, who is so virtuous (*sati*), should desire a second husband. It is true that when bad days come, even one's wife and son don't remain one's own." When Keshini points out that Nala had deserted Damyanti, he goes on to say: "no matter how much a woman suffers on account of her husband, it is not right to criticize him in front of others." It is the same sentiment he expresses to Damyanti when they meet: "However it might be, a *pativrata* woman, even when she sees faults (*dosh*) in her husband, does not criticize him (*ninda nahin karti*)."[55] While seemingly this is a story about Damyanti, at a closer look we see that Nala is the guide who lays down the qualities women must aspire to and cultivate: these include *satya dharma* (honor); *sati* (virtuousness); *pativrata* (husband worshipping).

---

[53] *Vamamanranjan*, pp. 4–5.
[54] Ibid., pp. 5–6.
[55] Ibid., pp. 6, 8.

Consider the second piece, *Ahilya Bai*. Ahilya's husband was Maharaja Rao Holkar, a man of lower caste. At his death (followed by that of their son), Ahilya Bai goes against the advice of Gangadhar Yashwant, a *rajpurohit*, to adopt a son. She decides to rule her kingdom and appoints Gangadhar as her prime minister (*divan*) and Tukoji Holkar as the head of the army (*senapati*). In a description of her routine as a ruler, this is what Shiv Prasad emphasizes: first she would have recitations of the *dharma-grantha* (scriptural texts). "She was highly skilled (*nipuna*) and accomplished (*padhna-likhna*, literally 'reading-writing')." She first fed the Brahmins, then herself. She did not eat meat or fish. Then putting on imperial clothes (*rajbesh*), she attended to the court until the evening.[56] Ahilya Bai, whom Shiv Prasad calls *dharmik stri* (virtuous woman), was noted as a ruler, albeit as a woman ruler who was highly disciplined, skilled, accomplished and a regular listener of the scriptures.

The next example, *Rani Bhavani*, is also a pious woman ruler. Shiv Prasad highlights the fact that Jagat Seth, his ancestor, helped Rani Bhavani at a critical time when her throne was threatened by Nawab Alivardi Khan of Bengal. In time, she was able to recover her estate. She used proceeds in good works, especially in Banaras. Shiv Prasad again describes her routine: after waking up at dawn, performing her ablutions and reciting the *Dharmashastras*, she would do the cooking herself, feed ten Brahmins, and only then would she eat anything. She attended to the matters of the estate, listened to the *Dharmashastras* again, followed by prayers and a meal. She was widowed at the age of thirty-two and lived until the age of seventy-nine, but never broke her discipline (*niyam*).[57] The emphasis is the same: discipline, virtue and regular absorption in scriptural texts. And again, man comes out on top.

Vidyottama, the wife of Kalidasa in *Kalidas ki Stri*, is lauded for her scriptural knowledge: she is called a *pandita*. Kalidasa, initially an illiterate (*murkh*) man, was lured into marriage with Vidyottama by several pundits. Getting Kalidasa to marry Vidyottama was a ploy of the pundits, none of whom could defeat her in scriptural debates and hence could not marry her: for that was Vidyottama's condition

---

[56] Ibid., pp. 9–11.
[57] Ibid., pp. 12–15.

of marriage. The story tells us that after his marriage to Vidyottama, Kalidasa, ashamed that the secret of his foolishness could not be hidden any more, works hard and becomes a wise poet.[58]

Finally, *Draupadi*: Shiv Prasad takes a moment from the Mahabharata when Ashvaththama, the son of the guru of Pandavas who had deserted and joined Duryodhana, beheads the five sons of Draupadi. Arjuna, seeing Draupadi's sorrow, vows to take revenge. When he brings Ashvaththama in front of her, however, she becomes compassionate and says: "this is the son of your guru Dronacharya. Why do you wish to kill him? You will bring dishonor to your dynasty." When Arjuna hears such compassionate words (*karunamai vaani*), he releases Ashvaththama.[59] Generosity and selflessness are highlighted: the ideals for superior women.

In Shiv Prasad's retelling of these five stories there is an emphasis on "womanly" virtues such as *satya dharma* (honor), *sati* (virtuousness), *pativrata* (husband worshipping) in Damyanti; and the idea of *dharmik stri* (virtuous woman) through a cultivation of discipline, skill (*nipuna*) and other vital accomplishments such as listening and reading of scriptural texts via Ahilya Bai and Rani Bhavani. The importance of scriptural knowledge is highlighted directly in the case of Vidyottama: but even a highly learned woman was an instrument for man's advancement.

Given the preexisting conditions in which girls and women were trained at home, and given the data suggesting a widespread resistance to girls being sent to schools, for Shiv Prasad to produce models in terms other than those familiar to his female (and male) audience would have been unthinkable – if indeed this can be done in any case, anywhere. What he did was to carry the tales of female exemplars from the space of the familial to that of the schools. Thus the girls could stand on known grounds, with recognizable illustrations and models (ancient and modern, Western and Indian) whom they could emulate. In this context, the question is scarcely one of reconciliation of the domestic and the public as proposed by Stark[60]: the *Vamamanranjan* simply reflects an extension of a former moral universe into a new

---

[58] Ibid., pp. 15–17.
[59] Ibid, pp. 17–18.
[60] See references to Stark.

space. A move towards "reconciliation," if that is the word, is charted out much later in the nineteenth century by educators and reformers such as Nazir Ahmad, Hali and Pandit Gauridatt, among others, as I demonstrate in the next chapter.

Let me turn to the remaining stories of the *Vamamanranjan*, from European sources. Consider what Shiv Prasad selects. Between the story of Vidyottama and Draupadi is a story entitled *Ma Baap ki Seva*: about the devotion of an unnamed American girl. Her parents were so poor that the girl decides to go to a dentist to sell her teeth so that she could provide for them. The dentist, on hearing the reason for her wanting to sell her teeth, is so moved that he gives her the money she needs to look after her parents.[61] Then there is a Bibi Jamieson narrating the story of a German bourgeois woman called Bibi Ambos, who struggles to get her brother Henry released when he is imprisoned on false charges. A countess named Elysee helps Bibi Ambos in arranging a meeting with the Czar (we are not told which czar) to obtain Henry's freedom. Shiv Prasad highlights the fact that it is Bibi Ambos who goes to Siberia in search for her brother, not her younger brother who had earlier taken a letter of appeal to St. Petersburg. Since then he had married and his wife was not willing to let him go. Moreover he was the only surviving male member (*mardon main ab vah akela ghar mein rah gaya tha*).[62] Women's highest goal, once again, was to be selfless.

In `Auraton ki Himmat (The Courage of Women)*, Shiv Prasad recounts the faithful lives of two second-century Christian martyrs, Vibia Perpetua and Felicitas (also known as Felicity), and the torture these women faced in keeping their faith, for which they were eventually put to death. (Perpetua was a married noblewoman and Felicitas was an expectant mother, a slave at the time of their martyrdom in Carthage, the Roman province of Africa.[63]) Shiv Prasad says, "There

---

[61] *Vamamanranjan*, p. 17.
[62] Ibid., p. 22.
[63] The record of the *Passion of St. Perpetua, St. Felicitas, and their Companions* is said to preserve the actual words of the martyrs and their friends. The detail of their martyrdom survives both in Latin and Greek texts. A lot has been written about these two women, including in several recent writings. See, for example, Erin Ann Ronsse, "Rhetoric of Martyrs: Transmission and Reception History of the 'Passion of Saints Perpetua and Felicitas.'" (PhD Dissertation, University of Victoria, 2008), 438 pages; Peter Dronke, *Women Writers of the Middle Ages* (Cambridge, 1984); Joyce Salisbury, *Perpetua's Passion* (New York, 1997).

is highest honor for them among the saintly Christian women (*sadhvi Isai striyan*)."[64] Here martyrdom emerges as the highest aspiration for women.

Pulcheria, the heroine of the next story, a fourth-century BCE East Roman empress, is noted for her intelligence (`aqlmandi`) and for the fact that she, along with her sisters, vowed in the interest of her empire never to marry.[65] There is a long discussion of her training her younger brother Theodosius II, his marriage, the death of Theodosius and his wife (Aelia Eudocia) and finally Pulcheria's rulership.[66] We are told Pulcheria married, albeit in "name only" (*naammaach ka vivaah*) at the age of fifty-one to the famous general Marcian, who respected her vow of chastity. Shiv Prasad concludes the story by noting Pulcheria's qualities: among others, intelligence (*buddhi*), patience (*vivek*), justice (*nyaya*), observance of a woman's fidelity and right ways (*dharma*).[67] And, one might add, another important virtue would be sacrifice.

Elizabeth Hungary Vali (Elizabeth of Hungary), is one of the longest stories in this part of the *Vamamanranjan*. Elizabeth (1207–1231) was a princess of Hungary, betrothed to the king of Thuringia's (in central Germany) son, Lewis. She was four at the time and Lewis eleven. Under the care of Lord Varila (in the service of the king of Thuringia), Elizabeth was sent to Thuringia to live. Whatever her father sent her each month she would spend on the poor and the needy. When she was nine, her father-in-law, who loved Elizabeth dearly, died. Lewis was enthroned, but he was only a titular head. At one point in the story, Lord Varila, in whose care Elizabeth's father had sent her to Thuringia, asked Lewis whether he intended to marry Elizabeth; if not, he advised him, it would be only appropriate to send her back to her father. Lewis replied that he would marry her; that he loved her because of her compassion and faith (*daya aur dharm*) and that the wealth of the whole world – even kingship – was nothing in front of her. At thirteen Elizabeth married Lewis.[68]

[64] *Vamamanranjan*, p. 30.
[65] "*Sarvshakti maan Jagdishvar ke saamne Brahmacharya palne aur sada kumari rahne ki saugandh khayi*"; *Vamamanranjan*, p. 30.
[66] Ibid., pp. 31–34.
[67] Ibid., p. 35.
[68] Ibid., pp. 35–38. The same year, 1221, Lewis was crowned as Ludwig IV. It is not clear why Shiv Prasad gives the name Lewis and not Ludwig.

Shiv Prasad emphasizes Elizabeth and Lewis's love for each other and the prosperous country and the subjects they ruled. He reminds the reader that Elizabeth never forgot her prayers and remembrance of God (*Ishwar ki stuti aur prarthana*).[69] She carried on working for the poor: she would visit them, pay their dues on their behalf, look after the women, give food to children and medicines to the sick. It was a time when leprosy was very widespread and people were scared of going near lepers, but Elizabeth would go to them fearlessly. She would bathe them, bandage their wounds. One day she bathed a leper boy and put him to sleep in the same bed as Lewis. When Lewis returned and heard about the episode from his mother, he went to his bed, pulled off the covers and saw Christ sleeping there. Lewis immediately gave orders to build a hospital for lepers.[70] Similarly in 1226, when Lewis was away, a famine devastated the kingdom. Elizabeth undertook many kinds of activities for the poor. Lewis and Elizabeth had three sons. Lewis died in a war that he joined: Christian kings against the Muslims to regain Bait-ul-Muqaddas.[71] The two brothers of Lewis, Henry and Conrad, threw Elizabeth out (with her three sons and a newborn) along with a proclamation that no one was to give shelter to her. All the people that she had helped turned away. In the end, Lewis's brothers and other relations had a change of heart and they invited Elizabeth back, giving her land and the throne to her son, Herman. She continued helping the poor.[72]

The next model, Chilonis, the daughter of King Leonidas of Sparta (254–235 BCE), is briefly mentioned for the devotion and care she gave to her father. Sybilla, the daughter-in-law of William the Conqueror (also known as William I), according to the following story, saved her husband by sucking poison from his wounds: he lives and she dies in this act of sacrifice, we are told in a paragraph on her. Gambar Karodhring, a Danish entrepreneurial heroine, in the next brief piece advises the Danish king (again unnamed) at a grave moment when there was no food to eat that instead of killing the children and old

---

[69] Ibid., p. 38.
[70] Ibid., pp. 39–40.
[71] This event occurred in 1227 when Ludwig, en route to join the Sixth Crusade, died of plague in Italy; Rainer Koessling (ed. and tr.), *Leben und Legende der Heiligen Elisabeth nach Dietrich von Apolda* (Frankfurt am Main, 1997), p. 59.
[72] *Vamamanranjan*, pp. 42–44.

people (as several of his advisors had proposed to him), he should order the young to go to other lands and find ways to live. Thus, came into being the settlement of Lombardy in Italy. In *Caroline* (the story of the wife of George II of England), we read how Caroline teaches her older daughter to inculcate kindness.[73] This daughter of Caroline, whenever she went to bed, would make her friends read endlessly even when they tired. Hearing this, one day, Caroline ordered her daughter to read a book as she herself lay down. The mother kept on asking her to read while the daughter, sleepy and tired, found it hard to continue. In this way, Caroline established a moral for her daughter and said to her: "Remember for your comfort, do not put others to discomfort. Do not trouble others because they have the same heart as you."[74]

In *Bhai ka Moh*, due to a crime, the entire family of Entopharnis receives a sentence of execution (As I mentioned earlier, we do not know who Entopharnis is.). The wife of Entopharnis begs forgiveness from the king, who asks her to choose forgiveness for one man from her family. She asks forgiveness for her brother. When the king asks why she chose her brother and not her husband, she replies, "if I live, I can always find a second husband since it is not forbidden to do so. But where will I find a brother? My parents are dead." The king not only forgives her brother, but also her older son.[75] *Pita ka Moh* tells the story of a woman in Nero's Rome, who begs forgiveness for her father, who was charged for no reason, but Nero orders them both killed. Finally, in *Pita Ka Moh*, bearing the same title as the previous tale, a man named Duc de La Roche-Foucould and his daughter are sentenced to be hanged to death.[76] The daughter hides herself and her father, but when she sees him weakening in hiding, she decides to write a letter to the concerned officer (*hakim*), saying that they had been in hiding, their land had been confiscated and that her father was dying for want of food and clothes. She adds that although she was unable to save her father from the cruelty of hanging, she was

---

[73] Caroline had four sons and three daughters: Princesses Anne, Amelia and Caroline. Presumably it is Anne that Caroline teaches in the story.

[74] *Vamamanranjan*, pp. 44–46.

[75] Ibid., p. 47. Like several stories in this collection, it is not clear who Entopharnis was and where and when the story is set.

[76] See my notes in the introduction to these stories on the possibility of two Ducs de La Roche-Foucould that could be the actors of this story.

sad that she could not even protect him from hunger. She urges the officer to hang her and spare her father; moved by her kindness, the officer forgives the father and the daughter and returns their property as well.[77]

While these stories are different from the earlier ones – in geographical and cultural setting, and in their wide-ranging chronology – there is a language of morals shared by both the Indic and non-Indic narrations. Women are noted for their devotion to parents or to other members of their families, brothers or fathers or husbands in a variety of ways. For example, in the case of the American girl and in the story of Chilonis, both stories entitled *Pita ka Moh* (*The Love of the Father*), selflessness almost becomes a form (without any content) for women to embody. The woman in Nero's Rome, as well as the daughter of the Duc de La Roche-Foucould work to protect their fathers: again, hollowed out of desire and intention. Sybilla saves her husband by sucking poison from his wounds, the ultimate example of the sacrificing wife.

Bibi Ambos is marked for her bravery and her tireless efforts to rescue her brother. In the stories of Vibia Perpetua and Felicitas, we learn about matters of faith through two saintly Christian women (*sadhvi Isai striyan*). Pulcheria the empress is noted for her intelligence (*`aqlmandi, buddhi*), patience (*vivek*), justice (*nyaya*) and correct ways (*dharma*). Likewise, Gambar Karodhring, the Danish woman, is celebrated for her advice to the king. Caroline, the queen and mother, teaches her older daughter the significance of important virtues such as kindness. The family, lineage and inheritance are constituted as male: women serve only to preserve and reproduce it, and in extraordinary moments, to make remarkable sacrifices.

The morals of these stories are crucial to the kinds of virtues that the schoolgirl would be expected to memorize and emulate: well-defined practices central to her worlds. Based on these stories, one might even tabulate the duties of women spelt out by Shiv Prasad: ablutions, cleanliness, keeping house, cooking (even for queens), filial piety, sacrifice of personal pleasure (in marriage), listening to the scriptures, performing acts of charity – all of which add up to a woman's *dharm*, which can

[77] *Vamamanranjan*, pp. 47–48.

be described, in short, as service and sacrifice, duty and a disciplined lifestyle in the interest of family and empire.

In these stories, Shiv Prasad captures a distinct ethics of female societies from different regions and times that were supposed to serve the purpose of educating his north Indian schoolgirl readers. Shiv Prasad's rendition of Damyanti might be said to speak to a *pativrata* model, but what he emphasizes through this story is Damyanti's commitment, loyalty and love for Nala. Nala makes the argument for a *pativrata* wife in two instances, yet Damyanti, as recounted by Shiv Prasad, is not quite the embodiment of the *pativrata* woman, in spite of her submissive mode. Elizabeth of Hungary and the Christian martyrs are remembered as *sadhvi Isai striyan*: that is, devout Christian women. Ahilya Bai and Rani Bhavani are virtuous monarchs, and Vidyottama, a highly literate woman.

There is a provocative tension in Shiv Prasad's selections. Various possibilities of reading and activity were made available to girls. By presenting and not editing the tales, Shiv Prasad left open what girls might read, what they might memorize and idealize. There were scores of models and a variety of virtues to choose from in the *Vamamanranjan*. But there is a disciplinary move too in the author's use of the term *Vama*, meaning women. In a moral universe pervaded by such a range of women models, for the schoolgirls who read the *Vamamanranjan*, there were also familial expectations and duties, specific tasks such as cooking and cleanliness, which are underscored. *Vama(manranjan)*, for the entertainment of women, is the sign of a text that leads the reader to consider the various activities of the home, especially the duties of women, which include reading scriptures, emulating the virtues of piety and so forth. For all that, as we can see, the models of *Vamamanranjan* are not tied exclusively to domestic domains. Practices of literacy, knowledge of the scriptures, the travels of women are all valued.

The important point that emerges in Shiv Prasad's *Vamamanranjan* is that while it was not exclusively concerned with an emphasis on domesticated women figures, nonetheless, the stories make clear that the "freedom of the forest" was not a message that girls and women were expected to absorb. In this context, Shiv Prasad's inclusion of Insha's tale of Rani Ketki in the *Gutka* and his exclusion of it from the *Vamamanranjan* presents an interesting puzzle.

SHIV PRASAD'S *KAHANI THETH HINDI MEIN* (*THE STORY IN PURE HINDI*)

In 1867, Insha's tale about Rani Ketki comes to sit in the middle of an impressive collection of stories, the *Gutka*, designed by Shiv Prasad as part of the Hindi curriculum for junior civil servants and army officers of the British Empire. According to McGregor, the *Gutka* was reprinted twice by 1876 and was probably Shiv Prasad's "most important contribution to the moulding of the emergent Hindi style."[78]

It is important to understand that Shiv Prasad's collection was intended for a Hindi syllabus.[79] What Insha allows us to read is altered significantly in this context. For a start, the *Gutka* or *Hindi Selections* (another title by which the collection was popularized) was designed to teach Hindi as a language to the officers of the Raj. The questions posed through this collection then would be: How to speak Hindi? What was the cartography of Hindi language? Which tales (*Gutka* includes tales) would provide the best examples of Hindi linguistic practice? What would be "pure" Hindi? Recall that the tale of Rani Ketki, in its new physical and contextual placement in the *Gutka*, is given a title: *Kahani Theth Hindi Mein* (*A Story in Pure Hindi*). Providing a title to Insha's tale immediately circumscribed it as an example of the perfection of the Hindi language. Perhaps, too, Shiv Prasad took Insha's prefatorial comments literally, which claim that the story contains no Persian or Arabic vocabulary or regional or local dialect.[80]

There is another question we might ask. The non-inclusion of a tale like that of Rani Ketki in the *Vamamanranjan*, as I have argued, was linked with the morals and values deemed necessary for the education of the schoolgirl, the reader of the *Vamamanranjan*. It is important to detail, therefore, what in Rani Ketki's tale might have been considered inappropriate, and the implications of this story that might not have been convergent with other stories included in the *Vamamanranjan*. To

---

[78] McGregor, *Hindi Literature*, p. 72.
[79] Talwar says Shiv Prasad's preface to the *Gutka* is the first written history of Hindi language from a "scientific and historical perspective (*vaigyanik aur sahityik drishti se*)." Talwar, *Bhartiya Sahitya*, p.31.
[80] Insha says: "*ek din … apne dhyan mein chadi ki koi kahani aisi kahiye ki jisme Hindi ki chuut aur kisi boli ka put na mile*; *Urdu Ketki*, I, p. 5; *Hindi Ketki*, p. 2.

clarify these points, it will help to turn for a moment to another story included in the *Gutka*, the legend of Shakuntala, more specifically, Laxman Singh's *Shakuntala*. Let me note in passing that the Shakuntala story was also *not* included in the *Vamamanranjan*, although it was at least as popular as the stories of Damyanti, Ahilya Bai and so on.

Laxman Singh (1826–1896) was a graduate in English and Hindi of the Agra College, and had been a deputy collector since 1855. He had collaborated with A. O. Hume in the development of education and journalism and began his rendition of *Shakuntala* in 1861. His style was unlike Raja Shiv Prasad's in that he avoided the use of Persian or Arabic vocabulary entirely. "This style was from now on to offer a viable literary alternative to Sivaprasad's, whose cultural experience had been so different from Laksman Simh's... In keeping with his interest in India's classical past, Laksman Simh works not from a Brajbhasa version of Sakuntala, but direct from a Sanskrit text."[81]

It has been suggested that the influence of M. Kempson, the director of public education of the NWP from 1861–1877, who was in favor of wider use of a Sanskritized Hindi, was fairly strong at this time. He supported the Bareilly Tattvabodhini Sabha, for example, in making Hindi versions of Sanskrit works available in schools; he also encouraged translations of English works and introduced a system of prizes for successful authors, translators and compilers. While the total volume of Hindi works rose sharply in the 1860s, "the proportion devoted to more strictly educational subject matter, which had earlier predominated, markedly fell, despite being boosted by a dramatic upsurge of Hindi readers and manuals." Along with Agra and Banaras, Allahabad, Delhi, Lucknow, Ludhiana and Lahore emerged as new centers of Hindi publication.[82]

In her stimulating study on Shakuntala, Romila Thapar details the earliest narration of Shakuntala that occurred in the epic Mahabharata in the form of poetry or *kavya*. She argues that "an expanded treatment of the narrative is best known as the play, *Abhijnana-sakuntalam* by Kalidasa which, although it borrows the story from the epic, nevertheless differs from it significantly." The character of Shakuntala changes with each new rendering: from the earliest narration in the

---

[81] McGregor, *Hindi Literature*, p. 73.
[82] Ibid., p. 74.

Mahabharata to the *nataka*/play *Abhijnana-Shakuntalam* by Kalidasa; then in several popular renditions and adaptations; and finally, in colonial and nationalist interpretations. What is striking, the author notes, is that "whenever Sakuntala is mentioned we think immediately of the play by Kalidasa which has been, and continues to be, valued both by Indian commentators as well as others who have read it in Sanskrit, or in translation."[83]

Here is an outline of the story. Raja Dushyanta goes on a hunt and arrives, without realizing where he is, at a hermitage set in a deep forest. Shakuntala receives him. Dushyanta, taken by Shakuntala, offers her marriage. She accepts it and it is endorsed by her foster father, Kanva. The king leaves for his capital. After an exceptionally long gestation, a son, Bharata, is born to Shakuntala in the hermitage. When he comes of an appropriate age, in accordance with Kanva's wishes, he is taken to the capital, Hastinapur. What follows is a question of paternity when the king meets his son and his wife, Shakuntala. How this is resolved differs in two versions, as do the manner and dialogue of the characters.

In the epic version, "Sakuntala receives him [Dushyanta] alone and is forthright and welcoming... Duhsanta, much taken by 'the flawless girl with the beautiful hips,' offers marriage and also what seems to be a kind of bride-price-jewels, gems, clothes and even his kingdom. Sakuntala makes the marriage conditional. The decision to marry Duhsanta is hers alone and is later endorsed by her foster-father." When Shakuntala meets Dushyanta, "she is forthright, free, assertive, high-spirited young woman who demands that her conditions, as stipulated at her marriage, be fulfilled... Sakuntala marks a counterpoint to the notion of the *pativrata*, the ideal wife, which is referred to elsewhere in the text in the later didactic sections." "Who in fact is Sakuntala?"[84]

In Thapar's excellent contextual layering of the society and the emerging political forms of this time, we begin to understand why

[83] Thapar, *Sakuntala*, p. 5. Thapar suggests that the bracket 400 BCE to 400 CE would be the most appropriate time frame of the epic. Likewise, she says the date for Kalidasa varies, but he is placed in the fourth century CE. Ibid., p. 7.
[84] Ibid., pp. 37, 39. Shakuntala's condition of marriage was that the son born to her and Dushyanta would succeed as the next king, with which Dushyanta immediately agrees. Ibid., p. 26.

Shakuntala's direct articulations are possible in the epic version. Thapar details the character of the lineage societies with chiefdoms moving to being incipient kingdoms; hunting as a mechanism for keeping control over grazing grounds; and the appearance of women as "strong personalities, cherishing their autonomy and willing to argue for their rights" in epics such as the Mahabharata.[85] Shakuntala thus belongs to the *atavika/vanvasi* society: society of the forest (at the center of which is the hermitage of Shakuntala's foster father), which is conditioned by different sets of norms than those of Hastinapur (the capital). She is not a "submissive subject," and sees herself "as equal in status to man, characteristic of the society of forest dwellers whose egalitarianism would be more evident than that of Hastinapur."[86] Thapar also notes the importance of celestial women to the mindset of such a society, the *apsaras* (Shakuntala was the daughter of an *apsara*), "who had their own codes of behavior and were not subject to the rules of human society, although quite a few played an ancestral role in genealogies." In the epic version, when Dushyanta is faced with the question of the paternity and the claim of his son on the father's clan, this issue is made clear to him in a celestial voice.[87]

What happens in Kalidasa's play is that while the central theme remains the same as that of the epic, the author introduces several sub-plots – as important as the main story – involving a curse and a signet ring (*nama mudra*).[88] Shakuntala is given the signet ring by Dushyanta and because of the curse of a saint, she loses it. Thus, when she meets the king, there is no evidence, and the king has forgotten his marriage with Shakuntala owing to the curse. Again Thapar provides excellent contextual detail about the courtly background of this time and its rather different principles – which then affects the way Shakuntala is presented – hunting and romantic love, pursuit, contesting emotions and ultimate submission; love-in-union and love-in-separation

[85] Ibid., pp. 13, 15.

[86] Ibid., p. 39.

[87] Ibid., pp. 15, 38. For a detailed discussion of the context that I have briefly outlined, as well as the place of the *apsara* in social arrangements and issues of sexuality, see Ibid., ch. 2, "The Narrative from the *Mahabharata*."

[88] Thapar suggests that the signet ring became popular with the coming of the Indo-Greeks and those associated with the Mediterranean trading communities. For the place of the ring and the curse in Kalidasa's play, see Ibid., especially pages 54–56, 58–60.

as important components in romantic plays and so on. Additionally, "the visibility of Brahmanical high culture is evident and was a dominant part of the classicism with which Kalidasa is associated." Thus his play reflects the "values of elite society, largely conditioned by upper caste mores."[89]

Now Shakuntala appears shy and "overawed by the king." The conversation between Dushyanta (Dusyanta, Thapar notes, as he is named in the play) and Shakuntala does not have the force of the epic. Her companions Priyamvada and Anusuya take the initiative: Priyamvada explains Shakuntala's birth and identity to the king. Shakuntala is shy and retiring, "the romanticized persona of a woman of upper caste culture." In this version, Shakuntala presents no conditions, and the initiative comes from Dushyanta.[90] Thus, in the epic version the issue of the treatment of Shakuntala is handled via the celestial voice; in the play, the introduction of several other issues "detract from commenting on the injustice of Dusyanta's treatment of Sakuntala." Shakuntala, helpless, calls for Mother Earth, and "Menaka (an *apsara*) whisks her away in a flash of lightning." When the ring is brought to the king, he regrets her departure and the loss of a son. In the end, Dushyanta travels via Indra's airborne chariot and comes to the *ashrama* of Rishi Maricha, where he recognizes not Shakuntala, but his son first. "Sakuntala does not hesitate to welcome him, continually referring to him as her noble husband, and addressing him as *aryaputra*."[91]

Laxman Singh drew on Kalidasa's version, which became most widely propagated (as Thapar has proposed) and available in many renditions. McGregor suggests that Laxman Singh worked from a Bengali recension of the text, an edition from 1859 and its Bengali verse translation in 1860; and that he appears to have made a partial collation of his original version with Monier Williams' edition of the Devanagri recension.[92] Shakuntala in Laxman Singh's version is decidedly shy. The plot of the story is exactly the same as that of the play: with the curse and the signet ring playing a major role, as well as other

[89] Ibid., pp. 44, 47, 49. For further contextual details, see Thapar's ch. 3, "The *Abhijnana-Sakuntalam of Kalidasa*."
[90] Ibid., pp. 48, 49, 52, 53.
[91] Ibid., pp. 60, 61, 62–63.
[92] McGregor, *Hindi Literature*, p. 73, and fn. 20.

signs of drama that Thapar discusses.[93] For example, when Dushyanta enters the hermitage, his right arm flickers, which he himself sees as a good omen.[94]

Most noticeably, Shakuntala remains submissive all through and rarely speaks. Anusuya and Priyamvada do most of the talking: starting with when Dushyanta enters the hermitage, to the ever encouraging playfulness and teasing among them, the *gandharva* marriage of Shakuntala and Dushyanta and so on.[95] Anusuya says to Dushyanta early on in the story that kings are loved by many queens. That he should treat their friend Shakuntala in a way that there is no heartache. Dushyanta replies: "There may be many queens in the residential quarters (*Ranibaas*), however, there are only two things in this world that I shall cherish most: the earth and your friend."[96] Even when Shakuntala is sent to meet Dushyanta, despite Dushyanta's forgetfulness (owing to the curse), and his condemnation and insult of her, she does not utter a word until much later on in the scene.[97] The story ends with Shakuntala's respectful reception of Dushyanta.

The 1803 tale of Rani Ketki (without the title) and the epic version of *Shakuntala* were unlikely to sit easily with the distinguished women models of the *Vamamanranjan*. As Thapar has so persuasively argued on the construction of "many Shakuntalas," and as I attempted to illustrate in the previous chapter, the "Woman of the Forest," Shakuntala and Ketki of the Insha and epic versions were playful characters. They spoke forthrightly and expressed their feelings openly for Udaybhan and Dushyanta. Both ensured that the difficulties that arose in the making of their relationships were dealt with by the heroines themselves – along with other characters. Ketki managed to get hold of the magical ashes, and Shakuntala confronted the king openly about his morality when he refused to recognize her.

Again, as I have demonstrated in the detailed discussion of Shiv Prasad's sociopolitical context (and Insha's in the last chapter), such a storytelling was centrally premised upon a universe created in folk

[93] Gutka, pp. 62–63.
[94] Ibid., p. 34.
[95] Ibid., pp. 34–43.
[96] Ibid., p. 59.
[97] This scene start on page 73 and in all the drama and dialogue, the first time she speaks is on page 81. The modern reader keeps on getting more and more impatient and wants Shakuntala to scream.

literature: here the hunt and the forest were vital, alongside a singular "woman of *atavika/vanvasi* society"[98] such as Shakuntala of the epic. Even though Ketki is not shown to inhabit such a forest society, which included the *ashrama* and the hermitage, it is in the forest that she meets Udaybhan. And it is to the forest that she returns to find him. It is in the forest that she expresses her freedom and her agency. As Thapar puts it evocatively, "The hermitage is set so deep in the forest that it is almost another world – a magical world of translucent green, lush growth... It is liminal space, the bridge between the two contrasting ecological cultures of the *grama*/settlement and the *aranya*/forest."[99]

Given the sensitive context of the beginning of new practices of instruction in the new space of the school, the question would be what kinds of stories and morals (and meanings) an author might find appropriate for his readers. How much discipline was required? How much freedom could they live with – respectably? Shiv Prasad will clearly have seen Insha's playfulness. The question was how to focus the readers' attention to particular effects and not to others. Let me reiterate that he simply reproduced the story in the *Gutka* without removing any materials of the tale. But he framed it differently for a different audience and mediated how generations of readers would see, notice and read the tale.

Returning to the *Vamamanranjan*, it is obviously not the case that there are no examples of strong women in the text: women models such as Ahilya Bai and Damyanti – and Elizabeth of Hungary and Pulcheria – among others were presented as strong yet praiseworthy women. However, there are two significant points to be noted about the selection – and the continual emergence of such figures in many collections such as the *Vamamanranjan*. The first is that these women were considered exceptional: their stories were cast as extraordinary over and over again.[100] Equally, their life stories were stories of sacrifices and incredible duties performed in the interest of families, kingdoms and other such well-guarded and valued domains (arguably, Laxman

---

[98] Thapar, *Sakuntala*, pp. 36–37, 39.
[99] Ibid., p. 36.
[100] Nur Jahan, Queen Victoria and Begum of Bhopal are other figures that are fairly extensively recalled in comportment tracts such as the *Mirat al-'Arus*, and in manuals of excellence and other such related literature.

Singh's Shakuntala would fit perfectly in the *Vamamanranjan*). They spoke of a moral society – which is also a point from which moral condemnation flows, and the girl reader must know this – in which the palace, the kingdom or the domestic world was the all-consuming center and the forest was clearly marginal.

In this milieu, the inclusion of the story of Ketki in the *Gutka* becomes possible primarily because of the emphasis on the Hindi language now provided in the title. In its new physical placement, the space of the forest recedes into the background, becoming no more than a setting: not as in Insha's tale, a vital space for a girl becoming woman with various desires, which are in turn elaborated, encouraged and held in check by different characters – Insha himself, the parents, the ascetic and the close woman friend. Shiv Prasad circumscribed the freedom and agency of Ketki by giving her tale a title and recasting it as a story about pedagogy and the Hindi language. The *Gutka* was meant for the junior officers of the Raj, and there was no danger of corrupting them through the inclusion of the tale of Ketki. And even if it was circulated as a textbook, as Dalmia suggests, the content of the tale had already been confined and presented as a story in Hindi excellence.

In the preceding pages, I have taken up the implications of the newly emerging idea of the school as a space for the education of girls in the context of the debates on the standardization and the homogenization of languages, scripts, religions and communities that emerged in the latter half of the nineteenth century. I have discussed the challenges thought to exist for girls expected to go to school, and the kind of life spaces someone like Shiv Prasad imagined for them. *Vamamanranjan* and *Gutka* both illustrate Shiv Prasad's concerns and bring to light the specific ways of learning and the activities girls and women would be required to take on as part of self-making – in the school and in the home.

If Insha allowed us to think of the palace and the forest as paradigmatic spaces of yearning, activity and wishes of the girl and woman, Shiv Prasad produced a different argument about the potential and needs of the female, to be cultivated in the institutionalized space of the school. In the next chapter, I deal with another domain that is significantly transformed at this time – the household – and with it, the changing conception of the girl-child/woman that became central to reformist debates in the late nineteenth century.

4

The Woman of the Household

Regarding the newly emerging circumstances of the late colonial encounter, scholars have written extensively about the sociocultural milieu of the north Indian literati and service gentry – the new *kachahri* milieu – lived out in urban settings and organized around the courts and the new urban neighborhoods and lifestyles. In this context, I believe, the household becomes a critical space that tells us a great deal about the altering environment and aspirations of the time: indeed, the household becomes the symbolic place for the girl-child/woman in the new reformist regime.

In order to ask the question about the domestic space, the meaning of the household and the relationship of these spaces to their surroundings such as the *mohalla* (neighborhood), I explore a number of significant texts concerned with the upbringing and training of respectable (*sharif*) girls and women. The first is Nazir Ahmad's *Mirat al-`Arus* (*The Bride's Mirror*) (1867–1868), which won a government prize in 1869, became a part of the school syllabus and a model for the ideas of the good woman/bad woman, was translated into many languages and has never been out of print since its publication. Alongside the *Mirat*, I work with Pandit Gauridatt's *Devrani Jethani ki Kahani* (*Tale of Sisters-in-law*) (1870), modeled after the *Mirat*; Khwaja Altaf Husain Hali's *Majalis-un-Nissa* (*The Assemblies of Women*) (1874); and among a corpus of his writings, Nazir Ahmad's *Taubat-al-Nasuh* (*Repentance of Nasuh*) (1873), and the *Banat-an-Na`sh* (*The Daughters of the Bier*) (1874) – texts that animate the women figures and the physical spaces that the writers believe they must inhabit. Figures and spaces in association with each other preserve the morals of these tales.

As suggested earlier, the attention to the girl-child and woman in the texts of the later half of the nineteenth century marks a departure from the focus on the noble males of the earlier distinguished "mirror of princes" genre, which dominated the elite circles and courtly societies of the preceding centuries. The "mirror of princes" literature continued to be an important part of the inheritance of the several writers considered in this chapter. Yet, there are significant new themes and emphases in the narratives on the girl-child and woman that become the centerpiece of many of their tales – the new manuals of comportment and conduct.

A conspicuous tendency in these texts is the overarching presence of the patriarch (the father figure, the male head and guide) in matters concerning respectable households. It is the fathers who emphasize specific forms of training; it is they who underline the principles of comportment; and it is they who tell the daughters what makes a good marriage and how to achieve good relations in their new homes once they marry.

In this rising emphasis on the woman and an adjacent engulfing male presence, the domestic world comes to be institutionalized in a new way. This institutionalization refers to more than the appearance of certain kinds of physical structures (such as schools and bungalows) or educational agendas (such as curricula and textbooks). A sign of this institutionalization is the emergence of a distinct domestic sphere, marked out as "domestic," peopled by women and children but dominated in a new, more insistent way by men. It is a domestic sphere in which men loom large, not always physically, but as a guiding presence – as teachers and philosophers of their wives, daughters and other women – showing them the "art" of marriage, what it takes to maintain a good household and good relationships with kinsfolk and elders and what constitutes the appropriate training and upbringing of children. Men as managers and mentors produce a reorientation in the fashioning of women subjects, especially when we compare this situation with many moments in the precolonial past.

My book on the early Mughal domestic world indicated that, although the public and private domains were closely imbricated, most noticeably in the alignment of the domestic and courtly in the making of the monarchy, the courtly and domestic remained homosocial spaces in which men and women retained their separate areas of influence and supremacy. Women were "in charge" of many things: they made marriages, prescribed the rituals and conduct in birth and training, spoke of the correct way in matters of visitations to the elderly, in arrangements of feasts and so on.[1] In the later nineteenth century, as I shall try to show, women and children lived in domestic worlds, but now much more clearly and continuously than before men tell them how they are to conduct themselves. Immediately, this detail alone complicates the simple progress narrative of women's increasing liberation over time.

In this women-centered albeit male-governed domestic world portrayed in several late-nineteenth-century texts, the household becomes the select physical realm where the girl-child, girls, women and older women belong. The *mohalla* (the neighborhood) remains a central aspect of the discussion of women's community, but its precise boundaries, how far one might go into the *mohalla*, who the girls and women of respectable families might mix with, who comes in, who goes out, all become debatable issues.[2] In the *Mirat*, for example, Asghari agrees to teach the spoilt Husnara (from a neighboring family), but makes clear that she will do so only in her own house. In the *Banat*, she sets up a *maktab* (school) for the girls of the *mohalla* in her own home. Again, in the *Mirat*, Akbari is condemned because she mixes with lower-class women of the *mohalla*; additionally, she wishes to set up a separate home. In a sense, the *mohalla* (and the school) now moves into the household, and this affects the texture of the respectable household, and with it, its women figures. What we notice in these texts is an increasing talk of household jobs, disciplined lifestyles, focus on filial piety, hygiene, management of servants and finances and practically no talk of play. Even where the discussion of pleasure arises, as it does in the *Banat*, the toys serve a purpose: inculcation of good virtues in the girl-child.

---

[1] Ruby Lal, *Domesticity and Power in the Early Mughal World* (Cambridge and New York, 2005).

[2] In a restricting domestic scenario, with clear boundaries regarding the outside world and interaction with the outsiders, it is likely that women's direct relationship with the *mohalla* (via rooftops, for example) increased. Ironically, the discussions of the access to such spaces – older and newer – are highly reduced in the texts of this time.

In the reformist tracts of the 1870s from the NWP under discussion, we note fathers emphasizing education, training and the accomplishments of their intelligent and literate daughters, seen as critical to their success in their lives and homes after marriage. What also underlies these texts is that in the production of reformed (or aspirationally reformist) social conditions, in which the literate woman is seemingly at the helm of domestic affairs, her agency is reduced to very little. This is in spite of the fact that the question of women's education, and with it the girl-child and her upbringing, now gets pointed attention.

In this chapter, I argue that there are striking ways in which the parallel emphasis on the woman and on the constant male presence (men are physically more regularly present as philosophers and advisors) affects the respectable household and what are considered the important physical spaces, as well as the duties and the expected demeanor of girls and women. My discussion is divided into several parts. In section II, I detail the context of the production of the five texts central to the writing of this chapter. In laying out the scholarly debates on the production of the relevant texts, I suggest that the *kachahri* milieu that several scholars have painstakingly written about in fact gets articulated in the domestic world of the *ashraf*: which is to say that the "class anxiety" of respectable Muslim men comes to be elaborated by way of the discussion on women, who now become central in their arguments about what I have called the resuscitation of respectability.[3]

What is arresting in the argument of the educators and reformers about women and respectability is the setting out of a lineage of conduct. Nazir Ahmad says in the preface to the *Mirat* that it was not a practice for girls and women to read and write, but the women of respectable families learned to recite the Quran and Urdu books connected with religious matters and instruction. According to the custom of his family (*khandan ke dastur*), Nazir Ahmad's daughters also learned the Quran and other relevant books from the older women. He argues that seeing the men read and write (*mardon ki dekha-dekhi*), however, the girls became desirous of knowledge (*`ilm*). He adds that he searched extensively for books filled with ethical

[3] A discussion of scholarly writings follows in the next section.

instructions and with issues that women faced in their everyday lives but because of their superstitions and ignorance were not able to think about improvement (*islah*). He did not find one and hence wrote the *Mirat*.[4]

Nazir Ahmad begins a trajectory of ethical digests for the improvement and manners of the girl-child and woman. As I noted at the beginning of this chapter, a large number of books were produced in the wake of the success of the *Mirat* – often replicating the same story (*Devrani-Jethani* that I investigate closely in this chapter, for instance, reproduces the storyline of the *Mirat* for a Hindu context). I reflect on the question of lineage of conduct in a variety of ways: in the (now) contested place of women in handing the protocols of womanhood; in the installing of patriarchs as advice givers, and, in section III, by discussing the making of a literary lineage in order to link the point about a textual genealogy of the manuals of reform. I take one example, Nasir al-Din Tusi's 1235 ethical digest, *Akhlaq-i Nasiri*, to make my point. Scholars have noted that texts such as Tusi's were a central part of the ethical worlds of Muslims. I read Tusi's book in relation to Nazir Ahmad's writings to consider what Tusi might have looked like for the *ashraf* of mid-nineteenth-century northern India; indeed, how do Nazir Ahmad's works in the nineteenth century animate the concerns and ethics of the literary landscape that he valued – in which works such as those of Tusi's were vital.

In sections IV and V, I discuss the roles that authors outline for the girl-child and women readers of their books: and the events, propositions and models through which they outline the practices of respectability for the imbricated figure of the girl-child/woman. In particular, I ask how the responsibilities and articulations of a new respectability were gendered through the terms for the articulation of girl-child/woman in the contemporary talk of reform: what *sharif* men and women, boys and girls were expected to do and what they were thought capable of doing. What was particular and distinctive about the ways in which the *sharif* girl-child was supposed to be trained, what models would be appropriate, as opposed to those for the *sharif* boy, to make them respectable Muslim women and men?

[4] *Mirat* Urdu edn., pp. 29–30.

RESUSCITATION OF RESPECTABILITY

A few words are necessary here about the context of the production of these texts. Nazir Ahmad and Hali's context was rather different from that of the Mughal courtly setting of an earlier generation, and their economic background far more modest than anything suggestive of a Mughal notable. Alongside this economic feature, we might add that their milieu was inflected by wide-ranging changes through which many Muslim publicists were becoming conscious of the end of "their glorious past": "the rise of a new and largely Hindu commercial class; the requirement of examination success to enter public service; the introduction of elections to municipal and district boards; the manifestation of increasing Hindu assertiveness across many social and political arenas" and so on.[5] Additionally, the importance of direct colonial intervention at this time in soliciting books on the subject of women needs to be borne in mind.[6]

This late colonial moment in northern India, with a variety of economic, political and social moves, has been described as one that witnesses a shift from a court to a *kachahri* culture. In this context, several scholars have written about the "class anxiety" on the part of the *ashraf* (respectable Muslims) to preserve respectability for themselves when there was very little access to well-established benchmarks of courtly/*sharif* behavior.[7]

---

[5] Francis Robinson, "The Memory of Power, Muslim 'Political Importance and the Muslim League,'" p. 9. (unpublished paper). For a more extended discussion of the changed nineteenth-century context, see Iftikhar Ahmad Siddiqi, *Maulavi Nazir Ahmad Dihlavi: Ahval-va-Asar* (Lahore, 1971), and the writings of C. A. Bayly, Mushirul Hasan and Francis Robinson. I am grateful to Francis Robinson for letting me see an advance copy of this paper, and to him and David Lelyveld on the issue discussed in this paragraph.

[6] In August 1868, the government of the NWP announced award prizes for Hindi and Urdu books best suited for educational use. "Books suitable for women of India will be especially acceptable, and well rewarded." The *Mirat al-`Arus* was awarded the prize in 1870. The *Taubat-al-Nasuh* won the prize in 1874. Naim, "Prize-Winning Adab," pp. 292–293, 299–301.

[7] This is one reason why Nazir Ahmad's claims to *sharif* status become grounded rather more on matters of conduct and learning than on ideas of descent. Faisal Devji's "Gender and the Politics of Space: The Movement for Women's Reform in Muslim India" *South Asia*, Vol. 14 (1991), is suggestive about the kinds of ideological changes in play in what he would argue is the creation of a new Indian middle class.

Nazir Ahmad (1830–1912), a Muslim publicist and a prolific writer who published numerous books in diverse genres, came from a family of distinguished *maulavis* and *muftis*. His father, a teacher in a small town near Bijnor (in present-day Uttar Pradesh), taught him Persian and Arabic. In 1846, Nazir Ahmad enrolled at the Delhi College and studied there until 1853. He began his career as a *maulavi* in Arabic, but soon (in 1856) became a deputy inspector of schools in the Department of Public Instruction. Later, after he had produced a superb translation of the Indian Penal Code in Urdu, he was nominated to the Revenue Service. He was posted as deputy collector in what was then called the North Western Provinces, from whence came the name "Diptee (Deputy) Nazir Ahmad" by which he is popularly known.

As a proponent of women's education, Nazir Ahmad was well aware of colonial projects on this issue and the British critique of the Indian family. At the same time, he was deeply immersed in Islamic literary culture. He was a sophisticated political translator for the colonial regime on one hand and a critic of empire on the other.

Scholars have described Nazir Ahmad as a "radical and far-reaching" proponent of women's education and social reform.[8] Mushirul Hasan notes that Nazir Ahmad's work sets apart his era as an "Age of Reform."[9] C. M. Naim remarks that the major concerns of Nazir Ahmad's writings are "the uplift of *sharif* women and the proper upbringing of *sharif* children."[10] Gail Minault writes about the "generation of reform," men "who were pivotal in responding to the changed conditions of British rule, in defining Muslim society and

---

[8] The phrase in quotation marks is from Naim, "Prize-Winning *Adab*," p. 306.

[9] Hasan, *A Moral Reckoning*, p. 157.

[10] Naim, "Prize-Winning *Adab*," p. 304. Or consider David Lelyveld's crucial point about education: "the well-rehearsed early history of English-style education in northern India is interesting as a piece of British intellectual history, but is largely peripheral to a social and cultural analysis of the region in the period before 1857. Only in the latter part of the century did these debates become relevant from an indigenous point of view." David Lelyveld, *Aligarh's First Generation: Muslim Solidarity in British India* (Princeton, 1978), pp. 68–69. If Nazir Ahmad was writing "A tale of life in Delhi a hundred years ago" as the subtitle to the translation has it, then the late-nineteenth-century models of education and schooling scholars invoke are rather anachronistic; centrally because these don't capture the ethos of "training and nurturing" but point to a rather institutionalized sense of education.

culture in the context of modern India, and in delineating norms and roles for women in that culture."[11] Nazir Ahmad, she argues, "realized that the older, home-based system was no longer vital, and he sought a way to revitalize it, or to evolve schools that maintained a base in sharif homes as an acceptable alternative. His syllabus combined a basic vernacular education, similar to that given to boys, and training in the domestic arts necessary for girls' future lives."[12]

Gauridatt (1836–1903), the second author examined in this chapter, was a teacher in the Mission School of Meerut, an ardent follower of Hindu reformer Swami Dayanand Saraswati and immersed in the development of Hindi language and literature (as part of the resuscitation of "Hindu" culture). He was described as the "Socrates of Hindi." Apart from establishing the Devanagri Pathshala in the Baidbara *mohalla* of Meerut, teaching Hindi to the children of various neighborhoods in Meerut, he also established several other schools to teach Hindi and composed numerous Hindi books for the education of children.[13] His major work, *Devrani-Jethani*, addresses the issues discussed, a little while before, in Nazir Ahmad's *Mirat*. Even if Gauridatt had not seen the *Mirat*, which is highly unlikely, he would have known that Kempson was its translator and that it had won a prize before *Devrani-Jethani*.[14] Mr. Kempson, the director of education of the NWP, had awarded Nazir Ahmad's *Mirat* a government prize: he also happened to be its translator. Gauridatt claims that Kempson liked the *Devrani-Jethani* greatly.

The broader historical context and the authorial concerns in Gauridatt's *Devrani-Jethani* are not dissimilar from that of the *Mirat*. Elite Hindu groups in Bengal and the North Western Provinces had turned to Western education much earlier than the corresponding

---

[11] Gail Minault, *Secluded Scholars*, p. 11.

[12] Ibid, p. 35.

[13] Kshem Chandra Suman, *Divamgat Hindi-Sevi (Pratham Khand): Sandharb-Granth* (New Delhi, 1981, 1st edn), pp. 189–190.

[14] For a discussion of the colonial invitation to write edifying texts that could help produce a Hindu and Muslim reading public in the colonial view, see, Naim, "Prize-Winning *Adab*," pp. 292–293, 299–301. A. S. Kalsi says that *Devrani-Jethani* emerged as a result of notification 791A of August 20, 1868 by R. Simpson, secretary to the government of the NWP, under which prizes up to one thousand rupees were offered for useful compositions in Urdu and Hindi. A. S. Kalsi, "Pariksaguru (1882): The First Hindi Novel and the Hindu Elite," *Modern Asian Studies*, Vol. 26 (1992): p. 765.

groups of Muslims. An urbanist impulse was seen among the Hindu elites, especially as it was manifested in their entry into the legal and bureaucratic professions.[15] It is not entirely obvious why Gauridatt chooses a *baniya* family for *Devrani-Jethani*, but some tentative suggestions may be made.

The gains that some sections of the Hindu landed and service classes (especially from Brahman and Kayastha, priestly and literary caste backgrounds) made were not shared by other sections of Hindu middle and elite groups. It may well be that Gauridatt felt the need to write about a different Hindu group, traditional but urban, that needed to turn to Western education. He thus chooses an urban setting, Meerut, a cantonment (associated with the modern colonial army), but locates his story in a traditional *baniya* (trading caste) family – where debates about the modern now take place. Thus there is a double move in *Devrani-Jethani*. One is found in the location of the text: not rural, but urban, specifically that of the colonial cantonment setting of Meerut, thus rather different from Nazir Ahmad's old Delhi of the *Mirat*, a traditional setting of the Muslim nobility.

Our third author, Khwaja Altaf Husain of Panipat, was popularly known as Hali (1837–1914), the pen name he adopted. Like Nazir Ahmad, he was what Gail Minault calls "a member of the transitional generation, men educated in the old way but aware of new forces at work in their society, ready to accept certain innovations that would improve their secular existence, like an English education for their sons, without altering their overall cultural allegiance." Hali advocated reform: his women characters reflect "on the backward condition of the Muslim community, the stagnation of vernacular learning, and the need for girls to be educated in order better to fulfill household and family duties." Further, "the women here are certain of their roles, and they do not question them, but rather seek to do better what they are destined for: marriage, motherhood, household management, relations with relatives, guests, and servants." Importantly, Minault notes: "this seems to the modern reader an extremely limited view of life and

[15] A point noted in the early debates between Francis Robinson and Paul Brass. For a further discussion, see Pandey, *The Construction of Communalism in Colonial North India*. For contextual detail in relation to history, gender and question of community, see Kumkum Sangari, *Politics of the Possible: Essays on Gender, History, Narrative, Colonial English* (New Delhi, 1999), especially pp. 184–187 and 192–193.

its possibilities, but to suggest that a girl in purdah in 1874 should get a full-fledged vernacular education, including learning to write, was very advanced."[16]

Nazir Ahmad's *Mirat, Banat* and *Taubat* and Hali's *Majalis* won prizes, enjoyed wide circulation and distribution and went on to become school textbooks.[17] In August 1868, the government of the NWP announced that it would award prizes for books best suited for educational use ("instruction, entertainment or mental discipline"). These had to be written in "one or other of the current dialects, Oordoo or Hindee." "Books suitable for women of India will be especially acceptable, and well rewarded." Nazir Ahmad wrote the *Mirat* as a reader for his daughter, which also became very popular among his female relatives. In 1869, it was awarded a prize of one thousand rupees, and the NWP government "purchased two thousand copies of the book for its institutions and recommended its inclusion in the school syllabi." In 1872, the *Banat* was awarded five hundred rupees. In 1873, the *Taubat* won the first prize. Matthew Kempson, the director of public instruction, liked the *Taubat* "so much that he translated it into English and published it in London in 1884."[18] Colonel Holroyd, the director of public instruction in the Punjab, who knew Hali's work, recommended the *Majalis* to the viceroy of India, Lord Northbrook. Hali was awarded four hundred rupees for his work (a very substantial sum at the time) and the *Majalis* was adopted as a school textbook for girls in the Punjab and the United Provinces and enjoyed that status for decades.[19] These texts have not been out of print since their publication, and, as Azra shows in the prelude to this book, they are still continually read.

All of these texts promoted the idea of learning and education for women as critical requirements of respectable life. The question

---

[16] Minault, *Voices of Silence*, pp. 4, 14–15. And further, Hali "favored the custom of purdah and the segregated social roles of men and women, but his advocacy of women's education and his sense of women's autonomy, dignity and importance within the family were quite revolutionary for 1874 when *Majalis-un-Nissa* first appeared." Ibid. Minault, *Voices of Silence*, p. 3.

[17] We are told that *Devrani-Jethani* wins a prize of 100 rupees at its publication, but it is not clear that it becomes a part of the Hindi curriculum in schools. The first copy of Gauridatt's book is preserved in the National Library, Calcutta. Kshem Chandra Suman, *Divamgat Hindi-Sevi*, pp. 190–191.

[18] Naim, "Prize-Winning *Adab*," pp. 292–293, 299–301.

[19] Minault, *Voices of Silence*, p. 12.

we need to ask concerns the nature of training prescribed for the nineteenth-century girl-child and woman, who read these books at home and later on in schools. What kinds of women figures emerge in these texts? What physical spaces are drawn as central to the construction of the girl-child and woman? What is the room for play, or contest, or inventiveness in the prescribed scenario?

Mushirul Hasan reminds us that "the 1870s [in India] had *not* witnessed the emergence of the so-called 'New Woman,' educated and individualistic or engaged in gainful employment, [although] changes of all kinds were beginning to transform millions of women's lives the world over."[20] The idea of the "new woman" suggests a rupture, a departure from the old. Yet, as several scholars have noticed, the new hardly supplants the old in any obvious or deeply substantive way in nineteenth-century India. Barbara Metcalf makes the point, for example, that "some women, like the heroine of ... *Mir`at al-`arus* ... did live in a home where the men of the family moved decisively outside the domestic domain for their livelihood. But that 'modern' characteristic of family life was still uncommon, and much else in the complexity of family life, both social and economic remained."[21]

The new reformist ideas in late-nineteenth-century northern India were articulated not to conform to some alien ("modern") standard, but to refashion and to finesse what were thought of as long-established ways of life for continued sustenance and vibrancy in a new economic and political context. In the idea of *sharafat*, as David Lelyveld has noted, a "cultural style" associated with the heritage of the Mughal court was as important – perhaps in the circle of Nazir Ahmad and Hali more important – as questions of descent. Dress, manners, aesthetics, "elaborate politeness formulas, familiarity with Persian and Urdu literary conventions, the art of elegant conversation, all these marked a person as *sharif*."[22] In the writings of Nazir Ahmad, Gauridatt and Hali that I look at, *sharafat* or respectability is a dominant motif: inherited

[20] Mushirul Hasan, *A Moral Reckoning*, p. 157.
[21] Barbara Metcalf, "Islamic Reform and Islamic Women," in Metcalf, *Moral Conduct and Authority*, p. 195.
[22] See David Lelyveld's piece on the word *ashraf* at the following website of keywords: http://www.soas.ac.uk/csasfiles/keywords/Lelyveld-ashraf.pdf. For historically changing connotations of the term *sharif*, see Lelyveld, *Aligarh's First Generation*, especially pp. 27–30.

notions of respectability (*sharafat*) are constituted and remembered in many ways.

I take the debate around *sharafat* and sociocultural practices to be a debate about the grounds for this reconstitution or what I call resuscitation of respectability. With all the earnest rethinking and rearticulation of the times, the self-conscious object of the reformers was to reproduce the familial and the values of a moral universe supposedly handed down through the ages. This affects profoundly the texts they wrote, but the point I wish to underscore is that what is presented as "old" and what appears as "new" is not unambiguous or self-evident. There is a double move, a playfulness if you will, in the reformist writings in which the old as well as the new are questioned. To put it differently, although the old is recuperated, yet it is not (cannot be), presented as old in the discourses on requirements of ethical life and the expectations for men and women. In the face of the fundamental political and ideological challenges brought by colonial rule in India, various kinds of adjustment and reconstruction became necessary. "Tradition" and "inheritance" – that which is in need of reform – itself came to be constituted anew.[23]

Several scholars have noted the influence of books from the West in the reimagining of the "old/new" world of the respectable Muslims in Nazir Ahmad's "reformative fiction."[24] Nazir Ahmad himself noted that he used Thomas Day's *History of Sandford and Merton* as a model for the *Banat*. Raja Shiv Prasad had translated Day's work into Urdu and Hindi around 1855. Muhammad Sadiq was the first to identify Daniel Defoe's *The Family Instructor* as the source for the *Taubat*. Setting out the context of Nazir Ahmad's writings, and by reading together some aspects of the *Taubat* and *The Family Instructor*, however, Naim makes some very important points about the context and the production of reformist texts: that colonial rule for Nazir Ahmad, and others like Sir Sayyid Ahmad Khan or Hali, was "by no means of unqualified goodness... They were not given to nostalgia the way the generation that followed them was." And critically, as far as Nazir Ahmad's writings were concerned, he was no "mere imitator."[25]

---

[23] As an initial articulation of this proposition, see Lal, "Gender and *Sharafat*."
[24] Both phrases are Naim's. Naim, afterword, *The Repentance of Nussooh*, pp. 128, 138.
[25] Ibid., pp. 128–129, 132.

Further, Naim says that "the distinction between the Inner [*batin*] and the Outer [*zahir*] has been for centuries the most powerful and pervasive way to prioritize and valuate both ideas and actions in all Islamicate societies at every level. It, therefore, becomes significant that Nazir Ahmad explicitly underscored the rejection of the Outer." Naim points out that the important task for Nazir Ahmad and other reformers was to "press individual community members to better themselves, and simultaneously convince them to do good to the community."[26]

What is evident even in this brief selection of comments that I have presented from Naim is the lack of fixity, undecidability even, and the variety of materials that an author draws upon in making proposals for the girl-child and woman of his times. Clearly, there is no one text that is likely to have inspired, shaped and structured all that Nazir Ahmad had to say about girls, women, community, household/ethical life. Naim's statement about inner and outer spaces and the placement of women subjects in appropriate physical domains is directly relevant to the concerns of this book. In the pages that follow, I link the issue of physical spaces with my argument about a genealogical move in the new didactic literature for a respectable girl-child and woman in mid-to-late nineteenth-century northern India, which lives on vibrantly in the twentieth century.

Many texts go into the construction of such a genealogy of books for women: the infamous chapter V from Sadi's *Gulistan*, the reader will recall from a discussion in Chapter 1, parts of which were erased by the lead character in the *Taubat* before his wife read it. Then there are books that were applauded by the very protagonists in the nineteenth-century texts under investigation: for example, the *Muntakhab-ul-Hikayat*, discussed and highly valued both in the *Mirat* and the *Banat*. The *Muntakhab*, a selection of seventy-seven stories, was written by Nazir Ahmad for his daughter in 1863.[27] And the women models invoked repeatedly in the *Mirat*, *Devrani-Jethani* and the *Majalis* that I explore in the last two sections. Additionally, there is the issue of the importance of older women in the protocols of womanhood, historically highly valued, but by the time of the writing of the books under investigation in this chapter, a contested contribution.

---

[26] Ibid., pp. 128, 136.
[27] Hasan, *A Moral Reckoning*, p. 145.

Let me turn at this point to an influential thirteenth-century ethical digest, Nasir al-Din Tusi's *Akhlaq-i Nasiri*, first published in 1235 in Alamut. We know that the cultural inheritance of Nazir Ahmad, Hali and their contemporaries included works concerned with *adab* and *akhlaq* (books that focused on ethical and moral behavior). Again, as pointed out in Chapter 1, writings such as the *Akhlaq-i Nasiri*, in which the father is the focus of the worldly domains, inner and outer, were very much part of the north Indian Islamicate milieu, as was Sadi's *Gulistan* (1258), concerned with ethical and moral issues; and the *Qabus-Nama* of Kai Ka`us ibn Iskander ibn Qabus ibn Washmgir (1082) that related to rules and practices with regard to specific occupations; and other courtesy books.[28]

From the section on the household in Tusi's book, I take the part on the upbringing of the girl-child to explore how Tusi's prescription on the training of children might travel across time and changing historical context (Note that Tusi wrote the *Akhlaq* in 1235 for an Ismaili prince. The sections on the household (*tadbir-i manzil*) and politics (*siyasat-i mudun*) were added subsequently.[29]). The question is: How does Tusi's text of the thirteenth century translate in sixteenth-century Mughal India when, as Alam points out, the emperor Akbar wanted the digest read out to him regularly?[30] And more centrally for my purposes, how does it get translated for the new salaried, respectable classes of the nineteenth century to which Nazir Ahmad and Hali belonged? What does Tusi read like in the nineteenth century? And what does this tell us about the "birth" of the girl-child of an eternal *sharif* (respectable) tradition at the hands of reformers and patriarchs?

---

[28] Naim, Afterword, *The Repentance of Nussooh*, p. 131.

[29] Consider these two *Akhlaq* recensions produced in the eighteenth century: *Akhlaq-i Muhammadi*, dedicated to Muhammad Shah, and the other written in 1857–1858 by Munshi Durga Prasad of Aligarh, commonly referred to as the *Akhlaq* from Sandila, dedicated to Queen Victoria. These were possibly the last time when the *Akhlaq* was reproduced. The more striking point is that the section on household is removed from these versions. I am grateful to Muzaffar Alam for this information and for a detailed discussion on *Akhlaq* materials in Chicago, May 2009.

[30] *Akhlaq-Nasiri*, Muzaffar Alam writes, was "certainly widely read in Mughal India... It is likely that the Mughals appropriated Nasirean ethics as a legacy of Babur... Tusi's book was not simply among the five most important books that Abu'l Fazl wanted Emperor Akbar to have read out to him regularly, it was among the most favoured readings of the Mughal political elites." (Alam, *Political Islam*, pp. 50, 51, 61).

In a section entitled "Concerning the Chastisement and Regulation of Wives (*ahl*)," Tusi propagates a domestic philosophy (*hikmat-i manzil*) that was supposed to work on the basis of specific links and relations among members of the household (*ta'lifi-yi makhsus*). While such pedagogy of households may appear highly particularized, there are universal rules here. The philosophy may be put into use by both kings and subjects, but the base of the household must remain as follows: father, mother, child, servant and sustenance. Here the child (as well as the servant) is a critical member, along with the father and mother. The man, not his wife, is the manager of the household (*mudabbir-i manzil*) and in charge of the training and education of children, specifically of sons. The male is addressed as the head of the household and the owner of property, wives, children, servants and slaves. The method of his governing the inhabitants of the household is based upon encouragement and chastisement.[31]

The motive for taking a wife, according to Tusi, is to preserve property and to have children, but male superiority must be preserved over both. A wife is an important participant in housekeeping (*qasim-i u dar kad-khuda'i*), the man's deputy (*na'ib*). Hence the "best of wives" is one adorned with intelligence, piety, continence (*'iffat*, emphasized repeatedly), shrewdness, modesty, tenderness, a loving disposition, in control of her tongue and shows "obedience to her husband, self-devotion in his service and a preference for his pleasure, gravity, and the respect of her own family." Further, she must not be barren. A virgin (*bikr*) was preferable, because she would more likely accept discipline (*bi-qabul-i adab*).[32]

There is an emphasis on disciplining the woman all along: otherwise the danger was that a "bad wife" could become a despot, enemy and thief. A worthy wife, according to Tusi, is one who takes on the role of mother, friend and mistress: "As for the worthy wife's attempt to assimilate to a mother, this means that she desires the husband's proximity and presence ... a friend means that the wife should be content with whatever the husband gives her or does not give her ... playing the part of a mistress involves humbling herself in the

---

[31] G. M. Wickens (tr.), *The Nasirean Ethics by Nasir ad-Din Tusi* (London, 1964), pp. 154–155.
[32] Wickens, *Nasirean Ethics*, pp. 161–162.

manner of a maidservant, giving the pledge of service, and enduring the husband's sharp temper."[33] The use of the word *kanizak* (mistress) is important: a servant girl "whose only function is to please her lord and master in every respect."[34] "The husband's procedure [*sic*] in ruling his wife should be along three lines," Tusi says: "to inspire awe (*haibat*), to show favour (*karamat*), and to occupy her mind (*shugl-i khatir*)."[35]

This section on wives is immediately followed by one entitled "Concerning the Chastisement and Regulation of Children." The two sections are seemingly in conversation with one another, not only because the man is the authoritative figure over both women and children. I shall return to the convergence between the two sections. Let me first turn to Tusi's instructions on the training of children. "When once the suckling is complete, one must concern oneself with the discipline and training of his character (*akhlaq*) before destructive dispositions (*akhlaq*) gain a hold," Tusi sets out writing. Expression of modesty is an indication of good breeding (*najabat*) in Tusi's view. Noble virtues such as intelligence, discrimination and piety are recommended: practices and duties of the faith (*sunan u waza'if-i din*) are deemed important. Greed, especially for food, drinks and other pleasures, including "brightly coloured and embroidered clothes [that] are fitting for women" should be avoided. Discourses on noble manners should be imparted to the child, but they should be kept away from "frivolous poetry, with its talk of odes and love and wine-bibbing ... for poetry can only be the corruption of youth."[36]

"Let gold and silver be presented to him in a contemptible light," says Tusi. "At times he may be given permission to play, but let his games be gentle (*jamil*)... He should be accustomed to obey his father, his mother and his tutor, and regard them with the eye of veneration... When he passes from the stage of childhood and reaches understanding of the purposes (*aghrad*) of men ... let it be brought home to him all that the true sense of 'bodily pleasures' is release from suffering and rest from fatigue."[37]

---

[33] Ibid., p. 165.
[34] Ibid., p. 302, note 1657.
[35] Ibid., p. 162.
[36] Ibid., pp. 167–168.
[37] Ibid., pp. 170–171.

It is the boys that are the beneficiaries of these instructions on the cultivation of noble values and selves. What about girls? Here is the one paragraph on them:

> In the case of daughters, one must employ in the selfsame manner, whatever is appropriate and fitting to them. They should be brought up to keep close to the house and *live in seclusion* (*hijab*), cultivating gravity, continence (`iffat*), modesty and other qualities *we have enumerated in the chapter on Wives. They should be prevented from learning to read or write*, but allowed to acquire such accomplishments as are commendable in women (my emphasis).[38]

For Tusi, the girl-child exists in the figure of the woman: the qualities to be aspired to, as well as the specific ways that will be denigrated, were all in place. The rights of the father and the centrality of the male

[38] Ibid., p. 173. In the *Qabus-Nama* of Kai Ka`us ibn Iskander (composed in 1082), a similar kind of juxtaposition of women and children may be seen. In the section entitled "Marrying a Wife," the author prescribes to his son, for who the book is written, that when seeking a wife, "he must refuse to be enslaved by beauty of face... A wife ... should be chaste and of sound faith, capable in household management, modest and God-fearing, brief-tongued, sparing and economical of materials." "Do not submit yourself entirely to her control... And you must marry a virgin... Marry a woman of honourable family... Your wife must be of sound health, of mature age and intelligent... Also, it is as well to know that women frequently destroy men of jealousy, but will sacrifice their persons only for very few [sic]." Further, "Once you have married a wife ... do not spend every night in her society. Let it be only from time to time, thus leading her to think that such is the universal custom. But if you customarily visit her every night, she will acquire a propensity for it... You must realize that a woman cannot steadfastly resist a man." [Reuben Levy (tr.), *A Mirror of Princes: The Qabus Nama by Kai Ka`us Ibn Iskandar* (New York, 1951), pp. 117–119]. This section is juxtaposed by the following entitled "On Rearing Children," in which the author first lays out the manner in which a son should be brought up. Starting with a good name that must be endowed on him, as the author puts it. He should be entrusted in the care of "intelligent and affectionate nurses." Then he should learn the Quran "by heart." When grows up, he should be instructed in the arts of wielding arms and of horsemanship; swimming; riding; javelin throwing; archery; wielding of spear. When the son reaches the age of puberty "then set about the task of seeking a wife for him." And now comes the prescription on daughters: "If you have a daughter, entrust her to kindly nurses and give her good nature. When she grows up, entrust her to a preceptor ... [to] learn the sacred law and the essential religious duties. But do not teach her to read and write; *that is a great calamity.* Once she is grown up, do your utmost to give her in marriage; it were best for the girl not to come into existence, but, being born, she had better be married or be buried." Further, "daughters are captives of their parents ... helpless and incapable of finding employment. Make provision for her ... fasten her about someone's neck so as to escape from anxiety for her." (Emphasis mine) *The Qabus-Nama*, pp. 119–125.

were declared. The duty of the mother, the role of the woman as a deputy (*naib*), albeit in subservience to the man, was set up as a natural arrangement. The direction here is straightforward: women must live in seclusion; they should be prevented from reading and writing; the girl-child should learn this from the start.

Afsaneh Najmabadi shows how in Iran, in the writings of Mirza Aqa Khan Kirmani (1853/54–1896), a contemporary of Nazir Ahmad and Hali, "the shifts in meaning from pre-modern to modern normative concepts reconfigured woman from 'house' (*manzil*) to 'manager of the house' (*mudabbir-i manzil*)."[39] A significant shift also occurred in the shrinking of a wider community of women, as the educated woman came to be confined rather more than before to the conjugal home – even as the domain of men's homosocial interactions was maintained or even expanded. The same kind of shift occurs in northern India in the nineteenth and twentieth centuries. In *Taubat al-Nasuh*, Fahmidah, now confined to a smaller home, is cast as a helper in the upbringing of children, as is Tahsidar's Saheb's unnamed wife in *Devrani-Jethani*. But there are other dimensions to the "helpmate's" condition (or the man's "deputy" to use Tusi's words) that the late-nineteenth-century reformers underline.

Nasuh and Fahmidah together take on the responsibility of "reforming" their children. However, it is Nasuh who becomes the "reformer"; Fahmidah can be no more than a helper (*madadgar*). While mothers are applauded for their tenderness (*shafaqat*) and deep devotion (*dil-sozi*) and are called upon to be central in the upbringing of girls and boys, it is the patriarchs who compose letters of instruction on married life for their daughters. In the *Mirat*, Durandesh Khan writes to Asghari immediately after her wedding about the rules of conduct expected of her, and adds: "Keep this [letter] with you as a rule of conduct, and if you follow the instructions (*nasihat*) contained in it... It is my wish that you should read this letter at least once a day, even when there is no necessity for it (*bila zarurat*), so that it's purport may always be kept in your view." In a parallel move in the *Devrani-Jethani*, Tahsildar Saheb elaborates similar rules for Anandi.[40] The fathers dominate

---

[39] Afsaneh Najmabadi, "Crafting an Educated Housewife in Iran," in Lila Abu-Lughod (ed), *Remaking Women: Feminism and Modernity in the Middle East* (Princeton, 1998), pp. 91–125.

[40] *Mirat* Urdu edn., pp. 103, 108; *Devrani Jethani*, pp. 17–18.

the stage, advising their daughters throughout their lives about their responsibilities in their married homes.

There is an irony here that I want to underline in order to push further the argument about the place of women in a domestic sphere that was being ordered differently. Fahmidah and Nasuh's arrangements towards an advancement of their children suggest that the involvement of women in the upbringing, training and improvement (*islah*) of children was central and essential. Not a small job, as Nazir Ahmad reminds us: "to refine ... children's morals (*akhlaq*), improve their natures (*mizaj*), amend their habits (`*adat*), and correct their thoughts and beliefs (*khayalat aur mu`taqidat*)... No one can meet the entire obligation of bringing up children unless he himself becomes a model of refined behavior for them."[41] The mothers can teach their children a lot in the course of their simple, daily interactions with them. "To begin with," Nazir Ahmad asks, "where is there anything like a mother's tenderness (*shafaqat*) and deep devotion (*dil-sozi*)?"[42]

At the same time, alongside this hope in a mother's devotion, tenderness, capability and responsibility, she remains the perpetual shadow of the man. Recall Durandesh Khan's admonition to Asghari cited earlier: "It is my wish that you should read this letter ... even when there is no necessity ... (*bila zarurat*), so that it's purport may always be kept in your view." And Asghari sends her own letter to her brother Khairandesh Khan, requesting him to go to Lahore and ask her father-in-law to come home for a fortnight to deal with Mama `Azmat's affairs, the caretaker who was misusing the finances and getting the family in debt. Asghari adds that if the men were present, the whole of this business would be settled admirably. The case of Nasuh, who makes the crucial decisions in regard to the improvement of his family (*islah-i khandan*), is another demonstration of the same hierarchy.

TEXTS OF REVITALIZATION

It is in a conversation between the authorial overture and the rest of the text that the *sharif* girl-child and woman, the domains in which they

---

[41] *Taubat* Urdu edn., pp. 8–9.
[42] *Mirat* Urdu edn., pp. 51–52. The second word, *dil-sozi*, literally means "burning of one's heart," that is, for someone's benefit or betterment, implying deep devotion or sacrifice.

must stay, and the cultivation of children and the responsibility of parents, come to life. This is to be especially noted in the prefaces to Nazir Ahmad's *Mirat, Banat* and *Taubat* and Gauridatt's *Devrani-Jethani*, which speak of the education required to produce "good" (or ideal) girls and women and serve as templates for what is to come.

Nazir Ahmad says that the stage of childhood is the best time in a person's life. At the same time, he emphasizes the importance of *parvarish*, nurturing or cultivation, for girls and boys (using *bachcheh* for both, and also *ladke* and *ladkiyan* in comments relating to girls and boys).

> Boys and girls ought certainly to consider how their life will be spent after they are separated from their parents. In this world the heaviest burdens fall upon the men of a family... But for all this you must not suppose that women have no share at all in the business of the world beyond eating and beautifying themselves. On the contrary, it is women who do the entire work of housekeeping... So if you look into the matter carefully, the world is like a cart which cannot move without two wheels – man on one side, and woman on the other.[43]

In the preface to *Devrani-Jethani*, Gauridatt remarks on a central difference between educated and uneducated women (*padhi aur be-padhi striyan*). He lays out what he sees as the ideal upbringing of children (*balakon ka palan poshan*) by women, detailing how women should spend their time and the kinds of tasks they should engage in.[44] Like Nazir Ahmad, Gauridatt suggests that the nurturing of the child is a crucial stage in laying down the ideal tracks to be followed in life. Closely tied to the upbringing of the child, in the authorial prescriptions, is the training of women, who will nurture the child as a nurturing of culture itself. The accounts that follow are stories of two kinds of married women – cultured and uncultured: *ladkiyan* and *striyan* as Gauridatt refers to the girl-child or girls and women in his book, and *ladkiyan, 'auratain, ma* (mother), *nani* (grandmother), *kunbe ki 'auratain* (women of the family), as Nazir Ahmad describes them.

In this play between girl-child and woman in the preludes and the texts, an imbricated girl-child/woman is proposed. In Nazir Ahmad's *Mirat*, especially, it is the preparation for the future that matters: "after

---

[43] *Mirat* urdu edn., pp. 33–34.
[44] *Devrani-Jethani*, pp. 1–2.

being married, they [girls/women] will have to live an entirely new kind of life, such as you see your mother and her mother living, as well as your aunt and all the women of the family... A new life, full of all kinds of perplexities and trials, is coming nearer."[45] Note the emphasis on life as lived by earlier generations: your mother and *her* mother. The girl-child must always think of the time that will follow her marriage and recognize the responsibilities that would inevitably be different. Thus the girl-child becomes only a preparatory image of the married woman.

The main part of the *Mirat* elaborates a model of education and desirable conduct for girls and women of *sharif* families. It is the story of two sisters named Akbari ("the great one") and Asghari ("the small one"). Akbari never lives up to her name, is never "great," because of her *behunari* (lack of talent) and *badmizaji* (ill-temperedness). Asghari becomes great in her "small," wise acts because she is gifted with *hunar aur saliqa* (talent and proficiency), *adab* (good comportment), *qa'ida* (the right way) and *nekdili* (kindness).[46]

In the *Devrani-Jethani*, Gauridatt illuminates the domestic life of a Hindu Agarwal *baniya* family in Meerut. Daulat Ram, the older son, is married to Gyano; the second son, Chote Lal, to Anandi; hence, *Devrani-Jethani ki Kahani*, the story of the sisters-in law. Here too, the women have oppositional characteristics: Anandi is sweet-natured; Gyano argumentative and contestatory; the first literate, the second uncultured; one intelligent, the other comparatively dull; one a good cook and manager of the house, the other distinctly inefficient at these tasks; and so on.

Although a separate stage of childhood is mentioned in these texts, and an appreciation of the need for education (read literacy) of the girl-child is marked, one may note a slippage whereby girlhood comes to be erased. While the training of the girl-child at the right time is emphasized, the results of her training, demeanor, future outlook and responsibilities (those that come with married life) are always fully anticipated. Foregrounded throughout the texts is the need for civil and modest behavior even in the girl-child. In the end, then, she only plays a bit part. What comes through in the stories found in these

45 *Mirat* Urdu edn., p. 39.
46 Ibid., pp. 65, 98.

educational treatises and manuals of conduct, as opposed to their prefaces or statements of authorial intention, is the portrait of the "ideal woman." And the ideal woman, in turn, is marked as ideal precisely by how she behaves in her married home, and by a prescribed lack of independent initiative and thought.

In describing the early days of Akbari's marriage to Muhammad `Aqil, Nazir Ahmad accentuates Akbari's unsuitability for a respectable married life. He details her *behunari* (lack of talent) and *badmizaji* (ill-temperedness),[47] her disrespectful relations with her mother-in-law and sister-in-law and her persistent, useless engagements with the younger women of the *mohalla* (neighborhood) who are not from *sharif* families. He notes finally her demand for a separate household, which turns out to be the most irresponsible demand of all. (Na`ima in the *Taubat al- Nasuh* is the equivalent of Akbari, the bad daughter-in-law, living in her father's house, fighting with her mother, strikingly irreligious and hence misguided.)

The author derides the desire for separate households, repeatedly emphasizing the importance of the togetherness of extended relations. Akbari's wish to have an independent household is a fundamental flaw. By contrast, Asghari is lauded for keeping her family together – as if this choice (or acceptance) itself constitutes the core of her *sharafat*. In this delineation of the two leading characters of the *Mirat*, Nazir Ahmad spells out his notion of the respectable woman: being the woman of the household, living with kith and kin, behaving in a respectful and dutiful manner.

Asghari triumphs in everything she does because she is gifted with *hunar aur saliqa* (talent and proficiency), *adab* (good comportment) and *qa`ida* (the right way).[48] Thus she successfully fosters good relationships with her mother-in-law and sister-in-law, efficiently arranges the daily chores and the domestic expenses, even exposes the trickery and wastefulness of Mama `Azmat, the long-time household helper. Strikingly, Asghari never mixes with the lower-class women of the *mohalla* or neighborhood. She educates the girls of the *mohalla,* but always in a controlled and guarded, not to say

---

[47] *Mirat* Urdu edn., p. 65.
[48] These are the adjectives with which Asghari is introduced in the *Mirat*, qualities with which she subsequently manages most affairs of her married life, as the author argues. *Mirat* Urdu edn., p. 98.

aloof way. She never appears irresponsible or casual, unthinking or carefree.

The *sharif* Asghari is educated (*padhi-likhi*) and very willing to teach the girls, but she will do so only in the restrained terms of the respectable: in her own house and without any monetary returns. It is important that she makes clear that she is not in any one's service (*naukri*). She will simply share a few words of knowledge that are "a blessing from the elders (*buzurgon ki `inayat*)."[49] Nazir Ahmad makes it plain that only *padhi-likhi* women who cultivate their talents (*hunar*) for the business of the world and who are aware of the need for good comportment (*adab*) and right ways (*qa`ida, tariqa*) can be the guardians of respectability.

This is a point, alongside teaching ethics (*akhlaq*) and good house-keeping (*khanadari*), that Nazir Ahmad elaborates forcefully in his *Banat-an-Na`sh* (*The Daughters of the Bier*). This book, though not a sequel, details several themes and episodes introduced in the *Mirat*. In the *Banat*, we have Asghari, now the *ustaniji*, teaching the girls of the *mohalla*. The story centers on Husnara, whom we encounter briefly in the *Mirat*, a young *sharif* girl, ill-behaved like Akbari, now being put in the hands of skilled Asghari for training and cultivation.

The technique of storytelling in the *Banat*, in fact, is very similar to that employed in the *Mirat*. The chapter entitled "*Husnara ki `Aadaat*" ("Ways and Habits of Husnara")[50] serves as the guide for what follows in the rest of the story. The author lists Husnara's ways: *shararat* (naughtiness), *badmizaji* (ill-temperedness), *khud-pasandi* (self-admiration), *laalach* (greed), *besabri* (impatience), *susti* (laziness), *behunari* (lack of talent) and so forth.[51] The rest of the story focuses on the gradual refinement of Husnara's `aadaat, first by gentle conversations with Mehmooda, Asghari's sister-in-law, again familiar to the reader from the *Mirat*. Mehmooda, a young girl from the *Mirat*, is now herself a trained young woman and takes up the initial task of enlightening Husnara on various subjects, including *sharafat*, importance of equality and kindness to servants, and introduces her to other subjects

---

[49] Ibid., p. 166.
[50] The first chapter of the *Banat* in which Asghari is invited to teach Husnara by her mother is also a chapter in the latter half of the *Mirat*. The *Banat* version is slightly more detailed.
[51] *Banat* Urdu edn., p. 466.

such as problems of wealth, the history of money and barter, different kinds of dolls, how to stitch and cook, the pleasures of reading, the mystery of colors and the law of gravity and mathematical calculations, among several other subjects.[52]

The *Taubat-al-Nasuh* (*Repentance of Nasuh*) has a very different outcome from the *Mirat* even though these works are superficially similar. *Taubat* is a tale set at the time of a deadly cholera epidemic in Delhi. Nasuh's (the hero's) aged father succumbs to the epidemic. Nasuh also contracts the disease, but before he recovers, he has a fateful dream in which his father warns him of the day of reckoning that awaits all human beings. The conversation between Nasuh and his father is set in a divine *kachahri* (judicial court), bringing out "an existential similarity," C. M. Naim notes, "between the British *kacehri* ... whose terror and justice they [Nasuh, his father and their contemporaries] had recently experienced in 1858, and the Divine *kacehri* that they must inescapably appear before one day with the rest of the humanity."[53]

In the dream, Nasuh's father tells him that he was accounting for his sins (*gunah*). Nasuh puzzles as to why his father, who had led a life of piety (*khudaparast*), would be guilty of sins. Nasuh asks his father whether he could help him in this troubled time. In a long conversation that follows between Nasuh and his father, the latter asks Nasuh whether the family had prayed for him after his death. Nasuh replies regretfully that they had mourned his death, done all the rites, but had not prayed for him.[54]

At the end of this conversation, Nasuh wakes up. In reflecting on the dream, he becomes convinced that it was his own sins that led to his father's agony: he had altogether neglected the five times of daily prayer; often feigned indisposition and went to physicians to get a certificate to escape the obligatory fasts; evaded the *zakat* (alms tax) by a temporary transfer of deed to his wife. Nasuh reproaches himself, saying just as his *badi* (bad deeds, sins) had impinged on his children, their children would be affected in a similar way. Hence, he decides to devote himself to setting things right in his household (*islah-i khandan*).[55]

[52] Ibid., pp. 471, 473, 484, 487, 504, 509, 521, 524.
[53] Cited from C. M. Naim's afterword to the English translation of the *Taubat*, p. 133. Hereafter, Naim, afterword.
[54] *Taubat* Urdu edn., pp. 22–24.
[55] Ibid., pp. 36–37.

To begin the process of setting his household "right," Nasuh has a conversation with his wife, Fahmidah. He makes her his *madadgar* or helper in this cause.[56] A series of conversations follow among the mother, the father and the children on a variety of subjects. Nasuh's wife, Fahmidah, talks to her eldest daughter, Na`ima, and to her youngest daughter, Hamida; Nasuh, to his sons: first to the youngest, Salim, then to the one in the middle, `Alim, and finally to the oldest, Kalim. Na`ima and Kalim, the eldest male and female children, may be seen as equivalents of Akbari, challenging and argumentative. The younger brothers and sisters are, by contrast, consenting and obedient.

Once again, Nazir Ahmad's narrative style in the *Taubat* appears similar to that found in the *Mirat* and the *Banat*: the juxtaposition of the behavior of a refined girl with that of a discourteous girl, and here additionally, of a *sharif* boy with one who is not so well bred, showing what the perfect *sharif* son or daughter should be. Yet the moral of the story in this instance turns out to be rather different, as we will see later in this chapter.

Altaf Hussain Hali's *Majalis-un-Nissa* (*The Assemblies of Women*), a well-known text from 1874, although similar "in intention" to the *Mirat*, is rather different in form.[57] It is based upon a literary style, that of the sufi *majlis* or assembly in which advice was given by the sufi *pir* (guide) to his *murid* (disciple). In the *Majalis* there is a strong plea for the education of women, for reasons not unlike those spelled out in the *Mirat*: that educated women would do a more accomplished job of looking after the family and training and upbringing children. Yet what immediately draws the attention of the reader is that this text, like the *Banat*, provides unusual detail about the education of a girl-child: the stages of learning, the texts, the values, the games, the skills and the *adab* that accompanies it all. The elderly Atuji tells the story of Zubaida Khatun, a young girl educated by her parents, in the first six *majalis*. The last two *majalis* tell the story of Sayyid

---

[56] This may again be seen as a slightly radical move in the text in that a partnership is urged between the man and the woman. In the preface to the *Mirat*, Nazir Ahmad invokes the analogy of a cart being drawn by a husband and a wife to provide the balance: suggesting that the world is like a cart which cannot move without two wheels – man on one side and woman on the other. Likewise in a letter discussed later in this chapter, Durandesh Khan invokes a similar metaphor for Asghari: of a cart of the world (*duniya ki gaadi*) being drawn by a husband and a wife.

[57] Minault, *Voices of Silence*, p. 10.

Abbas, the son of Zubaida, raised by his mother as the very model of a *sharif* man. Together, they add up to a full-blown treatise on the new conception of education for the girl-child. In the *Majalis-un-Nissa*, a book committed uncompromisingly to the girl-child's learning, a very clear picture of the highly regulated domestic life for female figures emerges.

In the very first *majlis*, when Atuji makes the case for the education of women to other women, old and young, who are present, she does so by emphasizing that an educated woman would recognize the "right and duties of both young and old." That she would respect and work to make sure that "the husband should be the master and she the mistress of the household." In the fourth *majlis*, we hear Zubaida Khatun's mother instructing Zubaida (coming to us via Atuji) that "When the food is prepared and ready to serve, and your father comes from the men's quarters, go to the kitchen and have the food dished out in front of you... You should send special food outside [outside the *zanana*] to any male guests, and then you should lay the cloth for your father and place the food before him with your own hands." In the fifth *majlis*, just before Zubaida Khatun turns thirteen, her mother lying ill, nearing death, says to her: "Although I realize that you do not need any further advice, still you don't know much about life. You have studied a lot but experienced little." Then she gives Zubaida Khatun lengthy advice on married life, relations with mother-in-law and sister-in-law and the importance of endurance in marriage, concluding her remarks as follows: "Never forget that husbands have the higher position." After this her mother dies. At the end of the fifth *majlis*, we are told that Zubaida Khatun gets married. Before her marriage, however, it is her father, not a woman from the household, who discusses with her the question of marriage, saying among other things that it "is not a matter for a few days, but rather bondage for a lifetime!"[58]

At its most general level, then, my argument is about the very different prescriptions that emerge in these texts regarding the training of *sharif* boys and girls, men and women. My proposition relates not only to matters of curriculum and correct behavior, but to an attitude of mind and a sensibility, which is where the chief difference between the sexes is seen — and intended — to lie. For it is the construction of

[58] Ibid., pp. 36, 72, 86, 89.

the self, even if the selves are meant to be entirely constructed from recurrent listing of prescriptions, which is at the heart of my argument about the girl-child/woman.

THE CURRICULUM FOR A GIRL-CHILD'S EDUCATION

"I do not deny that too much learning (`ilm`) is unnecessary for a woman," Nazir Ahmad wrote in his introduction to the *Mirat*: "but how many women are there who acquire even so much as is absolutely necessary?" Girls and women would perhaps never be able to read and write like boys and men, but they do need literacy "sufficient to meet your own requirements." "To keep all the accounts of the house – what there is to receive, and what there is to pay – entirely by rote is a very difficult matter," thus a matter for men alone. Besides basic reading and writing, two other talents (*hunar*) were essential for girls: needlework and cooking. Additionally, it was important to keep their daily habits (`aadaat`) up to the mark even in good times when the household wanted for nothing.[59]

What kind of education was Asghari, Nazir Ahmad's heroine, imparting? "It is not only their reading which I insist upon," Asghari states. "Apart from reading, I also teach them about the affairs of the world (*duniya ka kaam*), which will fall upon their heads before many days are over." And what was the business of the world? She taught the girls sewing, stitching, cutting out clothes, many ways of dyeing clothes, mixing unusual colors, housekeeping and all kinds of ceremonial functions. She argued that if the burden of running a prestigious house (*bada ghar*) fell upon their shoulders, they should be able to do it in the most proficient and experienced way (*mashshaq aur tajurbekar*).[60] Household at the center of life for the girl-child: discipline and accomplishment of tasks, the most desirable traits for a girl coming of age.

In the evenings the girls would entertain themselves, and tell stories, and ask each other riddles. But, as Asghari put it, the stories were not all about cock sparrows and hen sparrows. "We have an excellent book (`umda kitab`), *Muntakhab al-Hikayat*, in which there are a great

---

[59] *Mirat* Urdu edn., pp. 35–36, 37.
[60] Ibid., p. 175.

variety of very good stories, one better than the other, and in these the author has conveyed some piece of instruction."[61] (This book reappears in the *Banat*, as I mentioned before). In entertainment, instruction turns out to be the key.

The details of a respectable woman or girl-child's training, demeanor, future expectations and responsibilities of adult married life were at once known. Reading, writing, sewing, making up beds, arranging jewels, learning to make dishes such as fish, which are not of an overly rich character and yet to cook them nicely:[62] all these were things to be proud of. Nazir Ahmad emphasizes *khanadari* (housekeeping), *bandobast aur saliqa* (good management and proficiency), but also crucially *izzat aur nam* (credit and honor).[63] For the author, *khanadari* (housekeeping) and *duniyadari* (matters of the world) was the same thing. Everything in life fell under these heads: marriages (*shaadiyan*), the matter of giving and taking in relationships (*lena-dena*), the education of children (`*aulad ki tarbiyat*) and so forth.[64] Education was required to "climb the hill," the challenges that lay ahead.

For Hali's heroine, Zubaida Khatun, the vital tasks she learned as a girl-child were not that different. We learn about these in the second *majlis*: saying prayers properly, correct behavior in eating, drinking, getting up, sitting down, listening, respecting the elders. Also, avoiding "fraternizing with servants, talking too loudly, running around, looking someone boldly in the eye while talking to them, laughing boisterously, going about without head covered." All these things were taught to Zubaida Khatun at age five:

> When I was five years old, my mother turned me over to the *us`ani*... Until I was seven I studied only the Quran with her... At the beginning of my eighth year, all my time was taken up: in the morning... I studied the Quran with Ustani-ji, and then Mughlani taught me stitching for an hour. After eating at 10:00, Mother gave me free time to play. But frequently I went back to Mughlani of my own accord and sat and sewed with her... At 11:00 my father came into the interior of the house... He had me sit down on the floor next to his bed and practice *naskh* and *nasta`liq* calligraphy... When I completed the Quran and learned all the

---

[61] Ibid., p. 177.
[62] Ibid.
[63] Ibid., p. 34.
[64] Ibid., p. 51.

religious injunctions concerning prayer, fasting, bathing and cleanliness, Father began to teach me the translation of Shah Abdul Qadir and also began teaching me Persian and arithmetic. [Zubaida Khatun's father also advised her to read the *Tales of the Four Darvishes*, the *Bagh-o-Bahar*] ... Mother had drilled into me from the beginning that work was so important that, even in childhood, I didn't enjoy playing much.[65]

How was such training put into practice? Asghari successfully fosters good relationships with her relatives, managing the daily affairs of the household and its domestic expenses. As noted earlier, she does not mix with the lower-class women of the neighborhood. She educates the girls of the *mohalla*, but always in a guarded way. She is never irresponsible, unthinking or carefree (playful). No running to the rooftops, no frequent visits to or from women of the *mohalla*, no chit-chatting.

In a way, Asghari replicates the ways of the patriarch. In the *Banat*, she appears like Durandesh Khan: not physically there all the time, we know she is somewhere in the *makhtab* and is an overarching presence – in Mehmooda and other girls' constant references to her excellent ways, knowledge expertise and worldly wisdom. She appears and gets proactive at the perfect time – just like the patriarch's letters arriving at the momentous time in their daughter's life – as soon as Husnara has learned to read with Mehmooda and declares for the first time that she was ready to read a story in front of everyone.[66]

The beautiful Anandi of *Devrani-Jethani* is similarly literate, intelligent, a good cook and an efficient manager of the house. For Gauridatt, Anandi's literacy, her being educated, or *padhi-likhi*, was to be especially noted. The author refers to this accomplishment repeatedly. She reads Nagri, Gyano does not. She cooks twice a day, as a result of Gyano's inadequacy in this regard. Following the afternoon meal, she rests for an hour, then turns to stitching, knitting and embroidery. Girls of the extended kinship networks and the neighborhood flock around her. She teaches them knitting and reading, while she continues

---

[65] Minault, *Voices of Silence*, pp. 50–51. Shah Abdul Qadir was the son of the eighteenth-century reformer Shah Waliullah of Delhi, and he translated the Quran into Urdu. Gail Minault notes that Zubaida Khatun first read the Quran in Arabic and then read the translation (Ibid., p. 157, fn. 8). *Bagh-o-Bahar* by Mir Amman Dehlavi was originally written in 1801 for training European students of Fort William College in Urdu.

[66] *Banat* Urdu edn., p. 563.

other household tasks. She recites couplets from the *Bhagvad-Gita* so wonderfully that the other women are entranced. On days of festivals such as *Ekadashi, Janamashtami* and *Ramnaumi* (when the women are excused from stitching and other such chores) she sings devotional songs from the poets Tulsidas and Surdas.[67] Household tasks as well as breathing spaces are all confined to the boundary of the house.

Sukhdeyi, Anandi's sister-in-law, forms a special relationship with Anandi, and when she marries, she too begins to teach Nagri to the girls of her married household. In a letter that she sends home after her marriage, she requests Anandi to send a particular book, adding that "here too, we have something like a girl's *madrasa* (school)."[68] In the *Banat*, Mehmooda replicates Asghari's example. A chain of female exemplars and practitioners is thus established.

Anandi is highly successful in managing her daily household work and in having excellent relationships. Gauridatt says, "It is a blessing of God that the hearts of a man and woman meet in this way. It is not surprising that hearts do not meet if a man is educated (*padha-likha*) and the woman is not (*be-padhi*)." A further applaud: "When these two [Anandi and her husband Chote Lal] saw each other, they were very pleased. She would ask him about his tasks, and he was always concerned that nothing should happen that would hurt her. He would not do anything without consulting her." Chote Lal brings Nagri newspapers for Anandi to read. He reads her Urdu and English newspapers at night, and when he tires he asks her to read the Nagri ones. Anandi's section of the household (*chaubara*) is like that of other *baniya* families, but she uses her expertise to beautify it appropriately. She places two easy chairs alongside a shelf of books, and to make her household colorful she uses a lot of blue instead of gray. She throws rugs on the floor and hangs pictures on the walls.[69]

In the *Majalis-un-Nissa*, the whole point of the story that Atuji narrates about Zubaida Khatun is to show how an educated mother successfully raises her son, as Minault puts it, "to be a resourceful and forward looking individual, the very model of a modern *sharif* gentleman."[70] (In turn, Sayyid Abbas, Zubaida's son, narrates his

[67] *Devrani-Jethani*, p. 12.
[68] Ibid., pp. 8, 12.
[69] Ibid., p. 10.
[70] Minault, *Voices of Silence*, p. 15.

everyday training and the making of a *sharif* boy in the seventh *majlis*).

In all these texts, the reading and writing of women is equated with the care of household and kinsfolk by obedient women. The values of the training given to *sharif* women as girls was emphasized accordingly: cooking, sewing, cleaning and acquiring the learning necessary to keep household affairs in good condition. Household becomes the focal point to which the girl-child must arrive as a woman. Tahsildar Saheb is fairly candid in the letter he writes to Anandi in the *Devrani-Jethani* about her duties in her marriage and new home. Subsequently, we see that Anandi is applauded for her education in her new household, celebrated for reading newspapers with her husband, teaching Nagri to the girls of the *mohalla*, reciting devotional songs and couplets. Asghari's father writes a similar letter of comportment to her at the time of her marriage, and the outcome is the same: an emphasis on a respectfully married woman who should be terrific in the management of her household.

It was important that women were educated, but what does Nazir Ahmad mean when he says, "I do not deny that too much learning is unnecessary for a woman, but how many women are there who acquire even so much as is absolutely necessary?" Absolutely necessary for what? To improve their *hunar* (talents) so that they become experts in *khanadari* and *duniyadari* – ethics of household life.

Nazir Ahmad, Hali and Gauridatt drew portraits that girl-child and woman were supposed to bear in mind always (in the future, as in the past). These become part of a cultural repertoire, part of an accepted code of conduct that may be invoked when necessary. There is a compliance (and passivity) in Anandi's "wonderful" recitation of the couplets (*shloka*) from the *Bhagvad-Gita*. On days of festivals, again, her singing of devotional songs from the poets Tulsidas and Surdas is cast as a typical and customary part of a virtuous routine. Zubaida Khatun's passion for learning is evident, but what was crucial in her learning was to follow the ways laid down by her mother, father and teacher: the lessons of her girlhood formed the basis for the instruction she gave her son. There's a bit of a musical chairs game the reader encounters in the *Majalis-un-Nissa*, in that instructors and instructed seem to follow one another closely. But this is precisely the point about a chain of instruction established through these books and the figures that make distinct (and firm) prescriptions about the woman of the household.

Vital to these elaborations regarding the respectable household was the distinctly gendered training – *ta`lim-u-tarbiyyat*, translated as "education" by many modern scholars – for men and women in the respectable family. The message of Nazir Ahmad, Hali and others was that training that produced "good" women, mindful of correct behavior and the ideals of domestic life, was itself a sign of *sharif* tradition. Such training also produced "good" men, equally symbols of cultured *sharif* existence. But there was a disparity, for the men were variously invested in contemplative endeavors: thinking beings striving for noble values and the appropriate way of life.

"As soon as boys can speak," Nazir Ahmad says in his preface to the *Mirat*, "they have the capacity for instruction. If the mothers are talented, they can educate the child from an appropriate moment." Note the emphasis on "boys" (*ladke*), even though "child or children" (*bachche*) is sometimes substituted for the word. The writer adds that neither the children themselves nor the mothers particularly want them to go to the school (*madrasa*). Going to the *madrasa* is described by the author as being "*ustad ki qayd main*," literally imprisoned by the teacher! However, he says, if the mothers want they can teach their sons a great deal. Even when the boys go to the *madrasa*, they do so half-heartedly. The mothers can, in the course of their simple, daily interactions with their children, teach them a lot. "To begin with," the author asks, "where is there anything like a mother's tenderness (*shafaqat*) and deep devotion (*dil-sozi*)?"[71]

Thus, although Sayyid Abbas, son of Zubaida, goes through rigorous training, including a regular and binding everyday routine of reading and training in comportment, we see, that unlike for the girl-child, there is a constant emphasis on spaces of leisure and fun that seem important to his training: discussion of baths in hot water, regular meals, reading newspapers, playing, shooting, playing with bat and ball, *kabaddi*, horse riding, running races, wrestling and shooting.[72]

Consider, from the *Taubat*, the argument `Alim, Nasuh's second son, puts to his father in one of their conversations. There was no

---

[71] *Mirat* Urdu edn., pp. 51–52.
[72] Minault, *Voices of Silence*, 103–105.

doubt, he notes, that he had read the Quran from the time when he was very little: "From the beginning till the end, I read it, but I could not understand entirely (*mutlaq*) what was written in it and what its meaning was." For he read the Quran "like a parrot."[73] Later on, he tells Nasuh, he acquired a copy of a book of moral instruction from a missionary, a *Padri Saheb* whom he met in a crowd and saw responding to people's angry disputations without a wrinkle on his face. `Alim says that he did not know the name of the book, but as he read it, he found the book worthwhile. By reading it, he realized that his manner of living (*tarz-e zindagi*) had been worse than that of animals. Since reading the book, however, he had begun to understand the pains of others as his own[74] and thereby improved his own life. The quality of reflectiveness in this exchange is not found in any of the comments that Nazir Ahmad puts into the mouths of his female characters, such as Akbari or Na'ima. Through `Alim's articulation, Nazir Ahmad appears to suggest that it is necessary to *think*, to understand through reflection, what it means to be a good Muslim and to lead a cultured life.[75]

The question that follows is to what extent, and in what ways, the civilized Hindu or Muslim girl-child or woman would qualify as educated or capable of being educated. Is the girl-child/woman's education anything more than the consolidation of the condition and culture into which she had been born? That is to say, more than the addition of a certain minimal literacy to the other talents with which she was supposed to be naturally endowed?

In the next section, I push the argument about the seemingly static and non-agential role of women that the reader might note in the authorial prescriptions at a first glance. In the reformist discourses, alongside the respectable boys and girls, we have the argumentative Kalim and Na`ima of the *Taubat*, Akbari of the *Mirat* and Husnara of the *Banat*, among others, who were uncultured, wished to set up separate homes and mixed with women of lower classes. These figures allow subversive moves in the texts, cutting at the authority of the authors, the ideal male and female characters and along with them,

---

[73] *Taubat* Urdu edn., p. 86.
[74] Ibid., p. 88.
[75] Ibid, pp. 90–92.

the well-accepted social forms and prescriptions. Critically, it is in the arguments of these girls and women, boys and men that we begin to discern the room for contest and a vision for alternative models and lifestyles.

MODEL WOMEN

Accounts of exceptional women are important to all the books we have discussed in this chapter. Acts of exemplary women were repeatedly invoked by the authors as part of the prescription for women to perfect their lives. The exemplars set out for girls included the incomparable Mughal women, Nur Jahan and Zeb-un-Nisa Begum; the English queen, Victoria; and the Begum of Bhopal, Sikander Begum. To use Nazir Ahmad's words about the greatness of such models: "They are women who have organized the affairs of the nations, and of the whole world, not of just a little home and family (*ye voh ʽauratain hain jinhone ek chote se ghar aur kunbe ka nahin balke mulk aur jahan ka bandobast kiya*)."[76] But all at once, it is significant that Nazir Ahmad underlines that the "great" women were not women of the household.

In contradistinction, the author sets out the future of the girls in the following instructions for married life: "after being married, they [girls/women] will have to live an entirely new kind of life, such as you see your mother (*ma*), and *her* mother (*nani*) living, as well as your aunt (*khala*) and all the women of the (*kunbe ki ʽauratain*) family... A new life, full of all kinds of perplexities and trials, is coming nearer."[77] So the idea remains that from within the family, the "protocols of womanhood [were] being passed on, generation to generation."[78] However, it is the men who select the models that girls and women must admire.

In teaching the girls, Asghari emphasizes the example of outstanding women: the Mughal queens, Nur Jahan and Zeb-un-Nisa; the English queen, Victoria; and the Begum of Bhopal, Sikander Begum.[79] The models of greatness invoked by Nazir Ahmad are replicated by

---

[76] *Mirat* Urdu edn., p. 35.
[77] Ibid, p. 39.
[78] J. M. Coetzee, *The Slow Man* (London, 2005), p. 31.
[79] *Mirat* Urdu edn., p. 35; see also a reference to the same text in the *Banat* that Husnara learns to read; pp. 563–564.

his heroine. Yet it was also necessary, and natural, that such figures remained inaccessible, since the girl-child/woman had to follow the prescriptions for good domestic behavior laid down by the patriarchs. Or even when such exemplars come within reach, they do so in the terms that would fit a good wifely role. Gail Minault remarks astutely about Queen Victoria who appears in the *Majalis* several times:

> In fact, throughout the work, though she [Queen Victoria] is the ruler over her vast realm (and all women are, in a sense, queens in their own realms), the stories about her show her to be a woman who cares about her family, about those who are dependent upon her, and who exemplifies compassion and justice in her dealings with others. The queen thus provides a model of womanly and wifely behaviour. Hali has patterned Victoria according to his own criteria of the ideal woman, intelligent, competent, and patient.[80]

At one point in the *Mirat*, Asghari has a discussion with the girls she teaches about the rulers of Hindustan. Husnara, one of her pupils, says that Queen Victoria is their king. Asghari asks, "A man or a woman?" Husnara replies, "A woman." A little later Safihan asks, "[I]s a *woman a king?*" Asghari responds: "What is there to be amazed at that? ... She does exactly the same things as men do who are kings. She governs the country; she protects her subjects."

Safihan could not help wondering, as she puts it, how a woman was able to organize the affairs of a nation (*mulk ka bandobast*). Asghari explains to Safihan that her amazement comes from the fact that she considers the queen to be like herself or like Asghari. Asghari points out the important difference between them (between Safihan/Asghari and the queen) by saying that when God grants high ranks (*rutba bade karna*), he also grants the leaders who hold those ranks capacity (*haunsala*) and wisdom (`*aql*) accordingly.[81]

In the *Majalis*, here is what Zubaida Khatun's mother says about the two imperial models for her daughter, one from the "olden times," Raushanara Begum, the daughter of the Mughal king Shah Jahan, and the other from "more contemporary times," Queen Victoria.

> When Alamgir [Aurangzeb, son of Shah Jahan] imprisoned his father, Raushanara refused to desert her father and went to prison with him

---

[80] Minault, *Voices of Silence*, p. 23.
[81] *Mirat* Urdu edn., pp. 180, 181, 183.

and served him loyally... Raushanara, unlike her brother, performed her filial duty and is praised for it to this day. This was all by virtue of her learning... [Then she goes on to the second example] Your father once knew an Englishmen and I was acquainted with his wife. One day she told me that Her Majesty, Queen Victoria, had written a book of reminiscences about her husband and their children. In that book there are scores of examples to convince you that God is very wise to have created such a great woman in the world. Of course, it is difficult to imitate royalty. Still, a person should at least understand what is good for her and what is not. She should not just stick to what she has learnt from her ancestors.[82]

(This follows a long discourse on the importance of vaccination and the problems with customs and superstition). Thus the models that Zubaida Khatun drew upon exhibited virtues she was asked to inculcate; or rather, as Minault puts it, Hali underlined specific virtues in the models he chose and designed them accordingly for his readers. So the queens were cast as models with precise qualities that the girl-child/woman could (should) aspire to: filial piety via Raushanara; and "compassion" via Queen Victoria, as it is put to Zubaida Khatun later on. She is told "Pride and Arrogance never cross her mind." The point of the thinking, not just "what she has learnt from her ancestors," as Zubaida Khatun's mother explains was as follows: "Just as a king is worthless without a prime minister, so too knowledge without skill will not benefit the world in any practical way. Women should be educated so that they renounce evil customs and choose good habits ... be able to manage their household property ... learn how to raise children and sympathize with their husbands."[83]

Does this conversation indicate that women like Asghari or Zubaida Khatun's mother or the girls that they were teaching had the capacity, or duty, to work out what their aspirations and vocations should be, or what paths and models they should follow in order to be good Muslim women? Could the girls of the *mohalla* aspire to be like the compelling imperial examples about whom they were reading? Or was it simply that they could read the fables of great women "out there," but then make sure that they returned to their domain to continue practising to be the women of the household?

[82] Minault, *Voices of Silence*, pp. 63–64.
[83] Ibid., pp. 66–68.

In Nazir Ahmad's view what the girls and women could (and could not) do was linked deeply with the training of the different sexes: crucially, the responsibility of the mother and father in the education of children, including the right time for learning, thus ensuring specific outcomes for men and women of respectable families. The author accentuates the mother's (and other women's) responsibility in the training of children, yet simultaneously projects the father as the authoritative figure. Nazir Ahmad's philosophy of what constitutes a *sharif* life, and how one must bring up sons and daughters in a *sharif* family in order to reproduce and enhance respectability, is reflected, among several instances, in the way in which he depicts Nasuh and Fahmidah's sharing of the training of girls and boys in the *Taubat*. Although Nasuh and Fahmidah divide the responsibility of educating their sons and daughters, Nasuh is presented as the reforming head of the family. He made his wife a *madadgar*, a helper in this cause. Yet she was merely that – his helper. He remained the true rectifier, the man who could do repentance.

Consider an episode from the *Taubat* in which Kalim has an argument with his mother when she requests him to see his father, Nasuh. Following this exchange, Kalim leaves home without seeing his father. Nasuh, extremely agitated, goes to his son's quarters. Kalim occupies two rooms, the first of which he refers to as *ishrat manzil* or place of entertainment, which is luxuriously furnished with a dais, costly rug and pillows, a hookah and spitting vase, chairs of polished wood, a fan (*punkha*) with fringes of gold and silver lace, chandeliers and globes of colored glass and framed pictures and verses from several poets.

Nasuh gazes at his son's extravagance – cards and dice, musical boxes, flower jars, perfume, betel leaves, albums containing portraits of singers, dancers, wrestlers and eunuchs, jesters and gamblers. He next goes to Kalim's *khilvat khaneh*, or place of retirement, and is immediately attracted to a cabinet of books, Persian and Urdu. He finds the contents of these books false and degrading (*jhuthe qisse, behuda batain, luchche mazmun*). After Nasuh has examined them carefully, he resolves to commit them to the flames.[84] Nasuh's sons,

84 *Taubat* Urdu edn., pp. 163–163.

`Alim and Salim, join him; `Alim throws copies of *Divan-i Sharar* and *Kulliyat-i Atish* onto the burning book pyre.[85]

C. M. Naim has gone so far as to suggest that Kalim is the "true subject" of the *Taubat*. To many of the novel's earliest readers, he says, it must have been clear that it is Kalim's repentance that Nazir Ahmad was exemplifying.[86] There are other male figures in Nazir Ahmad's writings who are like Kalim, if not quite so "advanced." They interrogate, deliberate on and contemplate the meaning of the respectable life. Nasuh resolves on repentance. Even the obedient `Alim reflects on his lifestyle (*tarz-e zindagi*) and considers which books he might read to understand the pains of others and improve his own life.

What about Asghari, who is without question the ideal woman figure of the *Mirat* and an example replicated in several other books that follow the *Mirat*? Is there much sign of rethinking, interrogation or refashioning of ways of being in her behavior? Even in the instances when there are questions about appropriate conduct and models of behavior, her responses are knowledgeable but predictable – hardly based on reflection and self-questioning.

Asghari was fashioned to be free of any doubts regarding good conduct and the worthy life. There is no reflectiveness or questioning, let alone the daring and curious ways of Insha's Ketki. Or is it rather that these paths are laid down already – as it were by nature, with the only remaining task being that of refining and improving God-given, feminine talents? From all that we have seen of the *Mirat* and the *Taubat*, and indeed from direct comments that the author makes in these texts, it would seem that Nazir Ahmad's answer is clear. "It is ignorant if a woman considers a man her equal."[87]

What are the ways in which man was "naturally" superior to woman? Clearly, in Nazir Ahmad's construction, one of them had to do with the ability to interpret and challenge what was merely dictated by the elders or by tradition. In a passage already referred to, Naim

[85] *Divan-i Sharar*, probably of Mirza Ibrahim Beg, a Lucknow poet of the early nineteenth century. It cannot have been Abdul Halim Sharar, who was born in 1860 and has been called "the pioneer of the historical romance in Urdu"; Russell, *The Pursuit of Urdu Literature*, p. 99. Khwaja Haidar `Ali Atish wrote Urdu poetry in the first quarter of the nineteenth century. For details of his poetry, see Sadiq, *A History of Urdu Literature*, pp. 187–193.

[86] Naim, afterword, p. 140; and e-mail communication from the author.

[87] Ibid., p. 105.

makes a powerful observation regarding Kalim: "Arguably," he says, "Kulleem is the most memorable and complex character in TN [the *Taubat-al-Nasuh*], perhaps in all of Nazir Ahmad's novels ... we cannot help noticing that Nazir Ahmad gives Kulleem [the interlocutor] ample opportunities to argue his own case against Nussooh's imperious moralizing."

Naim quotes the last section of the *Taubat* to make the point: "There is no doubt that if Kulleem had survived he would have surpassed his brothers and sisters in virtue [*neki*] and piety [*dindari*]. He had changed his views after suffering hardships... Consequently, he was a *mujtahid* – [one who had striven and achieved sound views] – while others were *muqallid* – [mere imitators]."[88]

The suffering that Kalim (and Nasuh) had to go through, the questioning that accompanied their negotiation of a rapidly changing social and political environment, may be seen as one reflection of the class anxiety of the time. Both these male characters – and to a certain degree `Alim – strove to think through the most appropriate means of maintaining a *sharif* lifestyle in this time of change. And what should be emphasized in their upbringing, demeanor, speech, reading and more generally, their being. The crucial point to note is this: that the man consistently interprets what is given to him and what choices he needs to make in leading the *sharif* life.

Would the respectable woman have a comparable option of rethinking her position and needs? In what ways might the anxieties of the class to which they belong be expressed in the lives and thoughts of women? I ask this question not to suggest that the women figures of these texts are automatons simply executing the directives of the male order. However, what a girl should aspire to, how she should emulate models is not (cannot be) readily prone to quick answers.

Unlike the other texts, the *Banat* gives a different kind of possibility for the girl-child than we have encountered so far. On hearing that Husnara had learned to read, Asghari, feeling pleased, gives a long, unusual discourse on the subject of *Ghairat aur Gaur*: *ghairat*, meaning self-respect and/or honor; *gaur*, paying attention, thinking, being curious. These qualities, in Asghari's views were critical to cultivating *ilm*, knowledge. She recommends to Husnara that she cultivate a

[88] Ibid., pp. 138–139 (translation Naim's).

habit of paying attention (*gaur karne ki `aadat daalo*).[89] Where would reflection, thinking, cultivation of self-respect take the girl? What kind of figure becomes possible when virtues such as the ones that Asghari recommended are cultivated?

Whether it is Asghari, Anandi, Zubaida Khatun or Mehmooda, it is significant that their learning, even their reflections in the end are meant to address the question of respectable life: at the heart of which is the household weighed down by the prescriptions of the patriarch. The requisites of the domestic world become so overpowering that even the few moments of reflection, contest or play in the texts get overcast by the burdens of household discussions – which in turn leads to more or less one-dimensional figures in these texts. And one might add the strikingly reduced expressions for women. As the previous chapter and this one demonstrates, girl-child, girls and women (*ladkiyan, striyan, `auratain*) often appear within the terms of housekeeping (called matters of the world, *duniyadari*), that is, marriages, relationships with the kith and kin and education of children; or within the restrained, household-oriented literacy, central to which were their skills, talent, proficiency and good comportment. Additionally, women were centered as virtuous and chaste examples, especially so in the *Vamamanranjan* and in several other passages from texts mentioned earlier.

Let me turn to two further illustrations, from the *Majalis* and the *Banat* respectively, to further explore the point about what it meant to learn and reflect for girls. In a discussion with her son reported in the second *majlis*, Zubaida Khatun tells him about the toys she played with until she was six or seven years old.

> They had very strange names, and some had ugly faces which frightened me. Among them, there was one named Anger and one named Indecent Language, one named Slander and one called Lies, one named Insolence and one called Gossip, one Foolishness and another called Violence, one called Loquaciousness and one named Laziness, one called Idleness and another Sloth... The toys that had nice faces had names like Shyness and Modesty, Skill and Cleanliness, Virtue and Humility, Patience and Contentment, Kindness and Harmony and Obedience... There was also a pretty little fairy who seemed as if she were smiling about something, and you could not take your eyes off her. Her name was Smiling Face.[90]

---

[89] *Banat* Urdu edn., p. 565.
[90] Minault, *Voices of Silence*, pp. 47–48.

Toys were not meant for playing, and as Zubaida Khatun put it, their purpose was "to discourage me from evil habits and make me choose good ones."[91] Toys were teachers of values and qualities that a girl-child must imbibe. Even in her reading and learning, Zubaida Khatun tells us, as noted earlier, "if some of my girl relations were visiting and they insisted, I would go and play dolls with them. But mother had drilled into me from the beginning that work was so important that, even in child-hood, I didn't enjoy playing much."[92] *Ilm* (knowledge) itself was meant for the advancement of household skills, or as "the greatest treasure," Zubaida Khatun's mother explains, "Knowledge can bring you near to God and is necessary for salvation."[93]

In the *Banat* too, we have a detailed discussion about dolls. Husnara feels amazed looking at the dolls of Mehmooda: most of which were handmade (*apne hathon se kaadhi*), unlike Husnara's market dolls (*gudiyan bazaari*). The discussion that follows between Mehmooda and Husnara is not about the dolls themselves or how the girl-children played with these.[94] Their conversations are about talent (*hunar aur saliqa*), various kinds of embroidery, stitching and how Husnara might learn these skills. This leads to a chapter in which the reader is shown how Mehmooda teaches Husnara to sew.[95]

What was the status of the girl-child in the midst of these "practical ways"? Would the leisure available to Sayyid Abbas during his early years of training as a boy be possible for Husnara or Zubaida Khatun or other girls? Although Asghari recommends to Husnara that she cultivate a habit of paying attention (*gaur karne ki `aadat dalo*), would the possibility of reflection that Nasuh (or Kalim or `Alim) has be available to her as well? Could the *sharif* woman have the right to interpret the appropriate ways of conduct in her changing world? Could Asghari (or Akbari or Gyano or Na`ima) be a *mujtahid* or only remain a *muqallid*? The authors of these long-lived, well-circulated, much admired texts that I have investigated here, at least, do not seem to suggest such a possibility. What emerges in their narrations instead is not a girl-child or a woman with a possibility of reflection within

---

[91] Ibid., p. 48.
[92] Ibid., p. 51.
[93] Ibid., p. 58.
[94] *Banat* Urdu edn., pp. 471–472.
[95] Ibid., pp. 473–474.

the demands of the household, but simply a girl-child/woman of the household whose path and ways of being are clearly and unambiguously marked.

One needs to push the argument about the different roles assigned to men and women at this time a step further. Kalim, the contradictory "hero" of *Taubat*, was a thinker and interpreter, one who suffered anguish and made choices. Asghari, the "hero" of *Mirat*, merely followed the directions of the elders and the wisdom of tradition. The trained girl-child, now the married woman, caught up entirely in the "mindless" tasks of managing the household, raising children and preserving the honor of family and community. In a word, she is rendered static and non-agential.

For all that, the iconic Indian/Hindu/Muslim girl-child/woman could not be contained or frozen, even in the prescriptive texts of the Indian reformers. As my phrase girl-child/woman itself suggests, the figure of the respectable female in the late nineteenth century was always more than the neat subject that the upholders of the new patriarchy favored. Since education and improvement were hailed as signs of the time, and these had built into them the possibility, indeed the inescapability of change, growth and maturity (improvement), the girl-child/woman could not just be that. Such a figure was always liable to overflow the boundaries of the construction, girl-child or woman or both. And because Hegel's slave is forever restless, the subaltern (even the prescribed subaltern of reformist discourses) could not be completely tamed or constrained by the patriarchal and otherwise privileged overlords who attempted to construct and freeze them in sundry ways.

If Kalim stands out as a counter to the formal narrative of *Taubat*, so too the less reputable women of the *Mirat*, *Taubat*, and *Devrani-Jethani* – Gyano, Akbari and Na'ima – emerge as interruptions, signaling tendencies contrary to patriarchal prescriptions in spite of authorial intentions. These women are argumentative; they set up separate homes and mix with women of lower classes. And, as we know, Asghari and Akbari, Anandi and Gyano are two aspects of the same person, two possibilities inherent in all women, for the authors of these texts. I should also reiterate the point I have made repeatedly about the relationship between these "manuals" and "reality": that these texts are not "official" documents, speaking about "real" characters. These are books about what was desirable, and hence a reflection of the real.

These books are meditations on the window of the world, getting at sensibilities and figures, after which women and girls modeled themselves, as Azra so poignantly reminds us. What the contentious moments of these texts necessitate, then, are conversations and debates on conjugality and privacy, the promise of education and the claim of nationalism to universal citizenship, thus sowing the seed of future emancipatory endeavors. Already, in the spaces that these texts open up, the reader's glance may move forward to a time when women will deliberate and work to create a life informed by new notions of privacy and companionship, when they will no longer be content as the secondary educators of children under men's exclusive management. When they may aspire to be nothing less than equal partners with men – or "managers" alone, even to the exclusion of men from "the home and the world."

5

The Woman of the Rooftops

In the preceding chapters, I dealt with the emergence of the altered figures of the girl-child and woman brought into view through the new instruction and discipline of the institutionalized space of the school and the increasingly confined space of the household in the mid- and later nineteenth century. I have also argued that despite the constricting domestic demands for the girl-child and woman (which were perhaps heightened by the opening up of schools outside the home), it could never be the case that women would become completely docile: the literature (books, stories, characters) and the debates of the time make this all too clear. Women's negotiation of the prescriptive social and gender demands continued in subtle as well as obvious ways.

For a variety of reasons, not least the growing urban and semi-urban focus of respectable life for a traditional gentry increasingly drawn into the new *kachahri* (or colonial bureaucratic) complex, the space of the forest that brought with it multiple possibilities and choices of the kind depicted by Insha in his tale of Rani Ketki and in his Rekhti poetry – or found in the bardic narration of the story of Shakuntala – became less and less accessible over the nineteenth century. In the new urban and semi-urban cultural centers of colonial north India, however, the practices of the forest, the creativity and adventurism, the transgressions, the tasting of forbidden fruit, continued to be played out in other spaces – neither school nor household, forest or riverbank, nor even clearly defined as bounded spaces – that opened the lives of girls and women (and boys and men) to a wider world. I turn in this chapter to an investigation of these liminal spaces, which I refer to as "rooftops."

Ever since urban development, market towns and administrative headquarters made for significant, and dense, concentrations of populations of many different classes – and hence increasingly with the development of capitalism and the modern state in recent centuries – rooftops (or, more precisely, the terraces found on the tops of the houses of the well-to-do) have been a central organizing feature of women's spaces in the respectable, urban cultures of much of South Asia, the Middle East and North Africa. Rooftops, an important extension of domestic space, were the link between neighboring houses in these settings, so that women and children could hop from one to another, sometimes for miles. Rather than using the streets in front of the houses in the *mohallas* (neighborhoods) of urban north India, rooftops provided relatively protected avenues of movement for women from respectable homes. In addition, apart from allowing regular passage and communal interaction, the rooftops made it possible for women – and men (especially in male–male exchanges) – to access and cultivate, albeit for short whiles, aspects of forbidden life. This might be a glimpse of the loved one, a rendezvous, affectionate embraces that last a few hours of the night or a lonely communication with the sky.

Thus, rooftops were an extension of the domestic world, in part for reasons of practicality (family members sleeping on the terrace on hot summer nights, women and servants drying clothes, grains, pickles), in part when women *chose* to make them an extension. Women often did, in order to get away from the drudgery of the chores downstairs: upstairs, they looked over the drying grains, the pickles and wet clothes and dried their own wet hair. At the same time a woman got away from domestic chores on the rooftops, she spent time with friends or just went upstairs – escaping from the mundane – in a mode of self-introspection, wondering about her life, taking stock of all that was around her. In other words, rooftops provided a different, not-quite-domestic space, under the open sky: looking up at the endless stars and sky might even suggest an erasure of intermediaries between oneself and the infinite, between the devotee and the divine.

In the following pages, I use the term *rooftops* both in its literal sense (for rooftops); and, just as important, in a metaphorical sense to refer to spaces of adventure, experiment and transgression – openings, shadowy and less easily policed spaces, spaces between spaces, the connecting points between homes, and between homes and schools. Thus, I refer not only to the rooftops that form an extension of the home, a retreat and a passageway for neighbors and friends and lovers (young and old), but also to the passage from home to school and back again, on horse-drawn buggies or palanquins or (later) bicycles, through unfamiliar neighborhoods and markets that provided another space of adventure and exploration. Indeed, I extend this metaphorical application further, not only to the forests and other outdoor spaces accessed by respectable girls and women in an earlier time and to the alleyways and passages through urban and semi-urban neighborhoods that were an increasing part of their social world in more recent times, but also to other spaces of transgression such as dreams (which I discuss at some length in the later part of this chapter). For, needless to say, dreams are central to the making and self-making of girls and women in the later period as in the earlier, and in colonized countries as well as in the colonizing.

In this metaphorical sense, I want to suggest, the forest is often the rooftop in early-nineteenth-century Rekhti poetry, as well as in the tale of Rani Ketki: Insha, as we have seen, is a master at demonstrating the variety of exchanges between women that take place in the green spaces (gardens and forests) surrounding the neighborhoods. When we turn to the later nineteenth and early twentieth centuries in northern India, it is interesting to find that it is in the handful of women's memoirs and writings surviving from the period that the critical importance and place of the rooftops emerges most vividly. In what follows, then, I draw upon a variety of women's recollections – past and present – in order to consider how women (and men) of respectable households negotiated their everyday, in the home and the school, but even more in their margins.

I should stress that the women's writings I examine here emerge in the course of busy lives, led as they were meant to be led (so to speak). Yet, from those very practices of living there emerges a sense, one might even say an unself-conscious critique, of the structures they inhabit. I do not mean to suggest that the women concerned do not participate in the forms of exclusion and discipline that I discussed in the preceding chapters. But other aspects of their lives, other desires and struggles, emerge in their recollections, and it is the distinctiveness of their playful engagements, and their own unexpected efforts at closure, that I wish to explore in this chapter.

In this connection, I need to reiterate that in making Azra an important interlocutor throughout the book, I have attempted to break from a neat chronology in the writing of history. I continue with that mode of a "messy" time and space in this last chapter as well: not only in the choice of the authors and texts from different locations and periods, but also in the implicit suggestion that the articulations of these individuals are not limited to one clearly demarcated period or region, but resonate across cultures and historical times. Here, I make the claim about playfulness of the figure of the girl-child comparatively: *outside of the north in India* and *outside India* – by taking very provocative case studies. The texts in this chapter, crucially, echo Azra's concerns and speak back, as it were, to Azra – in solidarity. It is not a question of how this material informs us of women's lives in northern India: rather, my point is that women's experiences are sometimes shared and similar across the world – and certainly across different parts of a subcontinent with shared sociocultural inheritances.

Once we engage rooftops as a conceptual tool, and a paradigmatic space, we might open up a range of vistas into women's worlds, looking at many kinds of confinement, a variety of limits and numerous desires – and overt as well as covert ways of negotiating social and moral boundaries. I hope the exercise will lead readers to think of many other figures that demonstrate the propositions of this book. I can think of numerous well-known historical examples: the Begums of Bhopal, Begum Samru, the Rani of Jhansi, to mention three figures from nineteenth-century northern India. But my intention here is not to load the reader with an overflowing archive and examples of feminine criticism and creativity from each decade or century. Rather, it is to point to the fact that there are unusual ways of thinking about women's worlds, their aspirations and criticisms – even, or especially, when the argument seems to be that there are no texts or documents left behind by women.

The following texts from three different locations and times have been central to my engagement with, and amplification of, the metaphor of rooftops. I read, first, a rarely used memoir, the only known woman's "autobiography" from the Hindi-Urdu region, by a woman named Ashraf-un-nisa Begum (or Bibi Ashraf as her biographer calls her), who was born in 1840 in a small rural community of Bunhera, district of Bijnor in Uttar Pradesh. Muhammadi Begum (1878–1908), the compiler of Ashraf-un-nisa's biography, was the first woman to edit an Urdu magazine devoted to the welfare of Muslim women. Along with her husband, Sayyid Mumtaz Ali (1860–1935), Muhammadi Begum founded the first Urdu periodical for women, the *Tahzib un-Niswan*, a weekly magazine published from Lahore in 1898.[1] Bibi Ashraf was very close to Muhammadi Begum and wrote several poems and essays in the *Tahzib un-Niswan*. These include an essay on how she taught herself to read and write, which was originally published in two installments in March 1899.[2] The *Hayat-e Ashraf*, the Urdu text that I use, is a combination of Muhammadi Begum's observations based on her conversations with Bibi Ashraf and several of her interlocutors, interspersed with Bibi Ashraf's own writings on a variety of moments of her girlhood and womanhood (I clarify as I write whose narration I refer to).

I then turn to Bengali writer, teacher and propagator of girls' education, Rokeya Sakhawat Hossein's (1880–1932) work, *Sultana's Dream*. First published in 1905 in English, the story has been hailed as a "feminist utopia."[3] I read this story to suggest that the invocation of the concept of "Ladyland" employed in the tale contains not only the power of intellectual critique and political imagination, not

---

[1] For a discussion of the *Tahzib un-Niswan* and other Urdu magazines, see Gail Minault, "Making Invisible Women Visible: Studying the History of Muslim Women in South Asia," *South Asia*, Vol. IX. No. 1 (1986). Also by Minault, "Urdu Women's Magazines in the Early Twentieth Century," *Manushi*, No. 48 (September–October 1988); and "Sayyid Mumtaz Ali and 'Huquq un-Niswan: An Advocate of Women's Rights in Islam in the Late Nineteenth Century," *Modern Asian Studies*, Vol. 24, No. 1 (1990).

[2] I owe deep gratitude to C. M. Naim for giving me an Urdu copy of the *Hayat-e Ashraf*, the only autobiographical account of Bibi Ashraf, compiled by Muhammadi Begum (Lahore: Imambara Sayyida Mubarak Begum, n.d.). Translations of the text are mine. Cited as *Hayat-e Ashraf*. I use all the names of Bibi Ashraf in translating the *Hayat*: Ashraf-un-nisa for her girlhood, and Bibi Ashraf, Ustani, Ustani Sahiba, following Muhammadi Begum, in the accounts of her adulthood. See also C. M. Naim, "How Bibi Ashraf Learned to Read and Write," *Annual of Urdu Studies*, No. 6 (1987): 99–115. For a parallel account from Bengal, see the fascinating story of Rashsundari Debi by Tanika Sarkar, "A Book of Her Own, A Life of Her Own: The Autobiography of a Nineteenth Century Woman," in Tanika Sarkar, *Hindu Wife, Hindu Nation*.

[3] Barnita Bagchi (tr. and introduced), *Sultana's Dream and Padmarag: Two Feminist Utopias* (New Delhi, 2005).

just "utopia," but also clear signs of the resistance of women – something that Hossein's life and her achievements as a writer and educator exemplified.

And in the conclusion to this chapter, I use a late-twentieth-century memoir by distinguished feminist scholar, Fatima Mernissi, which speaks to the notions of girlhood, womanhood, and growing up in a *haram* in Fez, Morocco, in the 1940s. Mernissi's *Dreams of Trespass* (1994) not only helps to broaden and deepen my concerns about the question of boundaries and how women create a play in considering limits (*hudud*), it also shows, strikingly, the enormous importance and place of rooftops in the enactment of desires and the self-making of girls and women.

ASHRAF-UN-NISA'S ROOFTOPS

In the opening pages of the *Hayat-e Ashraf* we get a detailed sketch of Ashraf-un-nisa's ancestors and a full picture of her childhood. She was born on September 28, 1840 in a Shi`ah Sayyid family of Bunhera (district of Bijnor) in Uttar Pradesh. Her ancestors came from central Asia and served under the Mughal kings. Bibi Ashraf's father, Sayyid Fateh Hussain, left Bunhera and went to Agra and then to Gwalior to work as a lawyer – a move that his father (Ashraf-un-nisa's grandfather) was so disturbed by that he did not eat for several days. When people congratulated him, he would say, "God has given us so much that we have ten people in our service. Sadly this boy has insulted our family [by taking up a 'profession,' in this case the law]."[4]

Ashraf-un-nisa's grandfather's statements are a telling comment on the principles espoused by respectable Muslims in the early nineteenth century, people who had been employed at the Mughal court for generations and lived a life of a landed gentry, now moving into the ranks of a service gentry.[5] The tension that surfaces between Ashraf-un-nisa's grandfather and father due to the latter's move "to work" serves as an excellent entry point to consider the moral and

---

[4] *Hayat-e Ashraf*, pp. 1–3.
[5] This conversation is an early indication of what for the latter decades of the nineteenth century came to be referred to as the shift from the court to *kachahri* milieu. I discussed this milieu and texts that were much more firmly rooted in the *kachahri* milieu in the last chapter.

customary codes of this society and its implications for a respectable girl-child and woman.

When Ashraf-un-nisa's father left his ancestral home, he did not take his wife and children with him. As C. M. Naim notes, this was "more or less the rule at the time."[6] Bibi Ashraf was eight when her mother died. She and her brother were brought up by their grandparents and paternal uncle and aunt (who according to Muhammadi Begum were unkind to her). Muhammadi Begum, the editor and friend of Bibi Ashraf, suggests that from the time of her mother's death until her marriage, Ashraf-un-nisa's life was "colorless and sad" (*rukha pheeka aur udaas zamana*). Her grandmother was the only person with whom Ashraf-un-nisa shared matters close to her heart: the result, according to Muhammadi Begum, was that she was barely left with child-like desires and playfulness (*bachchon ki si batein aur bachchon ki si umangain*). There was little in the way of playing about or being part of children's fun. Education was also narrowly defined: it had to do with reading the Quran and selected Urdu texts that provided knowledge of the faith and the rules of fasting and prayers, in addition to reading books of *marsiya* (elegies that commemorated the martyrdom of Imam Husain, the grandson of Prophet Muhammad).[7] Bibi Ashraf writes as follows about the time of her girlhood:

> In our family (*khandan*), it was customary to teach the girls to read, but it was strictly forbidden to write. Girls were taught the Quran sharif and Urdu so that they could gain a knowledge of the faith and of keeping fasts and performing the *namaz*. We were six girls in our family. Our grandfather got an *Ustani* (teacher) for us... [The *ustani* lived with the family and was paid ten rupees a month in addition to being provided with food and clothes]. Some other girls from our kinsfolk (*biradari*) also joined us. In this manner, a school started. Although she belonged to a respectable Pathan family, our *Ustani* did not know Urdu... I had heard that the *Ustani* was eleven when she was first married, fifteen when she became a widow, and twelve years later she was married again... But when my grandfather heard this news [of the *ustani*'s second marriage] he was shocked and did not stir out of the house for many days. When people reasoned with him that she was only an employed teacher not a relation, he would respond: "She was nevertheless the teacher of our girls. It shames me if our girls' *Ustani* should marry a second time."[8]

[6] Naim, *Bibi Ashraf*, p. 100.
[7] *Hayat-e Ashraf*, p. 4.
[8] Ibid., pp. 5–7.

Ashraf-un-nisa's girlhood world was one in which there were clear limits to a girl's education and aspirations. The reasons for instruction were limited and strict, and the conventions of social and personal behavior firm. Thus, the *ustani* was dismissed after her second marriage. Ashraf-un-nisa's grandfather refused to employ another teacher, saying that it was not acceptable to him that any "outsider" should come to teach the girls. "It was better that the girls remained ignorant (*jahil*)."

On the other hand, Bibi Ashraf recalls that her mother was more disturbed by the lack of education in her daughter's life than by her own illness. Even in her ill health, the mother taught Ashraf-un-nisa the art of reading the *marsiya* aloud.[9] Within a year of her mother's death, Ashraf-un-nisa had learned to read the Quran. She had also developed a great desire to learn to read Urdu. As she puts it:

> Why was I so eager to read Urdu? In our house, during the forty day observance of Muharram, separate *majalis* [gatherings, in this context religious gatherings] for men and women were held each day. A *majlis* was held each Thursday as well to celebrate the fulfillment of someone's vow. That is why I was so eager to read Urdu. All the women of my family knew Urdu well, and when they gathered ... my female relatives would read aloud from books on issues of faith and religious observances. Listening to them, I learned a lot *by heart* [my emphasis] about these matters, just as one does with stories, but my heart only wanted that somehow I should be blessed (*ni`mat*) with the art of reading.[10]

What followed was much discouragement, along with bits of encouragement from a minority of elders. It is not clear who sought to obstruct Ashraf-un-nisa in her desire to learn with the dismissive remarks, "What will you do by reading?" And, "is it easy to read and to teach how to read?"[11] In all probability, it was with her aunt and grandmother that Ashraf-un-nisa discussed this matter. Her grandmother, as Bibi Ashraf tells the reader, was her main confidante. There is a reference to a conversation with a woman, who on seeing Ashraf-un-nisa cry asks her to leave, saying that if her grandmother saw her favorite girl crying, she would assume that she had been talked to in a severe

[9] Ibid., p. 8. On pages 8–10 we get a most moving account of little Ashraf-un-nissa coming to terms with her mother's death.
[10] Ibid., pp. 11–12.
[11] Ibid, p. 12.

manner (*sakht kaha hoga*). Given Muhmmadi Begum's report in the early pages of the text about the sternness of the aunt, it is likely that the exchange took place with the aunt. We learn later in the account that it was Bibi Ashraf's uncle who was most opposed to her reading. In fact, her father, who was away as mentioned earlier, expressed much pleasure when he came to know about her endeavors and how she taught herself to read.

Nevertheless, Ashraf-un-nisa made a determined and in the end successful effort to learn to read and write. The *Hayat-e Ashraf* records many details of the stipulated boundaries of learning laid down for a girl-child and how she imagined and dealt with the forbidden. It is an exceptional account in providing reflections on how a girl attempted to transcend prescribed limits, by pushing, while inhabiting, the confining structures – and expanding the little spaces that allowed her to cultivate her desires.[12]

> Late one night, as I was engrossed in these thoughts [of how to learn], it occurred to me that if I had a *marsiya* [an elegy, mentioned earlier] or a *salam* or a *mujra* [shorter poems honoring the Prophet and his family], I could put the words together and begin to read. After all, I knew the letters of the alphabet. Not a big thing. Let no one teach me! With this thought, I felt hopeful and courageous and in the morning sent *mama* [the domestic helper] to my friends to say that I needed a few *mujra* and *salam*. And that after having these copied, I would have them sent back. May God bless them for sending me these. But who was to copy them for me?[13]

Ashraf-un-nisa asked her grandmother to get some paper so that she could get her uncle to copy the poems for her. Then she wondered where to hide and make the copies. "If someone came to know of my writing that would be the end!" she tells us.

> I had no mother to cover up for me and writing was strictly forbidden to girls... My aunt was already so angry at my reading the Quran that she would say all sorts of things to me. Thinking all this, I decided that

---

[12] Much of the literature that concerns women's learning in prohibitive circumstances from later nineteenth-century Hindi-Urdu belt (and Bengal) is about mature women's accounts about how they struggled to write. While Bibi Ashraf's account is a retrospective one, it provides a rather unusual window into a girl's thinking, her growing up and her desires.

[13] *Hayat-e Ashraf*, p. 13.

at noon, when everyone was asleep, I would make some ink from the blacking of the griddle (*tawa*) and start copying. I did exactly this. I got the blacking from the kitchen, a lid of the clay pot, and a few twigs from the broom. Thus well equipped, I went up to the roof (*mahal par gayi*), acting as if I was going to rest there. Excitedly I began copying the words. *I cannot describe to you the happiness of that moment...* In this way, I would write every day and then break and throw away the clay pot lids. The women would find the water pots without lids, and wonder and grumble: "Who is this wretch who takes away the lids every day? May god break their hands."[14]

Of course, Bibi Ashraf could not understand, as she tells us, what she was writing. She says she was blinded by this intense desire, but would not stop her "foolish activity" (*nalayaq harkat*). She was scared that her bravery might be considered a sin. Moreover, she declares, she did not realize that one cannot learn without a teacher. "When I could not get anywhere, my crying spells started again. Then God gave me a teacher."[15]

At this time, a relative (the son of Ashraf-un-nisa's grandmother's sister) asked Ashraf-un-nisa's help in learning the lessons of the Quran. "The boy's coming to me for help was how God took pity on my despair and my luck took a turn for the better." One day a book fell out of his bag. Ashraf-un-nisa saw that the writing had no diacritical marks that would help correct pronunciation. It seemed like a book of *marsiya* to her; she asked the boy (unnamed) to read it. She liked it and asked whether he would teach her how to read the book. He refused saying, "I do not have the time. Moreover, the book is very difficult – you will never learn it." Despite Ashraf-un-nisa's gentle coaxing and promises of hard work, he refused. She then said to him: "If you will not teach me this book, I will not help you with your lessons." Given this ultimatum, he relented, and they began reading together. However, they had not even completed three pages of the book when the boy's father sent him to study in Delhi.

Ashraf-un-nisa had not grasped the basics at this point. "He never showed me the syllables and words, nor did he explain the text, but even the little he did was a lot for me." With incredible determination, Ashraf-un-nisa continued to read the book on her own. She would look

---

[14] Ibid., p. 14. Emphasis added.
[15] Ibid., p. 15.

at new words, and if she recognized any familiar letters, she would put them together. In this way, she says, she memorized a whole set of new words and read on, perhaps "half wrong at times."[16] Ashraf-un-nisa managed to read the entire book and used the same method to read other books. "Eventually," says Bibi Ashraf:

> I began to read Urdu fairly well. Then I turned to those *mujre* and *salam* that I had earlier copied down without understanding a word. When I read those copies, you cannot imagine my happiness... As I read my own handwriting, I felt more encouraged and so much more confident. I told myself, whatever a human being gets, it is on the basis of one's own efforts and desire... Then I turned to those broom twigs and the blacking, regarding them as my teachers, I began to copy from different books. After just a few days of practice, I could write from memory. No one, yet, knew the secret of my writing.[17]

Twigs and blacking are exceptional images: literal as well as metaphorical devices through which Ashraf-un-nisa dealt with the obstacles she faced in her desire to learn. Twigs and blacking, in other words, whatever there was at hand, served as her teachers. The terrace, while everyone was asleep downstairs, was the safest place to begin reading and writing. It is a remarkable statement of the initiative, independent thinking and resourcefulness of a girl who was adamant about the fulfillment of her desires. In Ashraf-un-nisa's stealing away of clay pot lids, quietly going away to the rooftops and keeping her talents hidden, the mischief of the girl-child emerges in a striking way: a powerful reminder that even while her girlhood was "colorless and sad (*rukha pheeka aur udaas zamana*)," to re-cite Muhammadi Begum, Ashraf-un-nisa's imagination and liveliness could not be contained.

In time, the fact that Ashraf-un-nisa had begun to read and write became known. "How long could I hide it?" "It was my uncle I had been most scared of, for he strongly disapproved of women learning to write. When he had gone to Gwalior [after the death of his wife, he joined Ashraf-un-nisa's father], I began to write openly. No one objected." "On the contrary," she says, "my writing skills were viewed as a novelty by my relatives. Whenever any woman had the need to send a letter, she would get it written by me..." And when she wrote

---

[16] Ibid. p. 16.
[17] Ibid., p. 17.

letters for them, she adds, "women would disclose to me their inner-most secrets (*poshida raz*), things that they would never speak in front of others... I could, however, understand only a tenth part of what I was told."[18]

Clearly, Ashraf-un-nisa was an excellent young learner. She helped the young boy with learning the Quran, and then wrote letters for women and shared their secrets – sensing through their demeanor per-haps that they were telling secrets, even though Ashraf-un-nisa did not fully understand what their confidential telling was about. A homoso-cial community of women comes clearly into view when Ashraf-un-nisa begins to write letters for women. And while she was busy using the exact same form of address (*alqab*) in the letters, regardless of the age and relationship of the addressee (which leads to a very funny exchange between a woman and her husband) – "*Barkhudar, nur-e chashm, rahat-e jaan, qurrat-ul-`ayn, tul `umra*, roughly translatable as "Young man, light of my eyes, comfort of my life, the core of my vision, may your life be long" – the women kept divulging their inner-most secrets (*poshida raz*) to her.[19] The reader of the *Hayat* can only imagine what these secrets might have been. (One more time, Azra's reminiscences are suggestive, as she describes how older aunts and cousins shared with young Azra the burdens of their marriages, among them the tough strictures their husbands laid down regarding money and the running of the households within a balanced budget!).

Bibi Ashraf was seventeen when the Mutiny against British colonial rule occurred in 1857. At this time, she mentions that all exchange of letters came to a halt. For nearly eighteen months, they received no news from her father, nor he from them. When peace returned, her father sent a man to get news of the family. When the man was return-ing to Gwalior, Ashraf-un-nisa's grandmother sent a letter for her son that she had had written by her brother. Ashraf-un-nisa gave a letter too, and wrote all that she had heard or seen during the Mutiny.

> My father was delighted when he read my letter. He wrote saying that the letter written by his uncle [Ashraf-un-nisa's grandmother's brother] gave him the news only of the family members. He did not write about other relatives or about the happenings of the Mutiny. The letter from

[18] Ibid., p. 18.
[19] Ibid., pp. 18–19.

the girl however made me very happy. She wrote all that she had seen or heard herself. Her letter gave me the pleasure that I get from a newspaper or a history book. I read her letter every day. But tell me who taught her to write?[20]

Ashraf-un-nisa's grandmother did the explaining: "Till this date, no one has taught her. She has learned through her own efforts and desire." Then, explains Bibi Ashraf, she wrote for her father the whole story of learning to read and write and of her "intense desire" to learn. He rewarded her by sending her an expensive quilt and several sets of clothes. "But my uncle was very angry when he found out that I had learned to write. He sent me a disapproving letter, and never forgave me so long as he lived."[21]

In Asraf-un-nisa's father's comments, we discern the unusualness of her writing. Clearly, her letters were nondomestic – he says they read like newspapers or history books: she had written everything that she had "seen or heard during the Mutiny." A firsthand, historical report. Conspicuously, her granduncle (grandmother's brother) gave Ashraf-un-nisa's father news only of the family. There is an attention-grabbing reversal of roles here. Classically, family news would be conveyed by the woman. Importantly, this episode also suggests – like Ashraf-un-nisa's inventive use of blacking and twigs and clay pots – her unusual thinking, reflection on the world around her and pushing the bounds as far as they could go, even while remaining within the confines of the domestic world. The *Hayat-e Ashraf* describes superbly how Ashraf-un-nisa continued to draw on her ingenious potential, negotiating inherited limits throughout her adult life.

When Ashraf-un-nisa was growing up, a girl-child from a respectable family was usually engaged to be married almost at the time of her birth. Numerous restrictions followed as she grew older. The passages that I have translated pertain to Bibi Ashraf's recollections of the period between 1840, when she was born, and 1859 when, at nineteen, she was married to her second cousin, Sayyid Alamdar Husain (the younger son of one of her grandfather's brothers), and went to Lahore to live with him. Her husband was a talented man and a good

---

[20] Ibid., pp. 19–20.
[21] Ibid., p. 20.

human being. They were both religious and observed their religious duties (*paaband-i shari'at*). Bibi Ashraf skillfully managed the domestic affairs (*khubi aur saliqe se*), as the later sections of her autobiography and biography make clear.

In the *Hayat-e Ashraf*, we learn that Bibi Ashraf had one son and three daughters. Of these, the son and one daughter died very young. Two daughters, Jafri Begum and Ahmadi Begum, lived until a few years after their father's death in 1870. Eleven years into her marriage, when Bibi Ashraf was thirty, she became a widow. Just before her husband's death, her beloved grandmother passed away. In 1871, her father died as well.[22] Captain W. R. M. Holroyd, the director of public instruction in the Punjab, a senior official in the same service as her husband, offered Bibi Ashraf a job and her two daughters a scholarship each to continue their education. She declined the job, but accepted the scholarships for her daughters. Muhammadi Begum gives us the particulars of these hard times in Bibi Ashraf's life. Events in the next few years increased her sadness enormously. Her two remaining daughters and a grandson also passed away. For years, Bibi Ashraf mourned the loss of her two daughters.

In 1878, she was offered a teaching job again. This time, she accepted. She became a teacher at the Victoria Girls School in Lahore, and strove to improve its reputation, eventually becoming its head teacher and helping expand the school to the Middle level.[23] Again, in the words of Muhammadi Begum:

> In those days ... the respectable [*shurafa*] families were cautious about sending their girls to school... As soon as she [Bibi Ashraf] arrived, the situation changed completely and those that condemned the school began sending their daughters with pleasure. Until now, there had only been a few younger girls in the school, and there was only one palanquin [*doli*] for transportation. When the number of girls increased ... the number of palanquins rose to seven... Until each girl reached home, Bibi Ashraf [whom now Muhmmadi Begum addresses as *Ustani* or *Ustani Sahiba*] would not leave... The superintendent of the school [a woman] always worked in consultation with her... And

---

[22] Ibid., pp. 20, 22, 23, 24.
[23] Ibid., pp. 26, 27, 31, 34. Middle level would mean beyond the primary and junior school, going as far as standard VIII. Standard IX and X would be high school.

respectable women visiting from London or America always came to her place to visit.[24]

Several changes took place during Bibi Ashraf's tenure as head of the school. Earlier, Muslim girls had to go out (perhaps to another location, although this is not stated clearly in the text) to learn mathematics from a Hindu teacher. Bibi Ashraf had a Muslim woman teacher employed in the school. Again, the inspectors who conducted the annual examinations as well as reviews of schools were often men: with Bibi Ashraf's efforts, several women (*ladiyan*, literally "ladies") came to serve as examiners and inspectors for Victoria Girls School. Muhammadi Begum notes that *Ustani Sahiba* treated her students just like her children. "I have seen myself how much she loved ʿUmda Begum. And once she told me that ʿUmda Begum is like my own daughter... Like mothers and daughters share the burdens of the world, exactly like that the *Ustani* and her students share their sorrows and joys (*dukh-sukh*) and discuss all kinds of matters with each other."[25]

On May 7, 1903, Bibi Ashraf passed away at the age of sixty-three. In noting her habits, lifestyle and everyday life, Muhammadi Begum helps create a picture of Bibi Ashraf as an unpretentious, religious, loving, open and compassionate human being.[26] If there is a term that captures Bibi Ashraf as an individual, it is the one that Muhammadi Begum uses for her in the discussion of the aftermath of the death of her two daughters: the phrase is *sabr-i jamil*. It is a difficult concept to translate, but let me attempt to convey something of its meaning by citing Muhammadi Begum's reflections while discussing this term. Who can we think of in the world who has had no troubles, and after much lamentation has not returned to silence, Muhammadi Begum asks. Rather than complaining endlessly, to face one's problems, to console one's heart by thinking about the difficulties of our ancestors, and to thank and accept the ways of God, to leave our fate in the hands of God, to forget one's hardships by thinking about others (*ghair*), and to participate in their joys and sorrows, is *sabr-i jamil*. "In all this, Bubu Sahiba [Bibi Ashraf] was an unparalleled model to be followed [*benazir aur qabil-i taqlid*] by the women."[27]

[24] Ibid., pp. 35–36.
[25] Ibid., pp. 36, 37, 38.
[26] Ibid., pp. 42–43. Translations of terms used by Muhammadi Begum.
[27] Ibid., p. 33.

Bibi Ashraf's *sabr-i jamil*, expressed in her relationships with a variety of women, stands out in her recollections as well as in Muhammadi Begum's parallel writing in the *Hayat*. Muhammadi Begum notes that when Bibi Ashraf's husband was alive, they did not host a very large number of religious gatherings: instead, he would give alms for religious purposes to the Imambara at Lahore. After his death, Bibi Ashraf began hosting religious gatherings for women (*zanani majlisain*) and their numbers increased rapidly. It was an expensive affair: the palanquins that brought women to the gatherings cost eighty to ninety rupees. Often, women stayed on after the event. Bibi Ashraf would look after them, providing meals and hospitality. The respectable families of the city would send their daughters and women to her place without any reservation; in fact, they felt special pride in doing so.[28]

Muhammadi Begum describes her own relationship with Bibi Ashraf with great tenderness. "She and I," says Muhammadi Begum, "have such love that it is like love between close relations." They met for the first time on March 20, 1898: in that first meeting, Bibi Ashraf met her with great affection, sat next to her and talked for a long time. And then their meetings became more frequent. They visited each other several times. "Whenever I went to Victoria Girls School," recalls Muhammadi Begum, "she would get up from her chair and insist that I sit on her chair. 'I will sit on the floor,' she would say. How could I make such a mistake in the majesty of this older Bibi that I should sit above and she on the floor. Finally, the decision used to be that we would both sit on the floor. As long as I stayed, she remained right next to me, not leaving even for a minute. And she was never happy at my leaving. 'Sit for a little longer,' she would urge."[29]

A close student of Bibi Ashraf's told Muhammadi Begum that people used to tell Bibi Ashraf that it is a sin (*gunah*) for a Shi'ah to love a Sunni person. But Bibi Ashraf would respond that she had a deep affection for Muhammadi: even if she was Shi'ah, "I will keep her in my heart." As I have mentioned, she wrote several pieces for the journal *Tahzib-un-Niswan*, edited by Muhammadi Begum.[30] Muhammadi

---

[28] Ibid., pp. 45, 46, 51.
[29] Ibid., pp. 52, 53.
[30] Ibid., p. 56.

Begum lists these in the *Hayat-e Ashraf*.[31] Bibi Ashraf also wrote a
glowing response to Muhammadi Begum when the latter sent her two
of her books, *Anmol Moti* and *Safia Begum*. Indeed, she bought fifty
copies of each of the books and had them included in the curriculum
of the Victoria Girls School.[32]

   Ashraf-un-nisa's journeys to the rooftop, teaching herself to read
and write with the aid of the twigs of a broom stick, blacking and clay
lids, was the beginning of her inching out of the familial and customary practices that commanded that girls and women must not read
or write. It is noteworthy how many women, with the exception only
of her aunt, as we are told in the *Hayat*, came to her side, marveling,
intrigued, yet celebrating her learning. The extraordinary strength of
mind and inventiveness that Bibi Ashraf displayed in learning to read
and write stayed with her throughout her life. As her autobiography
demonstrates, she continued to make passages for a better and creative
life – in her own familial life, in her school career, in her friendships
with women (*sabr-i jamil*, especially for women), and for us, in the
legacy of the writing that she left behind.

   Let me move from this portrait of the real life and struggles of a
girl-child and woman in the middle and later nineteenth century to the
imaginary world of another woman in the early twentieth century –
an imaginary world that nonetheless recalls for us many of the same
(small and hidden) spaces, and similar moments of everyday struggle
and freedom.

ROKEYA'S LADYLAND

   One evening ... I am not sure whether I dozed off or not. But, as far as I
   remember, I was wide awake... All of a sudden a lady stood before me...
   I took her for my friend, Sister Sara. I used to have my walks with Sister
   Sara, when we were in Darjeeling ...in the Botanical Gardens there. I
   fancied Sister Sara had probably come to take me to some such garden,
   and I readily accepted her offer and went out with her. When walking,
   I found to my surprise that it was a fine morning! The town was fully
   awake and the streets alive with bustling crowds. I was feeling very shy,
   thinking I was walking in the street in broad daylight, but there was not
   a single man visible. "I feel somewhat awkward," I said [to sister Sara]

[31] Ibid., p. 55.
[32] Ibid., pp. 61, 62, 63.

in a rather apologizing tone, "as being a *pardahnishin* [veiled] woman I am not accustomed to walking about unveiled." "You need not be afraid of coming across a man here [replied sister Sara]. This is Ladyland, free from sin and harm. Virtue herself reigns here."[33]

Sultana's story begins this way, with a dream – although we are not sure it is a dream, or a half-dream, whether it is day or night: and, by extension, whether the world Sultana is taking us to with Sister Sara is real or imaginary. It is such a play with borderlands that is at the heart of Rokeya Sakhawat Hosain's turn-of-the-century short story, *Sultana's Dream*, in which she juxtaposes two kinds of worlds with the roles of men and women strikingly reversed.

> By and by I was enjoying the scenery. Really it was very grand. I took a patch of green grass for a velvet cushion! "How nice it is!" said I. "Do you like it?" asked Sister Sara... "Yes, very much: but I do not like to tread on the tender and sweet flowers!" ... "The whole place looks like a garden," said I admiringly... "Your Calcutta could become a nicer garden than this, if only your countrymen wanted to make it so." ... I became very curious to know where the men were. I met more than a hundred women while walking there, but not a single man! "Where are the men?" [asked Sultana] "In their proper places, where they ought to be." ... "We shut our men indoors." "Just as we are kept in the zenana?" "Exactly so."[34]

In this setting, Sultana begins a contemplation on the condition of women in India. When she realizes that men and women had reversed roles in Ladyland, she says to Sara, "we have no hand or voice in the management of our social affairs. In India man is lord and master. He has taken to himself all powers and privileges and shut up the woman in the zenana." Sara asks Sultana why the women allow themselves to be shut up; Sultana gives an argument about male strength. Sara explains to her: "A lion is stronger than a man, but it does not enable him to dominate the human race. You have neglected the duty you owe yourselves and you have lost your natural rights by shutting your eyes to your own interests." Sara proclaims that men should be put in the *zenana*, but Sultana wonders what would happen to the business of the world: "even if this were done, would all their business – political and commercial – also go with them to the zenana!"[35]

[33] Mrs. R. S. Hossein, *Sultana's Dream* (Calcutta, 1908, Facsimile edition; rpt. Dhaka, 2005), pp. 1, 2–3, 4–5.
[34] Hossein, *Sultana's Dream*, pp. 5, 6–7.
[35] Ibid., pp. 9, 10, 11.

At this point in their conversation, Sultana and Sara reach the latter's house, which is neatly organized, and Sara explains to her how she manages embroidery as well as office work. Sultana says, "I [also] learnt that they [inhabitants of the Ladyland] were not subject to any kind of epidemic disease – nor did they suffer from mosquito-bites as we do! I was very much astonished to hear that in Ladyland no one died in youth except by rare accident."[36]

Beginning with this exchange in the story, Rokeya Sakhawat Hossein foregrounds the debates in late colonial India on civilization and reform, and issues of hygiene and health, by presenting Sister Sara as a symbol of colonialism. The name Sister Sara itself is a provocative device. Sister, a missionary woman: Sister Sara attempting to "convert" Sultana. As we shall see, the story centers on Sara's (colonialism's) influential attempts to have Sultana modify her thinking and consider possibilities for an altered set of gender relations.

The next steps in the story center on Sultana observing the vegetable garden, a "clean and bright kitchen [no smoke, since a proper chimney was installed]," the cooking carried out with the aid of solar heat, and so on.[37] On seeing Sultana's wonderment about solar heat and how the people gathered the energy of the sun, Sara recounts an episode prefaced by a reference to the reforms that were at center stage during the reign of Queen Victoria. (It is not surprising that the queen, the most visible symbol of women's power and inventiveness in many texts from late nineteenth century – especially notable in the texts in Chapter 5 – is important here too). As a preface to the story about solar energy, Sara explains how the queen believed in science and in girls' education. She notes that early marriage was stopped by the queen. "No woman was allowed to be married before she was twenty-one. I must tell you before this change we had been kept in strict purdah... But the seclusion is the same... In a few years we had separate Universities, where no men were admitted." Then Sara tells Sultana that in one of the two (women's) universities the students invented a wonderful balloon; attached to it were a number of pipes, by means of which they drew as much water as possible from the atmosphere. "The ingenious Lady Principal stopped rains and storms

[36] Ibid., pp. 11, 12, 13, 14.
[37] Ibid., pp. 14–15.

thereby." When the other university came to know about the balloon, its students tried something even more extraordinary. They invented an instrument and collected as much solar heat as they wanted. Sara continued, "While the women were engaging in scientific researches, the men of this country were busy increasing their military power." When they came to know of the inventions of the female universities, "they only laughed at the members of the Universities and called the whole thing 'a sentimental nightmare!'"[38]

Sultana was, however, still fascinated by the entrapment of men in the *zenana*. "But tell me," she asks Sara, "how you managed to put the men of your country into the zenana. Did you entrap them first? ... It is not likely that they would surrender their free and open air life of their own accord and confine themselves within the four walls of the zenana." "No, not by arms... By brain... Women's brains are somewhat quicker than men's." Sara then relates the episode about how the men went into the *zenana*.[39]

Ten years prior, when the military officers had ridiculed women's scientific discoveries, the women wanted to reply, but the lady principals advised them to respond not by word, but by deed, if they had an opportunity. The opportunity came soon. Sara recounts that on account of the queen's decision not to hand over political prisoners to a certain king, who demanded them from the "kind-hearted Queen," (it is unclear which king this is, we are only told that the political offenders came from his realm), he declared war "against our country." In this war, "nearly all men had gone out to fight; even a boy of sixteen was not left at home." So a meeting of wise women was held at the queen's palace to decide how to save the land. Finally, after much thinking, interspersed with moments of hopelessness, the lady principal who had devised the means of storing solar heat came up with a plan.[40]

This was the plan: "Before we [women] go out the men must enter the zenana," she said to the queen. "On the following day the Queen called upon all men to retire into zenanas for the sake of honour and liberty. Wounded and tired as they were, they took that order rather for a boon! They bowed low and entered the zenanas without uttering

---

[38] Ibid., pp. 16–19.
[39] Ibid., pp. 19–21.
[40] Ibid., pp. 22–25.

a single word of protest." Meanwhile, the lady principal marched with her two thousand students to the battlefield and "directed all the rays of the concentrated sun-light and heat towards the enemy... They all ran away panic-stricken... Since then no one has tried to invade our country any more." "And since then your country-men never tried to come out of the zenana?" asks Sultana. Sara answers, "Her Royal Highness sent them a circular letter intimating to them that if their services should ever be needed they would be sent for, and that in the meanwhile they should remain where they were."[41]

Sultana, on hearing this account from Sara, exclaims: "How my friends at home will be amused and amazed, when I go back and tell them that in the far-off Ladyland, ladies rule over the country and control all social matters, while gentleman are kept in the Murdanas [*mardana*, men's section] to mind babies, to cook and to do all sorts of domestic work!"[42]

Sultana's Dream was first published in 1905 in a Madras-based English periodical, *The Indian Ladies Magazine*. In 1930, years after the story was published, Rokeya recollected that her husband, Khan Bahadur Syed Sakhawat Hossein, a deputy magistrate, was away on a tour, and she wrote the story "to pass the time." Although she knew Urdu (spoken in the district of Bhagalpur, Bihar, where her husband was stationed), Bengali was her main language. She wrote the story in English to demonstrate her proficiency in the language to her husband who was always urging her to read and write English. Her husband read the story "without even bothering to sit down. 'A terrible revenge!' he said when he was finished."[43]

Rokeya's life story is important in understanding the vision she sets out in *Sultana's Dream*. She was born in 1880 in Pairaband, a small village in the north of present-day Bangladesh. Her mother, Rahatunnessa Sabera Chowdhurani, was the first of the four wives of her father, Zahiruddin Mohammad Abu Ali Saber, "an extravagant and extremely conservative zemindar." Zahiruddin, who knew seven languages, allowed his two sons to study Bangla and English, but

---

[41] Ibid., pp. 25–28.
[42] Ibid., p. 30.
[43] Roushan Jahan, "Sultana's Dream": Purdah Reversed, in Roushan Jahan (ed. and tr.), *Sultana's Dream and Selections from The Secluded Ones* (New York, 1988), pp. 1–2.

when it came to his daughters, he followed the practice among the elite
Bengali Muslims of the time: they recited the Quran and read a few
primers to do with ideal comportment of women "written in Urdu, the
language of Muslim elite in northern India." Rokeya and her elder sister, Karimunnessa, were not encouraged to read and write in Bangla.
"Karimunnessa used to squat in the inner courtyard of their house and
draw the Bangla alphabet on the ground with a stick, under the super-
vision of her younger brother... Once when she was deeply engrossed
in reading Bangla *Puthi*, her father discovered her. She nearly fainted
in fear."[44]

Karimunnessa, who had an avid desire for reading, was married off
at fifteen, but she continued to encourage Rokeya to read and write
Bangla. Rokeya also got great support from her brother, Ibrahim Saber,
in her efforts at educating herself. This education continued after her
marriage. Rokeya was married to Syed Sakhawat Hossein in 1896
when she was sixteen. They had two daughters, both of whom died.
"Sakhawat was a man of liberal attitude who wanted from his wife
not the traditional duty and obedience but love and sympathy; he not
only loved her, he was also proud of her." He died on May 3, 1909,
leaving Rokeya her share of the property and a "considerable portion
of his savings, to be spent on women's education." In 1911, Rokeya
opened the Sakhawat Memorial Girls School in Calcutta, with only
eight girls enrolled initially. By 1915, the number of girls had risen to
eighty-four.[45]

Rokeya's efforts in making sure that girls were educated – and
all that she went through as a teacher of Sakhawat Memorial Girls
School – can be usefully read alongside *Sultana's Dream*. In this early
literary moment, she seeks to negotiate the structures of power and
inherited prescriptions with the help of the potent and playful concept
of "Ladyland" – imagining the world upside down.

While "Ladyland" represents an allegory of the overturning of patriarchal society, Rokeya's "factual reportage" in the 1929 *The Secluded
Ones* (*Avarodhbasini* in Bengali), a collection of forty-seven anecdotes

---

[44] Roushan Jahan, "Rokeya: An Introduction to Her Life," in Roushan Jahan (ed. and
tr.), *Sultana's Dream and Selections*, pp. 37–38. *Puthi* usually contains religious literature written in the form of a pamphlet. It can also be a tale written in verse.
[45] Roushan Jahan, 'Rokeya', pp. 38–41.

documenting *purdah* customs among Hindu and Muslim women, presents the oppressive, "real-life" difficulties of girls and women in seclusion.[46]

When *The Secluded Ones* appeared, it shocked many people who were unfamiliar with the strictness of *purdah* customs, as well as sections of Muslim society who had prided themselves on the supposedly more liberal treatment of Muslim women when compared to the Hindus. "Yet," as her editor Roushan Jahan puts it, "within a short time, the detractors lost the battle. Rokeya's cause was upheld by younger, educated Muslims, both male and female. *The Secluded Ones* became a sourcebook to them while Rokeya became a source of inspiration."[47]

Report 47 of *The Secluded Ones* is instructive when placed by the side of *Sultana's* (Rokeya's?) *Dream*. In this juxtaposition, we have on the one hand the "real" testimony of women's incarceration, and on the other the dream of their freedom in the literary construction of Ladyland – a metaphorical space (a rooftop) that harbors the hope of converting a dream into a reality. It was only three years earlier, Rokeya tells us in Report 47, that they got their first school bus. "The day before the bus came, one of our teachers, an Englishwoman, had gone to the auto depot to inspect the bus. Her comment was, 'This bus is horribly dark inside. Oh, no! I'll never ride that bus!'"

Indeed, except for a narrow latticework on top of the back and front entrances, the bus was "completely airtight." On the first afternoon, when the bus took the girls to their homes, "some of them vomited." Others "were whimpering in the dark." That evening, writes Rokeya, Mrs. Mukherjee, a Hindu friend who came to visit, said mockingly, "What a fine bus you have! The first time I saw it, I thought a huge chest was being drawn on wheels. My nephew ran out and said, 'The moving black hole of Calcutta is passing by! ... How can the girls possibly ride that bus?'" On the afternoon of the third day, the mothers of several of the pupils complained, "You are burying the girls alive!" To Rokeya's rejoinder that she was at a loss – "If the bus was not such, you would have been the ones to criticize the bus as 'purdahless'" – they retorted angrily, "What? Do you want to maintain purdah at the

---

[46] Roushan Jahan, *Sultana's Dream and Selections*, p. viii.
[47] Roushan Jahan, *The Secluded Ones*, pp. 22–23.

expense of our children's lives? We are not going to send our daughters to your school anymore!"

The next evening, however, brought a completely different response. Rokeya received four letters, one in English, signed "Brother-in-Islam," the other three in Urdu. Two of the four were anonymous, and one of them had five signatures. "For the continuing welfare of my school," writes a harried Rokeya, "they were informing me that the two curtains hanging by the side of the bus moved in the breeze and made the bus purdahless. If something better was not arranged by tomorrow, they would be compelled, for the benefit of the school, to write in the various newspapers about this purdahlessness and would stop the girls from riding in such a purdahless bus."[48]

It is not entirely clear whether Rokeya Sakhawat Hossain was seeking to make a comment here on the greater liberalism of the English and of educated Hindus when compared with Muslims. What is clear is that she was pointing to the continuous difficulty of confronting inherited patriarchal structures and gender expectations. While Rokeya's aspiration (dreams) for the education of girls turned into a notable reality, the challenge of finding the appropriate conditions for that education remained constant. In Report 47, Rokeya compels the reader to see the impossibility of the demands made by society, strikingly presented in the women's complaints as well as in the letters. Nothing suffices: there is too much *purdah*, and there isn't enough!

For Rokeya, Ladlyand was a conception of men and women being together in difference while reversing the traditional gender roles. In Report 47 as well as in *Sultana's Dream*, the reader sees Rokeya's playfulness in bringing together critique, norm and utopia, and the importance of working with all three. Rokeya struggles with the idea of alternatives for women in *Sultana's Dream*: Sultana is both amazed and impressed by Ladlyand, and at the same time does not quite find the idea of men's incarceration viable. The end of the story is staggering precisely because it remains inconclusive and open-ended, thereby suggesting several possibilities for the future. Sultana opened her eyes: "I found myself in my own bedroom lounging in the easy chair."[49] A dream thus becomes a space – like the forest and the rooftops – where

---

[48] Roushan Jahan, *The Secluded Ones*, pp. 34–35.
[49] Hossein, *Sultana's Dream*, p. 38.

people's hopes are lived out, but from where they, especially women, have to turn back to spaces of discipline and pedagogy.

FATIMA'S FORBIDDEN TERRACE

"Happiness ... is inconceivable without a terrace," writes Fatima Mernissi in *Dreams of Trespass*, a girlhood memoir about her growing up in a *haram* in Fez, Morocco, in the 1940s, at the same time as Azra. However, she goes on to note, "not all the terraces of Fez were meant to be accessible; the highest ones normally were declared off-limits, because you could die if you fell off of them. Nonetheless, I dreamed constantly of visiting our forbidden terrace, which was the highest one on our street, and one where no child had ever been seen, as far as I could remember."[50]

The point that Fatima Mernissi draws attention to in this seemingly simple recollection of what she calls "The Forbidden Terrace," the title of her chapter, is that there was a lot at stake in the idea of terraces for the girl-child, girls – and women – living within the boundaries of tradition, in many kinds of physical, mental and communal confinements in Fez. The terrace, a spatial metaphor for freedom, for accessing denied spaces, for the exercise of individuality and choice, has at its core the principle of *hudud*: the "sacred frontier ... trespassing [of which] leads only to sorrow and unhappiness," as Fatima was reminded again and again.[51] In the opening chapter of her memoir of girlhood, entitled "My Harem Frontiers," she introduces the subject of prescribed limits for a girl-child growing up in a *haram*. "When Allah created the earth, said Father, he separated men from women... Harmony exists when each group respects the prescribed limits of the other; trespassing leads only to sorrow and unhappiness." "But," she recalls, "women dreamed of trespassing all the time."[52]

Around Fatima, it was not just men, but women too who expressed their views clearly on *hudud* or the sacred frontier. Fatima greatly admired Aunt Habiba, "who had been cast off and sent away suddenly for no reason by a husband she loved dearly, said that Allah had sent the Northern armies to Morocco to punish the men for violating the

[50] Mernissi, *Dreams of Trespass*, p. 145.
[51] Ibid, pp. 1–2.
[52] Ibid.

hudud protecting women. When you hurt a woman, you are violating Allah's sacred frontier." Lalla Tam (*lalla*, a title of respect for women), the headmistress of the Koranic School that Fatima joined at age three, explained that education meant learning all about *hudud*. Cousin Malika, two years older than Fatima, said "she knew for sure ... that everything would work out fine" if Fatima obeyed the teacher. Then there was Fatima's "rebellious" mother who "rejected male superiority as nonsense and totally anti-Muslim – 'Allah made us equal.'" When the events and exchanges around Fatima troubled her, she would often talk with Yasmina, her maternal grandmother, who lived on a "beautiful farm with cows and sheep and endless fields of flowers, one hundred kilometers west of us, between Fez and the Ocean."[53]

Lalla Thor, the co-wife of Yasmina, intrigued Fatima. "I asked Yasmina what that meant, to be stuck in a haram, and she gave me several answers, which of course only confused me." Fatima's grandfather, Yasmina's husband, had eight co-wives, "which meant," as Fatima puts it, "that she [Yasmina] had to sleep alone for eight nights before she could hug and snuggle with him for one. 'And hugging and snuggling your husband is wonderful,' she said. 'I am so happy your generation will not have to share husbands anymore.'"[54] Her paternal grandmother, who lived in the *haram* with Fatima and her parents in the city, was, on the other hand, a feared figure. She "appreciated being respected, that is to say, being left alone to sit elegantly dressed in her bejeweled headdress, and look silently out into the courtyard." She was the matriarch whose authority Fatima's mother strongly contested.[55]

Thus there were many kinds of frontiers, the meanings of which unfolded for Fatima in the conversations among women and in the discussion of various dramatic events during her girlhood years in a Fez *haram*. Apart from the women noted earlier, Fatima's cousins, Malika, Samir and Chama, were central to her thinking about frontiers, as were the storytelling sessions with her mother and those that Aunt Habiba led "upstairs." As Fatima puts it:

> I would sit on our threshold and look at our house as if I had never seen it before... When you lifted your eyes towards the sky, you could see

[53] Ibid., pp. 3, 9, 24.
[54] Ibid., pp. 33–34.
[55] Ibid., p. 7.

an elegant two-story structure with the top floors repeating the square arched colonnade of the courtyard... And finally, you had the sky – hanging up above but still strictly square-shaped, like all the rest, and solidly framed in a wooden frieze of fading gold-and-ocher geometric design. Looking at the sky from the courtyard was an overwhelming experience ... the movement of the early morning stars, fading slowly in the deep blue and white, became so intense that it could make you dizzy ... oh, I almost forgot the stairs. Lodged in the four corners of the courtyard, they were important because even grownups could play a sort of gigantic hide-and-go-seek on them, running up and down their glazed green steps.[56]

The open, limitless sky, access to the roof through stairs, journeys upstairs/downstairs – and the "invisible wings" Fatima was told that all women had[57] – all these are vital metaphors in Fatima's memoir about her girlhood. *Hudud* remains a constant presence in her consciousness, as does the idea of a girl-child growing up too quickly (*itni badi*) in Azra's. Fatima encounters the idea of the sacred frontier or the *haram* in the mind ("The Harem Within" is the title of chapter 7 of her memoir) in a variety of ways. The following exchange between Fatima and Yasmina, her grandmother, illustrates the point powerfully.

The word "harem," she [Yasmina] said, was a slight variation of the word *haram*, the forbidden, the proscribed. It was the opposite of *halal*, the permissible. Harem was the place where a man sheltered his family... The farm ... was a harem, although it did not have walls. "You only need walls, if you have streets!" But if you decided ... to live in the countryside, then you didn't need gates, because you were in the middle of the fields and there were no passersby... Any space you entered [however] had its own invisible rules, and you needed to figure them out. "And when I say space," she continued, "it can be any space – a courtyard, a terrace, or a room, or a street for that matter. Wherever there are human beings, there is a *qa'ida*, or invisible rule. If you stick to *qa'ida*, nothing bad can happen to you." ... Then she added something which really scared me: "Unfortunately, most of the time, the *qa'ida* is against women."[58]

Fatima witnessed how women challenged the frontiers and the *qa'ida*. She tells the reader how much her mother hated communal

[56] Ibid., pp. 4–5.
[57] Ibid., p. 22.
[58] Ibid., pp. 61–62.

life, especially eating at fixed times. "She would nag Father constantly about the possibility of breaking loose and taking our immediate family to live apart. The nationalists advocated the end of seclusion and the veil, but they did not say a word about a couple's right to split off from their larger family. In fact, most of the leaders still lived with their parents."[59] Two important decisions that Fatima's mother made challenged the traditional, behind-the-walls setup – and the authority of the matriarch who was at its center, enforcing strict guidelines and order.

> Mother especially disliked the idea of a fixed lunch hour. She always was the last to wake up, and liked to have a late, lavish breakfast which she prepared herself with a lot of flamboyant defiance, beneath the disapproving stare of Grandmother Lalla Mani. She would make herself scrambled eggs and *baghrir*, or fine crepes, topped with pure honey and fresh butter, and, of course, plenty of tea. She usually ate at exactly eleven, just as Lalla Mani was about to begin her purification ritual for the noon prayer. And after that, two hours later at the communal table, Mother was often absolutely unable to eat lunch. Sometimes, she would skip it altogether, especially when she wanted to annoy Father, because to skip a meal was considered terribly rude and too openly individualistic.[60]

Fatima's mother had revolutionary dreams: living alone with her family was one of them. "Whoever heard of ten birds living together squashed into a single nest?" she would ask. She argued endlessly with her husband. "What a waste of time ... these endless discussions about meals! Arabs would be much better off if they let each individual decide what he or she wanted to swallow." But Fatima's father would say that he "just could not break away." He would reason with Fatima's mother: "we live in difficult times, the country is occupied by foreign armies, our culture is threatened. All we have left is these traditions." And Fatima's mother would retort: "Do you think that by sticking together in this big, absurd house, we will gain the strength we need to throw the foreign armies out? ... This tradition is choking me." "So Father kept offering compromises," Fatima recalls. "He not only arranged for mother to have her own food stock, but also brought her things he knew she liked... She could make all the desserts

59 Ibid., pp. 75–76.
60 Ibid., p. 76.

and cookies she wanted, but she was not supposed to prepare a meat dish or a major meal. That would have meant the beginning of the end of the communal arrangement. Her flamboyantly prepared individual breakfasts were enough of a slap in the face to the rest of the family." Every now and then, Fatima's mother got away with preparing a full meal, but "she had to not only be discreet ... but also give it some sort of exotic name. Her most common ploy was to camouflage the meal as a nighttime picnic on the terrace."[61]

These "moonlight nights of laughter" are recounted tenderly by Fatima Mernissi:

> We would be transplanted to the terrace, like nomads, with mattresses, tables, trays, and my little brother's cradle... Mother would be absolutely out of her mind with joy. No one else from the courtyard dared to show up, because they understood all too well that Mother was fleeing from the crowd... Before long, she would start acting foolishly, like a girl, and soon, Father would chase her all around the terrace... Sometimes both of them made up games which included my sister and Samir [her cousin's brother] who was the only one of the rest of the family allowed to attend our moonlit gatherings and myself. More often, they completely forgot about the rest of the world... After these blissful evenings, mother would be in an unusually soft and quiet mood for a whole week.[62]

Fatima's mother's "yearning for privacy" was actualized week after week on the terrace. Yet it is striking to note that, in Fatima's words, "what she enjoyed most was trying to get Father to depart from his conventional self-controlled pose."[63] And she did. On moonlit nights the roof of the *haram* turned into a place of play and joy where the mother had the chance of being a girl and making her husband a playful boy. And by their side were the young Mernissi children, joyful witnesses to the games of the playful elders. This moment of pleasure and privacy was critical to Fatima's mother. As she often said to her after the picnics on the roof, "I want my daughters' lives to be exciting ... very exciting and filled with one hundred percent happiness, nothing more, nothing less."[64]

---

[61] Ibid., pp. 76, 78–79.
[62] Ibid., p. 79.
[63] Ibid.
[64] Ibid., pp. 79–80.

Fatima's activities as a child in the *haram* reinforced her desire to understand and get "one hundred percent happiness." Her perceptive observations of the spaces of freedom in her *haram* girlhood, and the sophistication with which she ties such spaces to everyday life, as we have noted, is only one demonstration of the rich resources she had as a girl-child: how she thought, how she accessed ideas through lived spaces and participation in nondomestic affairs. Her mother explained to Fatima what happiness could mean. "A happy woman," said her mother, "was one who could exercise all kinds of rights, from the right to move to the right to create, compete and challenge, and at the same time could feel loved for doing so." And: "happiness was also about the right to privacy, the right to retreat from the company of others and plunge into contemplative solitude. Or sit by yourself doing nothing for a whole day, and not give excuses or feel guilty about it either."[65]

In addition, there were the stories that were vital to her becoming. "Upstairs was also the place to go for storytelling." This is where magical tales were told by Aunt Habiba: "we loved her, and could hardly sleep on Thursday nights, so excited were we at the prospect of her Friday storytelling sessions... Sometimes when the story lasted for hours, the mothers did not appear ... we would beg aunt Habiba to let us spend the night with her... So on these graceful nights, we would fall asleep listening to our aunt's voice opening up magic glass doors, leading to moonlit meadows." Fatima's mother had already told her the story of Scheherazade, of the famed *Thousand and One Nights*. Subsequently, along with other women, she came to know about a variety of exceptional women singers. The women of the Mernissi *haram* would jump to the radio, as soon as the men left the house, and listen to Princess Asmahan of Lebanon and Oum Kelthoum of Egypt. The *haram* even went to the movies. The heroines of cousin Chama's plays were Asmahan, Scheherazade and *ra-idates*, pioneers of women's rights. Three of them were among her favorites: Aisha Taymour, Zaynab Fawaaz and Huda Sharawi, important (inter)national, feminist figures of the time.[66]

---

[65] Ibid., p. 80.
[66] Ibid., pp. 17, 18, 19, 103–104, 127–128. For details of the three feminists mentioned, see the chapter entitled "Egyptian Feminists Visit the Terrace."

"On the terrace," writes Fatima, "we loved the 1919 women's street march." This was a key moment in cousin Chama's play, in which all participants invaded the stage, jumped up and down, shouted insults at imaginary British soldiers and tossed away "their scarves, symbols of the despised veils." The forbidden terrace was where the plays were staged. And it was here, "upstairs," that Fatima found that magic, pleasure and what her mother might have called "one hundred percent happiness." As Fatima put it after her mother's picnics on the terrace:

> So every morning, I would sit on our threshold, contemplating the deserted courtyard and dreaming about my beautiful future, a cascade of serene delights. Hanging on to the moonlit terrace evenings, challenging your beloved man to forget about his social duties, relax and act foolish and gaze at the stars while holding your hand, I thought, could be one way to go about developing muscles for happiness. Sculpting soft nights, when the sound of laughter blends with the spring breezes, could be another.[67]

THE EXTENDED WORLD OF THE GIRL-CHILD AND WOMAN

In the lives and recollections I have outlined, we return, I am arguing, to the forest of Ketki and her playmates' swings, to Rokeya's dreams, and – indeed – to Akbari and Gyano's unacceptable rebellions. The point I wish to highlight through my exploration of these narratives is that the life of the girl-child and woman could never be limited to the physical, social and psychological spaces prescribed for her. This is where the metaphor of rooftops is particularly important. Rooftops are real places of escape and abandon, of creativity and negotiation. They are also imaginary domains (realms of dreams and daydreams) where girls and women play out imagined lives, fantasies, emotions and even a certain rationality – as in the conception of Ladylands that were radically different from the prescriptions in the bounded *zenana* and the *haram* that they inhabited.

Fatima Mernissi's memoir of girlhood set in Morocco in the 1940s foregrounds the question of boundaries and the generational negotiation of them in profound ways. In her reminiscences of growing up

---

[67] Ibid., pp. 131, 81.

in Fez, the actual physical spaces as well as lives lived in the mind are woven together in intricate ways. Rokeya Sakhawat Hossain deals in a fictional form with similar issues of boundaries, prescriptions and the negotiation of social order, inviting her readers to consider the dreams that girls and women had at the turn of the twentieth century, even though much of the articulation of their quest for freedom had to be confined to no more than the realm of dreams. Nevertheless, after Sultana wakes up from the dream of her travels in Ladyland, the reader may turn to Rokeya, the author, to journey with her and see how she worked to make her dream of education for girls come true.

Bibi Ashraf's recollections poignantly depict the ways in which a girl-child coming of age in nineteenth-century northern India negotiated the limits placed on her self-making. In her incredible story of learning to read and write, what stands out is the determination, the undying desire and the sheer perseverance that went into the attempt to realize her dreams in the face of forbidding circumstances. In our present time, again, as I indicated in Chapter 1, Azra alerts us to the fact that beside the burdens of women's domesticity, aspirations, dreams and playfulness continue to mark, and even rule, the lives of girls and women – even if they live on in subterranean form, which makes them often invisible in our texts, our national memories and our histories.

A Retrospect

In Pursuit of Playfulness

History writing concerned with the subject of women, education and reform in nineteenth-century India has critiqued – powerfully and appropriately – the objectification of women. In the available later nineteenth-century texts from north India and Bengal, female figures are presented largely, if not exclusively, as objects of reform and discipline. It is hardly surprising, therefore, that scholars have focused on these issues and interrogated the various sites of colonial and reformist contest, and with it, the emergent discourses on the place and the anticipated future for women. The outcome is that "disciplined" women figures, strictly confined within a variety of sharply delimited domains, have become the central strand of historical inquiry. Fuller pictures of women's lives, their becoming, their playfulness and visions have practically disappeared from our historical imagination and from public view.

While scholars would readily acknowledge that pleasure, joy and creativity are as much a part of the self-making of the girl-child and woman as are disciplinary constraints, prescribed rules of behavior and enforced silence, nevertheless, given the inheritance of the later nineteenth-century obsession with civilization and reform, it has not been easy to write a history that animates these aspects of the making of the girl-child and woman. It is a pursuit of playfulness – the multi-layered creativity of female figures within the constraining structures which remains critical in their becoming – that I have attempted to detail in this book.

Two questions that I have been asked by a number of people in the course of my writing this book have been central to my thinking about the girl-child coming of age. The first inevitably concerns sources or the imagined lack of these – a classic argument that feminist writers encounter, as do those thinking about other historically marginalized groups such as blacks, conquered indigenous populations, impoverished underclasses, sexual minorities and so on. When it comes to attempts to write minority histories, the problem of the "absent" archive is raised very quickly. The question seems ill-directed in many instances, for evidence is plentiful if we ask the right questions and explore a range of inherited sources. Thus, in the present instance, I have chosen to write a history of women figures as they are presented in a variety of nineteenth-century discourses, and argued at the same time that the various "literary" imaginations (and figurations) speak to the history of "real" girls and women.

My interest in using literary images and spatial metaphors all through the book arises from recognition of an obvious detail. The fact is that male authors wrote the vast majority of the texts that we must use in excavating a history of girls becoming women in nineteenth-century northern India. This calls for a number of different moves. As I argued in Chapter 1, I take the absence of women critics in the early nineteenth century as a challenge to think what kind of history one might write to explore feminine cultures and the making of women. Men birth women, I have said. But as I demonstrate, this articulation does not imply a complete erasure of women's agency, critique or playfulness.

Through an analysis of the production of each text (conduct manuals, novels, textbooks, readers, stories, reformist treatises and so on) taken up in this book, I have attempted to show something of the struggle – and playfulness – of the male authors themselves in the writing of their books for different kinds of female audiences. The choices that Raja Shiv Prasad or Nazir Ahmad made in writing the first textbooks for schools in the NWP, or conduct manuals (through the device of the story of two kinds of girls, a "mirror" for respectable women, *The Bride's Mirror*, for example), were far from straightforward narrations about what a woman "ought to be and to do."[1]

---

[1] Shaw, *What a Woman Ought to Be and to Do*, p. xi. Cited in Chapter 1.

In fact, none of the characters, even of didactic texts such as the *Mirat* or the *Banat* or the *Vamamanrajan*, would be viable for the readers of the time without some suggestion of contestation of what the authors were recommending: not surprising, the favorite character of my students is always Akbari, the spoilt girl-child/woman of *The Bride's Mirror*. Likewise, Husnara of the *Banat* compels us to witness a girl's thought process before she decides to learn to read: she asks questions of her *ustani* and expresses her views candidly about the subjects and the tasks that she does not enjoy. Several women models in other texts alert us to the possibilities of critical engagement that are implicit in the texts, even though the books were centered on the making of conformist and hence ideal women of the household.

Much of this ground and unfolding of women's unexpected and contestatory agency has been explored in Chapter 5. Deeply entangled in the life of nineteenth-century didactic works and their long-lasting circulation are colonial as well as reformist views about appropriateness, decency and respectability, which I have charted in the preceding chapters. Azra's narrative is a powerful reminder of the continuing centrality of this literature to a respectable girl-child's upbringing several generations later.

Following from the analysis of these colonial and reformist endeavors, I have gone on to argue that there are only certain kinds of books or stories – and certain kinds of female figures and subjects (girl-child, girl, woman) – that have survived in our more recent histories and memories. Given this finding, I have, as a historian of premodern times, followed my impulse to go back in time. And going back in time has been redemptive!

Here Insha's 1803 tale of Rani Ketki opens up a rather different history. With its versatile use of metaphors and allusions from a multifaceted and multilayered Indic and non-Indic literary inheritance, the tale neither fits the newly emerging colonial urge to classify folk wisdom into the Hindi or Urdu curriculum, nor does it appeal to the respectable ethics of the reformists for whom women were meant to be seen and not heard.

In Chapters 2 and 3 especially, I have suggested that numerous Hindi and Urdu texts of the early nineteenth century, exclusively read as sources for a contest around languages, were clearly marginalized in the historiographical inheritance and imagination. With their marginalization disappears their potential power in pointing to lives and worlds of girls and women very different from the ones that the colonial milieu of the later nineteenth century celebrated (and demanded).

Through texts such as Insha's, or the bardic narration of Shakuntala, and also several stories in the *Vamamanrajan*, as just a few examples, I have sought to "resuscitate" and describe the playfulness and creativity of women that the later nineteenth century sought to confine: the potential, the emotions, the adventures and the friendships of women. Looking to these earlier, "open" lives, not quite so sharply bound by the elaborate strictures and stipulations of later times, and not yet confined to a physically narrowed domestic world, at once challenges our view of the progress of women's increasing liberation with the passage of time, where *later* is, somehow, always *better* – to repeat a phrase from Chapter 1.

In this connection, I would like to return briefly to the question of the texts that have been used – and some that have remained unused – in this book. Some readers may wonder particularly why I have not analyzed the *Bihishti Zewar* and the *Sunlight on a Broken Column* in detail –both books important to our historical memory and thinking.

A few words about the two books are in order. *Bihishti Zewar* (*Heavenly Ornaments*), a multivolume guidebook published in the early 1900s, was written by the Deobandi reformer Maulana Ashraf 'Ali Thanawi (1864–1943). The second, Attia Hosain's novel, *Sunlight on a Broken Column*, was published in 1961.

As the excellent translation and commentary of the *Bihishti Zewar* by Barbara D. Metcalf makes clear, the book intended to provide "a basic education for a respectable Muslim woman. It rapidly became a classic gift for Muslim brides, who 'entered their husband's home with the Holy Qur'an in one hand and the Bihishti Zewar in the other.'" It was translated into several languages, including English for Muslims in the West. The key argument of Thanawi was that "true knowledge ... [was] the basis of a properly ordered society." His "goal in this work is to communicate correct teachings from the *shari'at*"[2] because the social order rested upon correct teachings and the control of the self in

---

[2] Barbara D. Metcalf, *Perfecting Women: Maulana Ashraf 'Ali Thanawi's Bihishti Zewar. A Partial Translation With Commentary* (Berkeley and London, 1991), pp. 3, 6.

any situation in which a woman might find herself. His emphasis was in accordance with the Deobandi theory of the person, which posed the *nafs*, or lower self, in opposition to *'aql*, or reasoned discrimination, and proposed that true self-fulfillment could be achieved only by cultivating the latter. "What is it, then, that the *Bihishti Zewar* seems to reform?" asks Metcalf. "Women have often, explicitly or implicitly, been deemed innocent of knowledge, *juhhal*, like children or those who lived in pre-Islamic times. Thanawi and his fellow reformist *'ulama* sought to do nothing less than bring women into the high standard of Islamic conformity that had been the purview of educated religious men." The result? Standardizing a "respectable morality throughout a large population during a period of social change ... [while encouraging] female competence and self-confidence in a domestic sphere."[3]

The novel, *Sunlight on a Broken Column*, begins with the protagonist, Laila, an orphan living with her grandfather along with a female cousin, a couple of aunts, two sons of one of the aunts and an aunt and uncle in the family's ancestral home, Ashiana – also the name of Hosain's family's house. The women live in *purdah*, and even when they go out, they have curtains covering the windows of their car. The grandfather dies and the household is broken up, with Laila going to live with her liberal, British-educated uncle and his family. The story follows Laila through her schooling, her friendships and first romance with a young man of no means for whom she ends up defying her family so that she could marry him. The final part of the novel is Laila's return from England years later, to see her now abandoned family home before her cousin sells it. The two brothers have been separated by Partition; the elder stayed in India, trying to represent Muslims and his family rights, while the younger moved his family to the new country of Pakistan. In all the political upheaval, they have been effectively isolated from one another for many years, unable to cross the border back and forth between the two countries. Laila looks back on what their life was like then; a privileged and very different world though at the cusp of change both politically and socially, especially for women's lives.[4]

<hr>

[3] Ibid., pp. 7, 13.
[4] In chapter 4 of her book, *Dwelling in the Archive: Women Writing House, Home, and History in Late Colonial India* (New York, 2003), "A Girlhood Among Ghosts: House, Home, and History in Attia Hosain's *Sunlight on a Broken Column*," Antoinette

Two issues need to be underlined about my selection of the texts in this book. As argued in Chapter 2 as well as in the preceding chapter, it is not my intention to overwhelm the reader by listing and analyzing everything there is on the respectable worlds of the Muslims and Hindus in the Indian subcontinent. In fact, no scholar can ever provide an entirely exhaustive list. There will always be more: paintings, records, architectural sites, stories, legends. Human creativity and playfulness knows no bounds.

Having said that, as far as the *Bihishti Zewar* and *Sunlight on a Broken Column* are concerned, let us remind ourselves that it is precisely these and other such *later* texts, in which a morality and a whole world and its way of being is standardized, that we immediately think of and repeatedly invoke. These are the "classics" in our imagination for an understanding of Azra's world (Hosain was from the Gadai branch of the Kidwai family). I have made the argument that *The Bride's Mirror* (central to Chapter 5) similarly acquired an elevated, almost revered, status. Looking to these classics has firmed up certain pictures of the girl-child and woman – and their spaces – in our minds. As detailed in Chapter 5, my quest is to consider a genealogy of these texts and to reclaim an extensive and varied textual tradition that animates the girl-child's coming of age. I have turned therefore to other texts and figures that are not automatically part of our inheritance and historical consciousness.

In an exploration of the history of the production of diverse nineteenth-century texts in which the girl-child and woman emerges in different guises and narrations, physical spaces as literal and metaphorical devices have been crucial to my investigation of the production of feminine figures. While each chapter in this book foregrounds the idea of one kind of space as a heuristic device for my investigation – forest, school, household and rooftops – it is my argument that in fact these spaces coexist and flow into one another. There is potential for contest in every space. Even the carefully disciplined school and household may provide unexpected avenues of freedom.

Burton places Hosain within a broader context of "Partition fiction" (p. 105) and oral histories of 1947, and analyzes the significance of spatial descriptions of home in such narratives and considers the ways in which the process of remembering is often expressed through architectural idioms (p. 105).

In the extended use of the metaphor of rooftops in Chapter 5, I bring together this idea of overlapping and contested spaces for a girl-child/woman. Ashraf-un-nisa's life, the story of the "real" girl-child's learning in secrecy, one of the most provocative moments in the *Hayat-e Ashraf*, is much more than a simple story about gaining literacy in forbidding circumstances. Her recollections foreground a girl's coming of age: making her own life even while she lived within the confines of respectability and inevitably followed the blueprint deemed suitable for her class and community. Like Ketki of Insha's story, Ashraf-un-nisa nurses many unfulfilled desires. She works to overcome the hurdles that obstruct her in learning to read and write. Ashraf-un-nisa's drawing on blacking, the clay lids, the broom twigs, her going on the roof to teach herself when everyone was asleep, is parallel to Ketki's playful use of the magical ashes that aided her in her search for Udaybhan. Ashraf-un-nisa finds a love of reading on the roof, away from everyone, as Ketki finds her lover in the forest by leaving the palace. The forest of Insha is in this sense the roof of Ashraf-un-nisa. It is this spirit of openness and adventure, of being inventive and making adjustments within given limits, that is characteristic of the fictive figure of Ketki and of the historical girl-child/woman subject found in Bibi Ashraf, Rokeya Sakhawat Hossein, Azra Kidwai, Qurratulain Hyder and Fatima Mernissi.

Women's marginality has been long-lasting: in their namelessness, in the wiping out of their contestation and engagements with inheritance, in the acceptance of innumerable prescriptions by which they must abide – where they can play, as Azra says, and where they can't; when they can laugh, and yet not too freely; or again, as Rokeya reminds us, where there is too much *purdah*, and not enough of it. While marking the confinements of the girl-child/woman in the nineteenth century, this book has been equally concerned with the ingeniousness of girls and women in constrained circumstances: their mischief, disobedience, their inching out of incarcerated worlds, their escape to the rooftops and to forbidden terraces. I have sought to make the point that these irreducible acts of play and laughter, as much as pain and suffering, are a central part of the drama of the patriarchal regimes that women inhabit.

If the struggle against marginality is the everyday of girls and women, I hope this book will serve as a reminder that margins, like rooftops, are potent spaces. It is in the margins that we negotiate the structures of power, the prescriptions, the notions of the bold and the beautiful, that have been handed down to us. It is at the margins of history, and politics, of the school and the household – as of all regulated machines – that the greatest possibilities of play lie.

Bibliography

Hindu, Urdu and Persian Manuscripts, Printed Books and Translations

Ashraf-un-nisa Begum, *Hayat-e Ashraf*, Muhammadi Begum (compiled), (Lahore: Imambara Sayyida Mubarak Begum, n.d.).

Bagchi, Barnita (tr. and introduced), *Sultana's Dream and Padmarag: Two Feminist Utopias* (New Delhi: Penguin Books, 2005).

Clint, L. "Rani Ketki ki Kahani," *The Journal of the Asiatic Society of Bengal*, Vol. 21, 24 (1852, 1852; Urdu text): 1–23.

Das, Shyamsundar (ed.), *Rani Ketki ki Kahani* (Varanasi: Nagri Pracharini Sabha, 1966, 6th edn.).

Pandit Gauridatt, *Devrani Jethani ki Kahani* (Patna: Granth Niketan, 1870; rpt. 1966).

Mrs. R. S. Hossein, *Sultana's Dream* (Calcutta: S. K. Lahiri and Co., 1908, facsimile edition; rpt. Dhaka: Liberation War Museum, 2005).

Jahan, Roushan (ed. and tr.), *Sultana's Dream and Selections from The Secluded Ones* (New York: The Feminist Press, 1988).

Levy, Reuben (tr.), *A Mirror of Princes: The Qabus Nama by Kai Ka`us Ibn Iskandar* (New York: E.P. Dutton and Co., 1951).

Maulvi Nazir Ahmad, *Banat-an-Na`sh*, in *Kulliyat-e Diptee Nazir Ahmad* (Lahore: Al-Karim Market, Urdu Bazar, 2004).

Mirat ul-`Arus, in *Kulliyat-e Diptee Nazir Ahmad* (Lahore: Al-Karim Market, Urdu Bazar, 2004).

Taubat-al-Nasuh, in *Kulliyat-e Diptee Nazir Ahmad* (Lahore: Al-Karim Market, Urdu Bazar, 2004).

Trans. *The Bride's Mirror, Mirat ul-`Arus: A Tale of Life in Delhi a Hundred Years Ago*, G. E. Ward (tr.) (New Delhi: Permanent Black, 2001).

The Repentance of Nussooh (Taubat-al-Nasuh): the Tale of a Muslim Family a Hundred Years Ago, M. Kempson (tr.) (Delhi: Permanent Black, 2004).

Metcalf, Barbara D (tr.), *Perfecting Women: Maulana Ashraf 'Ali Thanawi's Bihishti Zewar. A Partial Translation With Commentary* (Berkeley and London: University of California Press, 1991).

Minault, Gail (tr.), *Voices of Silence* (Delhi: Chanakya Publications, 1986).

Muhammad Husain Azad, *Ab-e hayat: Shaping the Canon of Urdu Poetry*, Frances Pritchett and Shamsur Rahman Faruqi (tr. and ed.) (New Delhi: Oxford University Press, 2001).

Raja Shiv Prasad, *Balabodh* (Allahabad 1867); British Library, OIOC 14160.a.3 (3.).

Gutka or Selections, Part I, II, and III (Allahabad: Printed at the N.W. Provinces and Oudh Press, 1882); India Institute Library, Oxford, Hindi Misc. B 17/1–3.

Ladkon ki Kahani (Banaras 1861, 2nd edn.); British Library, OIOC 14156.h.10.

Vamamanaranjana or Tales for Women (Ilahabad: Government ke chapkhane main chapi gayi, 1860). India Institute, Oxford, Hindi Shiv P1.

Siddiqi, Iftikhar Ahmad, *Maulavi Nazir Ahmad Dihlavi: Ahval-va-Asar* (Lahore: Majlis i Taraqqi i Adab, 1971).

Slater, S., "Rani Ketki ki Kahani," *The Journal of the Asiatic Society of Bengal* 24 (1852): 78–119.

Suman, Kshem Chandra, *Divamgat Hindi-Sevi (Pratham Khand): Sandharb-Granth* (New Delhi: Shakun Prakashan, 1981, 1st edn.).

Talwar, Veer Bharat, *Bhartiya Sahitya ke Nirmata: Raja Shivprasad 'Sitara-e Hind'* (New Delhi: Sahitya Academy, 2005).

Wickens, G. M. (tr.), *The Nasirean Ethics by Nasir ad-Din Tusi* (London: George Allen and Unwin Ltd., 1964).

Encyclopedias and Dictionaries

Dehkhoda, Aliakbar, *Loghatnāme, 1879–1955, Encyclopedic Dictionary* Vols I–XIV, Mohammad Mo'in and Ja'far Shahidi, (eds.) (Tehran, 1993–1994).

Haim, S. (ed.), *The Shorter Persian-English Dictionary, 3rd edn.* (Delhi: Languages of the World Publications, 1998).

Joseph, Suad et. al. (eds.), *The Encyclopedia of Women & Islamic Cultures, Vol. 1: Methodologies, Paradigms and Sources* (Leiden: Brill, 2003).

The Encyclopedia of Women & Islamic Cultures, Vol. 2: Family, Law and Politics (Leiden: Brill, 2004).

The Encyclopedia of Women & Islamic Cultures, Vol. 3: Family, Body, Sexuality and Health (Leiden: Brill, 2005).

The Encyclopedia of Women & Islamic Cultures, Vol. 4: Economics, Education, Mobility and Space (Leiden: Brill, 2006).

The Encyclopedia of Women & Islamic Cultures, Vol. 5: Practices, Interpretations and Representations (Leiden: Brill, 2007).

The Encyclopedia of Women & Islamic Cultures, Vol. 6: Supplement & Index (Leiden: Brill, 2007).

McGregor, R. S., *The Oxford Hindi-English Dictionary* (New Delhi: Oxford University Press, 1993).

Platts, John T., *A Dictionary of Urdu, Classical Hindi and English, Vol. 1* (London: Sampson Low, Marston & Co., 1884; rpt. New Delhi: Munshiram Monohar Lal, 2000).

Steingass, F., *A Comprehensive Persian-English Dictionary, 2nd edn.* (London: Routledge & K. Paul, 1892; rpt. New Delhi: Oriental Books Reprint Corp., 1981).

Urdu-Hindi Dictionary (New Delhi: Anjuman-i Taraqqi-Urdu, 1982).

English Primary Works

Mrs. Meer Hassan Ali, *Observations on the Mussulmauns of India*, W. Crooke (ed.) (Karachi: Oxford University Press, 1973, rpt.).

Mill, James, *The History of British India Volume I* (1817; rpt. London: Routledge/Thoemmes Press, 1997).

Parks, Fanny, *Wanderings of a Pilgrim in Search of the Picturesque with Revelations of Life in the Zenana*, 2 vols. (London: Pelham Richardson, 1850; rpt. Karachi: Oxford University Press, 1975).

Select Readings

Abu-Lughod, Lila, *Veiled Sentiments: Honor and Poetry in a Bedouin Society* (Berkeley and Los Angeles: University of California Press, 1999, 2nd edn.).

Writing Women's Worlds: Bedouin Stories (Berkeley and Los Angeles: University of California Press, 1993).

Alam, Muzaffar, *The Language of Political Islam in India, c. 1200–1800* (New Delhi: Permanent Black, 2004).

Altorki, Soraya and Camilla El-Solh, *Arab Women in the Field* (Syracuse: Syracuse University Press, 1988).

Aries, Philippe, *Centuries of Childhood: A Social History of Family Life* (New York: McGraw Hill, 1962).

Arondekar, Anjali, *For the Record: On Sexuality and the Colonial Archive in India* (Durham and London: Duke University Press, 2009).

Auerbach, Erich, *Scenes from the Drama of European Literature: Six Essays* (New York: Meridian Books, 1959).

Banerjee, Prathama, *The Politics of Time: 'Primitives' and History-Writing in a Colonial Society* (Delhi: Oxford University Press, 2006).

Bayly, C. A., *Empire and Information: Intelligence Gathering and Social Communication in India, 1780–1870* (Cambridge: Cambridge University Press, 1996).

Beck, Lois and Nikkie Keddie (eds.), *Women in the Muslim World* (Cambridge, MA: Harvard University Press, 1978).

Behar, Ruth, *Translated Woman: Crossing the Border with Esperanza's Story* (Boston: Beacon Press, 1993).

Berlant, Lauren, *The Female Complaint: the Unfinished Business of Sentimentality in American Culture* (Durham and London: Duke University Press, 2008).

Blake, Stephen P., *Shahjahanabad: The Sovereign City in Mughal India 1639–1739* (Cambridge and New York: Cambridge University Press, 1993).

Borthwick, Meredith, *The Changing Role of Women in Bengal, 1849–1905* (Princeton, NJ: Princeton University Press, 1984).

Burton, Antoinette, *Dwelling in the Archive: Women Writing House, Home, and History in Late Colonial India* (New York: Oxford University Press, 2003).

Butler, Judith, "Desire" in Frank Lentricchia and Thomas McLaughlin (eds.), *Critical Terms for Literary Study* (Chicago: University of Chicago Press, 1995): 369–386.

Chandra, Sudhir, *Enslaved Daughters: Colonialism, Law and Women's Rights* (Delhi: Oxford University Press, 1998).

Chatterjee, Partha, "The Nationalist Resolution of the Women's Question," in Kumkum Sangari and Sudesh Vaid (eds.) *Recasting Women: Essays in Indian Colonial History* (New Brunswick, NJ: Rutgers University Press, 1997): 233–253.

Coetzee, J. M., *The Slow Man* (London: Secker and Warburg, 2005).

Dalmia, Vasudha, *The Nationalization of Hindu Traditions: Bhartendu Harischandra and Nineteenth-Century Banaras* (New Delhi: Oxford University Press, 1997).

Das, Sisir Kumar, *A History of Indian Literature, 1800–1910* (New Delhi: Sahitya Academy, 2005, rpt.).

Deleuze, Giles and Felix Guattari, *A Thousand Plateaus*, Brian Massumi (tr.), (Minneapolis: University of Minnesota Press, 1980).

Demons, John, *Past, Present, and Personal: The Family and the Life Course in American History* (New York: Oxford University Press, 1986).

Devji, Faisal, "Gender and the Politics of Space: The Movement for Women's Reform in Muslim India," *South Asia*, Vol. 14 (1991): 141–153.

Diba, Layla S. and Maryam Ekhtiar, *Royal Persian Paintings: The Qajar Epoch, 1785–1925* (New York: I. B. Tauris Publishers, 1998).

Doniger, Wendy, *The Hindus: An Alternative History* (New York: The Penguin Press, 2009).

The Laws of Manu (New York: Penguin Books, 1991).

Doniger, Wendy and Sudhir Kakar (trs.), *The Kamasutra* (New York: Oxford University Press, 2009).

Dronke, Peter, *Women Writers of the Middle Ages* (Cambridge: Cambridge University Press, 1984).

Ehlers, Eckart and Thomas Krafft (eds.), *Shahjahanabad/Old Delhi: Traditions and Colonial Change* (New Delhi: Manohar, 1993, 2nd edn.).

Fisher, Michael, *The Inordinately Strange Life of Dyce Sombre: Victorian Angol-Indian MP and 'Chancery Lunatic'* (London: Hurst and Company, 2010).

Forbes, Geraldine, *Women in India* (Cambridge: Cambridge University Press, 1996).

Graven, Phillip, *Spare the Child: The Religious Roots of Punishment and the Psychological Impact of Abuse* (New York: Knopf, 1991).

Grierson, George A., "The Modern Vernacular Literature of Hindustan," *Journal of the Asiatic Society of Bengal*, Part I (1888).

Guha, Ranajit, *History at the Limit of World-History* (New Delhi: Oxford University Press, 2002).

Gupta, Charu, *Sexuality, Obscenity, And Community: Women, Muslims, and the Hindu Public in Colonial India* (New York: Palgrave Macmillan, 2002).

Hasan, Mushirul, *A Moral Reckoning: Muslim Intellectuals in Nineteenth-Century Delhi* (New Delhi: Oxford University Press, 2005).

Hunt, David, *Parents and Children in History: The Psychology of Family Life in Early Modern France* (New York: Basic Books, 1970).

Irigaray, Luce, *Conversations* (New York: Continuum Books, 2008).

Speculum: Of the Other Woman, Gillian C. Gill (tr.), (Ithaca, NY: Cornell University Press, 1985).

Jauss, Robert, "Literary History as a Challenge to Literary Theory," in Timothy Bahti (tr.), *Toward an Aesthetic of Reception* (Minneapolis: University of Minnesota Press, 1982): 3–45.

Kakar, Sudhir, *Indian Childhood: Cultural Ideals and Social Realities* (R.V. Parulekar Lecture; Delhi: Oxford University Press, 1979).

Kalsi, A. S. "Pariksaguru (1882): the First Hindi Novel and the Hindu Elite," *Modern Asian Studies*, Vol. 26 (1992): 763–790.

Kidwai, Riaz-ur-Rahman, *Biographical Sketch of Kidwais of Avadh: With Special Reference to Barabanki Families* (Aligarh: Kitab Ghar Publishers, 1987).

Koessling, Rainer (ed. and tr.), *Leben und Legende der Heiligen Elisabeth nach Dietrich von Apolda* (Frankfurt am Main: Insel Verlag, 1997).

Kristeva, Julia, *Desire in Language: A Semiotic Approach to Literature and Art*, Leon S. Roudiez (ed.), (New York: Columbia University Press, 1984).

Kumar, Nita, *Lessons from Schools: The History of Education in Banaras* (New Delhi and London: Sage Publications, 2000).

Lal, Ruby, *Domesticity and Power in the Early Mughal World* (Cambridge and New York: Cambridge University Press, 2005).

"Gender and *Sharafat*: Reading Nazir Ahmad," *Journal of the Royal Asiatic Society*, Vol.18, No. 1 (2008): 15–30.

"The Lure of the Archive: New Perspectives from South Asia," *Feminist Studies*, Vol. 37, No.1 (Spring 2011): 93–110.

"Recasting the Woman Question: the 'Girl-Child/Woman' in the Colonial Encounter," *Interventions*, Vol.10, No. 3 (2008): 321–339.

Lather, Patti, "Postbook: Working the Ruins of Feminist Ethnography," *Signs*, Vol. 27, No. 1 (Autumn 2001): 199–227.

Lelyveld, David, *Aligarh's First Generation: Muslim Solidarity in British India* (Princeton: Princeton University Press, 1978).

Lorde, Audre, *Sister Outsider: Essays and Speeches by Audre Lorde* (Berkeley: Crossing Press, 1984; rpt. 2007).

Mani, Lata, *Contentious Traditions: The Debate on Sati in Colonial India* (Berkeley: University of California Press, 1998).

McGregor, Ronald Stuart, *Hindi Literature of the Nineteenth and Early Twentieth Centuries* (Wiesbaden: Otto Harrassowitz, 1974).

Mernissi, Fatima, *Beyond the Veil: Male-Female Dynamics in a Modern Muslim Society* (Cambridge, MA.: Schenkman, 1975).

Dreams of Trespass: Tales of a Harem Girlhood (Reading, MA: Addison-Wesley Publishing Co., 1994).

Metcalf, Barbara D. "Islamic Reform and Islamic Women: Maulana Thanawi's Jewelry of Paradise," in Barbara Metcalf (ed.), *Moral Conduct and Authority: the Place of Adab in South Asian Islam* (Berkeley: University of California Press, 1984): 184–195.

Perfecting Women: Maulana Ashraf 'Ali Thanawi's Bihishti Zewar. A Partial Translation With Commentary (Berkeley and London: University of California Press, 1991).

Minault, Gail, "Begmati Zuban: Women's Language and Culture in Nineteenth Century Delhi," *India International Center Quarterly*, Vol. 11, No. 2 (June 1984): 155–70.

"'Ismat: Rashid ul Khairi's Novels and Urdu Literary Journalism for Women," in C. Shackle (ed.), *Urdu and Muslim South Asia* (London: School of Oriental and African studies, 1989): 129–138.

"Making Invisible Women Visible: Studying the History of Muslim Women in South Asia," *South Asia*, Vol. IX, No. 1 (1986): 1–13.

"Other Voices, Other Rooms: The View from the Zenana," in Nita Kumar (ed.), *Women as Subjects: South Asian Histories* (Calcutta: Street Publications, 1994): 108–124.

'Urdu Women's Magazines in the Early Twentieth Century,' *Manushi*, No. 48 (September-October 1988): 2–9.

"Sayyid Mumtaz Ali and `Huquq un-Niswan: An Advocate of Women's Rights in Islam in the Late Nineteenth Century," *Modern Asian Studies*, Vol. 24, No.1 (1990): 147–172.

Secluded Scholars: Women's Education and Muslim Social Reform in Colonial India (Delhi: Oxford University Press, 1998).

Naim, C. M., "How Bibi Ashraf Learned to Read and Write," *Annual of Urdu Studies*, No. 6 (1987): 99–115.

"Prize Winning Adab: A Study of Five Urdu Books Written in Response to the Allahabad Government Gazette Notification," in Barbara D. Metcalf (ed.) *Moral Conduct and Authority: The Place of Adab in South Asian Islam* (Berkeley: University of California Press, 1984): 290–314.

Najmabadi, Afsaneh, "Crafting an Educated Housewife in Iran," in Lila Abu-Lughod (ed.), *Remaking Women: Feminism and Modernity in the Middle East* (Princeton: Princeton University Press, 1998).

Nelson, Cynthia, "Public and Private Politics: Women in the Middle Eastern World," *American Ethnologist*, Vol. 1, No. 3 (August 1974): 551–563.

Orsini, Francesca, *The Hindi Public Sphere, 1920–1940: Language and Literature in the Age of Nationalism* (Oxford: Oxford University Press, 2002).

Print and Pleasure: Popular Literature and Entertaining Fictions in Colonial North India (New Delhi: Permanent Black, 2009).

Pandey, Gyanendra, *The Construction of Communalism in Colonial North India* (New Delhi: Oxford University Press, 2006, 2nd edn.).

(ed.), *Subaltern Citizens and their Histories: Investigations from India and the USA* (London: Routledge Press, 2010).

(ed.), *Subalternity and Difference: Investigations from the North and the South* (London: Routledge Press, 2011).

Petievich, Carla, "Gender Politics and the Urdu Ghazal: Exploratory Observations on Rekhta versus Rekhti," *Economic and Social History Review*, Vol. 38, No. 3 (2001): 223–248.

Philips, Robert, *Garden of Endless Blossoms: Urdu Ramayans of the 19th and Early 20th Century* (PhD Dissertation, University of Wisconsin-Madison, 2010).

Powell, Avril A., "History Textbooks and the Transmission of the Pre-colonial Past in North-western India in the 1860s and 1870s," in Daud Ali (ed.), *Invoking the Past: The Uses of History in South Asia* (New Delhi: Oxford University Press, 1999): 91–133.

Raheja, Gloria Kirin Goodwin and Ann Grodzins Gold, *Listen to the Heron's Words: Reimagining Gender and Kinship in North India* (Berkeley: University of California Press, 1994).

Rai, Alok, *Hindi Nationalism* (New Delhi: Orient Longman Limited, 2000).

Rajan, Rajeswari Sunder, *The Scandal of the State: Women, Law and Citizenship in India* (Durham: Duke University Press and New Delhi: Permanent Black, 2003).

Rich, Adrienne, "Compulsory Heterosexuality and Lesbian Existence," in Henry Abelove, Michele Aina Barale, and David M. Halperin (eds.) *The Lesbian and Gay Studies Reader* (New York: Routledge, 1993): 227–254.

Richman, Paula (ed.), *Many Ramayanas: The Diversity of Narrative Tradition in South Asia* (Berkeley: University of California Press, 1991).

Robinson, Francis, *The Ulama of Farangi Mahall and Islamic Culture in South Asia* (New Delhi: Permanent Black, 2001).

Ronsse, Erin Ann, "Rhetoric of Martyrs: Transmission and Reception History of the 'Passion of Saints Perpetua and Felicitas.'" (PhD Dissertation, University of Victoria, 2008).

Russell, Ralph, *The Pursuit of Urdu Literature: A Select History* (London and New Jersey: Zed Books Ltd., 1992).

Sadiq, Muhammad, *A History of Urdu Literature* (Delhi: Oxford University Press, 1984).

Salisbury, Joyce, *Perpetua's Passion* (New York: Routledge, 1997).

Sangari, Kumkum, *Politics of the Possible: Essays on Gender, History, Narrative, Colonial English* (New Delhi: Tulika, 1999).

Sarkar, Tanika, "A Prehistory of Rights: The Age of Consent Debate in Colonial Bengal," *Feminist Studies*, Vol. 26, No. 3 (2000): 601–622.

Hindu Wife, Hindu Nation: Community, Religion, and Cultural Nationalism (London: Hurst and Co., 2001).

"Enfranchised Selves: Women, Culture, and Rights in Nineteenth-Century Bengal," *Gender and History*, Vol.13, No. 3 (2001): 546–565.

Sedgwick, Eve Kosofsky, *Epistemology of the Closet* (Berkeley: University of California Press, 1990).

Shackle, Christopher and Rupert Snell, *Hindi and Urdu Since 1800: A Common Reader* (London: SOAS, University of London, 1990).

Shaw, Stephanie, *What a Woman Ought to Be and to Do: Black Professional Women Workers During the Jim Crow Era* (Chicago and London: University of Chicago Press, 1996).

Shulman, David and Narayana Rao, "Nala: The Life of a Story," in *Damayanti and Nala: The Many Lives of a Story*, Susan Wadley (ed.), (New Delhi: Chronicle Books, 2011): 1–12.

Sinha, Mrinalini, *Specters of Mother India: The Global Restructuring of an Empire* (Durham and London: Duke University Press, 2006).

Spivak, Gayatri Chakravorty, *A Critique of Postcolonial Reason: Toward a History of the Vanishing Present* (Cambridge, MA: Harvard University Press, 1999).

Stark, Ulrike, "Towards a New Hindu Woman: Educational Ideals and Female Role Models in Shivprasad's *Vamamanranjan* (1856)," in Ulrike Roesler and Jayandra Soni (eds.), *Aspects of the Female in Indian Culture* (Marburg: Indica Et Tibetica Verlag, 2004): 167–180.

Stearns, Peter N., *Childhood in World History* (New York and London: Routledge, 2006).

Steedman, Carolyn. *Strange Dislocation: Childhood and the Idea of Human Interiority, 1780–1930* (Cambridge, MA: Harvard University Press, 1995).

Stone, Lawrence, *The Family, Sex, and Marriage in England, 1500–1800* (New York: Harper and Row, 1972).

Thapar, Romila, *Sakuntala: Texts, Readings, Histories* (London: Anthem Press, 2002, rpt.).

Vanita, Ruth, "Different Speakers, Different Loves: Urban Women in Rekhti Poetry," in Gyanendra Pandey (ed.), *Subalternity and Difference: Investigations from the North and the South* (New York and London: Routledge Press, 2011): 57–76.

Gender, Sex and the City: Urdu Rekhti Poetry in India, 1780–1870 (New York: Palgrave-Macmillan, 2012).

"Married Among their Companions: Female Homoerotic Relations in Nineteenth-Century Urdu Rekhti Poetry in India," *Journal of Women's History*, Vol. 16, No. 1 (2004): 12–53.

Vanita, Ruth and Saleem Kidwai (eds.) *Same-Sex Love in India: Readings from Literature and History* (Delhi: Palgrave-Macmillan India Ltd., 2000).

Visweswaran, Kamala, *Fictions of Feminist Ethnography* (Minneapolis: University of Minnesota Press, 1994).

Wakankar, Milind, *Subalternity and Religion: The Prehistory of Dalit Empowerment in South Asia* (London and New York: Routledge Press, 2010).

Walkowitz, Judith R., *Prostitution and Victorian Society: Women, Class, and the State* (Cambridge: Cambridge University Press, 1980).

Weinbaum, Alys Eve, Lynn M. Thomas, Priti Ramamurthy et al. (eds.), *The Modern Girl Around the World: Consumption, Modernity, and Globalization* (Durham: Duke University Press, 2008).

Index

Hegel, Georg Wilhelm Friedrich, 166
Hindi,
    didactic texts, 41, 48–49, 50n40, 61,
        85–86, 88–89, 94, 102, 117–18,
        124, 130n6, 132, 134
    literature, 1, 49n34, 61, 64–66, 68, 91,
        118, 132
    politics of, 62, 68, 88, 90–91, 94–97,
        132, 202
    standardization, 54, 62, 65, 85,
        90–91, 95–97, 117n79, 118,
        132, 202, *See also* Hindustani;
        language; Sanskrit; scripts;
        Urdu
Hindi-Urdu region, 32, 171, 176n12
Hindu Child Marriage Bill (1929), 44,
        See also Child Marriage Restraint
        Act; reform; Sarda Act
Hinduism, 35, 47n32, 80n53, 84–85, 90,
        96–97, 100, 190
    historiography, 93, 101–2
    reform, 33, 40, 43–48, 54, 92, 97n26,
        99, 132, 157, 166, 191
    religious identity, 52, 57, 62, 66, 68,
        90–91, 96
Hindustani, 66n16, 95, 99
historiography, 5n6, 30, 33, 37, 39, 42,
        106, 200, 202
    colonial, 35, 93–95
    feminist, 55
    Indian, 85, 93–95
    periodization, 4–5, 171
    teleology, 33, 127, 203, *See also*
        archive
History of British India, 35, *See also*
        Mill, James
History of Sandford and Merton,
        104n46, 136, *See also* Day,
        Thomas
hommosexuality, 56n50, *See also*
        Irigaray, Luce
homosociality, 29, 127, 142, 179, *See
        also* friendship
honor, 35, 163, 166
    familial, 10–11, 72, 110, 166
    gendered, 10–11, 14, 23, 76, 108, 110,
        112, 152
Hosain, Attia, 203–5, *See also Sunlight
        on a Broken Column*
household
    institutionalization, 28, 126

management, 7, 20–22, 103, 126–27,
        133, 139, 141n38, 142–43, 145,
        151–55, 166–67
    as pedagogic space, 75, 98–104, 110,
        125–67
    pre-colonial, 126–27
    privacy, 15, 28, 167, 196–97
    relationship to neighborhood, 22,
        28–29, 103, 125, 127, 146–47,
        153
    respectable, 1, 11, 27, 49, 60, 75,
        125–67
    as sacred space, 23, 28–29
    as symbolic space of girl-child/
        woman, 125, 127, 151, 155,
        See also family; reform;
        respectability
Hume, A.O., 118
Hunter Commission (1882), 90, 98,
        See also colonialism; education;
        reform; school
Hurston, Zora Neale, 57n51, *See also
        Their Eyes Were Watching
        God*
hybridity, 67, 92
Hyder, Qurratulain, 7, 22n17,
        36–37, 206, *See also Naam
        ka parda*

Indian Mutiny (1857), 33, 46, 94, 95n21,
        140–43, 148, 179–80
industrialization, 52
Insha-allah Khan, 24–26, 48–52, 56,
        59–86, 89–93, 116–17, 122–24,
        162, 168, 170, 202–3, *See also
        Darya-e Latafat; Rani Ketki ki
        Kahani*
Irigaray, Luce, 38n12, 39n13, 56n50
Islam
    historiography, 94, 130
    Islamicate culture, 50, 131, 137, 138
    reform, 33, 45–48, 54, 99, 104n45,
        153n65, 157, 166, 189–91,
        203–4
    religious identity, 52, 57, 62, 66, 68,
        90–91
    Shi`ah, 173, 183
    Sufism, 3, 3n2, 149
    Sunni, 183, *See also* Quran
'Ismat (modesty), 23, 29, *See also*
        Rashid-ul-Khairi

sharafat (respectability) (cont.)
  sharif manhood, 28, 150, 154, 156,
    163
  sharif womanhood, 10, 23, 28, 54,
    125, 131, 143–45, 156, 165
Shulman, David, 106–107
Singh, Laxman, 118, 121–24, *See also*
  Shakuntala
space, physical
  as heuristic device, 154, 171, 205
  constraint, 4, 7, 11, 15, 28, 32, 62, 75,
    84n67, 85, 168, 192
  liminal, 62, 70, 74, 123, 124, 169, 170,
    206
  negotiation of, 11, 91, 98, 176, 194,
    198, 205
  ordering relations, 11, 27, 28, 34,
    52, 54
  paradigmatic spaces, 4–5, 34, 171
  shaping life, 1, 3–5, 8–19, 27–30, 59,
    70, 73, 135, 197–99
  spaces of freedom, 16, 26, 30, 48,
    62, 70, 75, 93, 116, 123, 192,
    197, 205, *See also* gardens;
    forest; household; neighborhood,
    rooftops; school
Spivak, Gayatri, 5n6, 37
Stark, Ulrike, 88n1, 91–92, 95n20,
  98–99, 110
storytelling, 38, 57, 62, 69n24, 100,
    106–7, 147, 193, 197
  Hellenic, 106
  Indic, 48, 60, 106–7, 122–23
  Urdu *dastans*, 60, 66
  variations of story, 106–7
subjectivity, 37, 38n13, 47, 54
Sultana's Dream, 172–73, 184–91, *See
  also* Rokeya Sakhawat Hossein
Sunlight on a Broken Column, 203–5,
  See also Hosain, Attia
Surdas, 103, 154, 155
Swami Dayanand Saraswati, 97n26,
  132

Tahzib un-Niswan, 172, 172n1, 183, *See
  also* Muhammadi Begum
Talwar, Veer Bharat, 88n1, 90, 93–95, 96,
  117n79
Taubat al-Nasuh (Repentance of Nasuh),
  21n13, 49–50, 125, 130n6,
  134–37, 142–44, 146, 148–49,

  156–57, 161–63, 166, *See also*
    Nazir Ahmad
Telugu, 84n67
Thapar, Romila, 46n32, 70, 70n26, 93,
    118–23, 119n83, 120n88
Theosophical Society, 96
transgression, 4, 11n8, 48, 51, 60, 168,
    170, 178, 194–95, 206
Tulsidas, 89, 103, 154–55, *See also*
    Balkhand; Ramacharitramanas
Turkish, 64

upbringing, 3–4, 9, 20, 27, 35, 41–42, 49,
    125–26, 141n38, 144, 202
  training, 9–10, 19–21, 28–29, 53, 59,
    87, 98–103, 125–67, 128–29,
    131n10, 138–44
urbanization, 28, 52, 125, 133, 168–70
Urdu, 24, 54, 61, 66, 94–95, 97n26,
    104n45, 153n65, 188
  didactic texts, 21, 41, 50n40, 66n16,
    128, 130n6, 132n14, 134, 174, 189
  educational use, 14, 19, 174, 175, 178,
    202
  government use, 94, 131
  grammar, 64, 68–69
  literature, 1, 7, 20n12, 49, 51n43,
    60–61, 64–66, 74, 94, 135, 161,
    162n85
  magazines and newspapers, 21, 23,
    154, 172, 172n1
  poetry, 51, 62–68, 74, 83, 162n85,
    168, 170
  politics of, 68, 88, 90–91, 94–95, 202
  standardization, 62, 68–69, 90–91,
    94–95, 202, *See also* Hindi,
    Hindustani, language, Persian,
    scripts
ustani (semi-trained teacher), 9, 100, 103,
    147, 152, 174–75, 181–82, 202,
    See also education, girls', women
Uttar Pradesh, 2, 3n2, 20n12, 61, 131,
    172, 173, *See also* North Western
    Provinces

Vamamanranjan (Tales for the
    Entertainment of Women), 27,
    49, 88–92, 98–99, 101, 104–18,
    122–24, 164, 202, 203
  `Auraton ki Himmat* (Courage of
    Women), 105, 111–12